THE ST. JOHNS

A Parade of Diversities

THE
RIVERS OF AMERICA

Edited by

STEPHEN VINCENT BENÉT
and CARL CARMER

As Planned and Started by
CONSTANCE LINDSAY SKINNER

Art Editor

RUTH E. ANDERSON

THE ST. JOHNS

A PARADE OF DIVERSITIES

by

BRANCH CABELL

and

A. J. HANNA

Illustrated by DORIS LEE

"And a voice heard from heaven said, Take
the little book which is open."
—*The Revelation of St. John the Divine*

FARRAR & RINEHART, INC.
New York   *Toronto*

To the memory of

Stephen Vincent Benét

—inasmuch as, after having been the first to select the theme and to invent the collaboration from which springs this book, he aided in its shaping throughout the course of two years, and upon the last day of his life found time to commend the finished work—so now, at outset, this account of his forefathers' homeland has been dedicated, not unbefittingly, in affection and homage from us both.

Contents

PART ONE: THE ROYAL RIVER

PART TWO: THE REPUBLICAN RIVER

What though Welaka's name this changing world has lost?
I'll sing of thee, St. Johns, and of thy glories boast . . .
Thy current moves, like Time, with long imprisoned souls
Who mark how much their life, like thine, has tides and shoals;
And though procrastination is of Time the thief,
Full well we know, to those thus bound, Time brings relief . . .
And that is why, St. Johns, I sing of thee,
Calling to friends up north, "Come down and see!"

—"The Glories of the St. Johns," by Solon Robinson

Part One

THE ROYAL RIVER

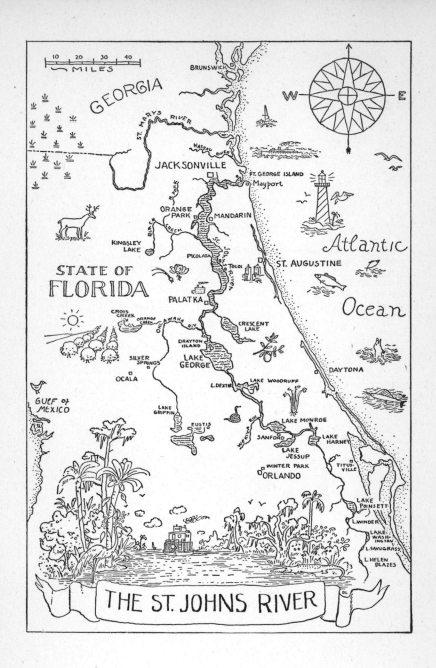

THE ST. JOHNS RIVER

Touching, from Afar, the Welaka

WILLIAM CULLEN BRYANT, the more thanks to his native American talent for dwelling upon the obvious in the tones of a major prophet, was neither the first nor the last person to observe that the St. Johns ranks as "one of the noblest streams of the country." It is likely that, in common with yet other observers, he also found in its great width, in its placidity, and in the darkness of its waters passing with an infinite and funereal leisure among tall forests made somber by incalculable stalactites of Spanish moss, an enchantment just slightly sinister.

Neither the Mississippi nor the Nile exceeds the average

expanse of the St. Johns between shore to shore for a full
hundred miles above its mouth; and with corpulence, you
would say, it combines laziness. Indeed, the fact that this
river's gleaming, broad surface so much more frequently
resembles the superficies of a lake than a moving current
very long ago led the adjacent Indians to call the St. Johns
"Welaka"—which meant The Chain of Lakes.

Howsoever tardily, science has here justified rhetoric.
Here, in full measure, the impressiveness of fancy would
seem to be buttressed by logic, inasmuch as thousands of
lakes are now known to cluster about this river basin; and
the contents of many of them find their way into the St.
Johns—of which the main stream passes through eight lakes,
and is immediately connected with five more lakes. This
curious configuration took shape, in a continent as yet under
course of construction, when the peninsula of Florida was
being composed (in polite accord with the nursery rhyme)
out of little grains of sand, which washed down continually
from the higher lands northward; and were so united with
countless layers of marine sediment formed by the skeletons
of no less countless generations of microscopic deep-sea
creatures.

Floridian rocks are not old enough, in a thus literally
upstart land, to contain any dinosaurian remains. Yet many
fossils have been garnered from the bottom of wells, by the
industry of learned persons (in a common-sense search after
truth at her proverbial home), and from rock quarries and
phosphate mines, from dredging operations, and from the
digging of canals, to afford proof that, in bygone eras,
animal life about the St. Johns has included members of such
fairly old families as the saber-toothed tiger, the four-tusked
mastodon, the imperial mammoth, the giant wolf, the water

hog, and a species of dog about as large as a Shetland pony—
along with the more parvenu lion, the rhinoceros, and the
hippopotamus.

The likelihood that, about twenty-five thousand years
ago, divers Americans were distressed by these unfriendly
and far stronger powers is accepted today, as a more or less
painful possibility, by those scientists who have analyzed
the skeletal remains and yet other human souvenirs un-
earthed at Vero Beach, within but a few miles from the
sources of the St. Johns. It may be declared with caution, in
any case, that human beings, in addition to the afore-mentioned and perhaps more practical animals, did infest the
banks of this river rather early. The aboriginal American
was living there, it is certain, in the twelfth century, a bit
more than five hundred years before the murderous inter-
jection of European politics, for the first time, assumed control of America's complaisant inhabitants; and his race, if
not of Japanese stock, was descended from the mongrel
Mongoloid peoples of Central Asia. Just how or when he
reached Florida remains unsettled.

In strange, if not wholly unexplainable earth-mounds—
which, standing upon the banks of the St. Johns or in
near-by swamps, still parallel this river for about three-
quarters of its course—are to be found human relics from
which has been reconstructed a fragmentary and very dim
notion of the prehistoric Floridian. Varied in size and shape,
these mounds are at times crude circular heaps, ranging from
fifteen feet in diameter to three hundred feet in perimeter,
whereas in other places beside the river they are builded like
long ridges. Their height varies from a few inches to twenty
feet; and being overgrown with seemingly antediluvian oaks

—along with many maples, palmettos, bay trees, wild orange trees, and magnolias—these mounds had stayed untroubled until late in the last century, when the intrusiveness of science, through a long series of excavations, parcelled out these earth-mounds into four classes: they being, severally, the foundation, the ceremonial, the refuse, and the burial mound.

Inside these mounds have been found skeletons, household and farming implements, weapons, and a gratifying extensiveness of pottery. Some of the dug-out urns and pitchers have the form of a man or an animal, while yet others are decorated with geometric designs. From other Floridian earth-mounds research has disinterred also, in a fair degree of numerousness and of preservation, its clues in the way of wood carving—very many of these being so incised with a cross and with a circle conjoined as to depict, symbolically and in a perfectly refined manner, that union of the male and the female principle from which proceeds all life. Such carvings (say scientists, quite as if it could possibly matter to anybody except their laborious coteries) may well indicate a direct connection with either Antillian or Mexacoid cultures. Yet (it is added) the remnants of certain artificial harbors and canals south of the St. Johns would appear— upon second thought, and in traits such as one should not disregard wholly—to relate the mores of early Florida to some artifacts of the West Indies and of Yucatan. Thus far declare the learned, uncontroverted by the intelligent, as to the first known inhabitants of the St. Johns valley.

—So that, upon the whole, our knowledge as to these prehistoric peoples upon the banks of the Welaka—who called themselves Timucuans—is both vague and unvigorous. They existed; and for a little while this fact seemed, to them, of a noticeable importance, an importance which interested Heaven. Love (with an inadequate outcome) and decay and many vain regrets, and death too, went among them, like tyrants; and yet always hope remained, along with one's self-condonation, to whisper about a rather more just future and a much more superb tomorrow. In brief, the Timucuans so far resembled all the rest of us as to honor man's unique power, the power to reason, by not using it very often. We can know that only, with any certainty, about those first Floridians, who were human beings.

During the sixteenth century, an estimated ten thousand of their descendants were in residence near the valley of the St. Johns—throughout the remainder of this chapter to give, for convenience sake, to the river its modern name; but just when, or which, Europeans first saw these Timucuan Indians is not beyond dispute. Eleven years before Ponce de León landed, in 1513, on the Atlantic coast near the mouth of the St. Johns, and claimed everything within eyeshot or the reach of Christian artillery for Spain, the eastern coast line of North America had been rudely mapped; the chance is not unlikely that the explorers whose knowledge had made possible this map knew about the existence of the St. Johns. Some historians have declared it was discovered, in 1521, by Gordillo and Quexas; but the fact now appears certain that the stream which these Spaniards christened the St. Johns lay north of the Savannah River. As the record stands, the St. Johns was first sighted by European eyes upon the Walburga's Eve of 1562, when the French discovered it; and upon the south bank of what the French termed the River of May, they established a colony, forty-three years before the more widely advertised landing of 104 English settlers at Jamestown.

Nor is it known just when the dispossessors of these Frenchmen—the Spanish—who, to begin with, called this river the San Mateo, saw fit to rename it in honor of St. John. It is assumed generally that this fluvial tribute was accorded to the Beloved Disciple during the last years of the sixteenth century; and that the name was derived from the Franciscan mission of San Juan del Puerto (St. John of the door, or harbor, or haven) which at this period was founded near the mouth of the river.

A similarly uncompromising silence chills speculation as to when the current name of the St. Johns River made its début upon maps. So far as is known, the first map to display the name was the anonymous *Mapa de la ysla de la Florida* [1680-1700?], of Spanish origin. And miles of the St. Johns as yet await their cartographer, for none knows how many miles, among the ambiguous and lonely, wild huge bogs about the river's source waters, where these waters take form, so imperceptibly as to seem evoked (fancy might here suggest) by the forces of an enchantment just slightly sinister, from out of impenetrable swamplands—veiled levelly and monotonously, so far as vision reaches, by the serrated pale-green leaves and by the brown flowering of sawgrass, and not changed at all (one imagines) since hippopotami sought hereabouts, in these mile-long desolate marshes, the comforts of home life.

2

Combines Instruction with Brevity

To OUTLINE, as briefly as may be, the general course of the St. Johns as it today exists, in marked contrast with the Welaka, seems needful, inasmuch as the St. Johns got its national, or to speak strictly, its international, importance from this same eccentric course, which is in Florida unique, and which in any part of the world would be labeled extraordinary. In contour, one may dare assert, the St. Johns resembles no other known river.

Not merely is the St. Johns shaped with such oddness as to progress, directly, through eight lakes. For near three hundred miles, it runs northward, as do but an exceedingly few other rivers upon this planet. It runs northward, as does not any other river (except only, for a space, one of its tributaries, the Oklawaha) in all the Floridian peninsula. With its confluents, it ascends the middle of this peninsula, in the form, should the inconsonant simile be permissible, of a liquid backbone; and precisely where the excrescent peninsula unites with the continent, just there, with an insane sort of abruptness, does the river turn east toward the Atlantic, so as to amputate from the mainland almost half Florida. The northward flowing of the St. Johns system, along the middle of a peninsula in which all the other water-courses lapse either toward sunrise or to the west, made of the St. Johns, during the first week that men employed canoes, the main highway of Florida's traffic; whereas the river's sudden and inexplicable-seeming bend to the east has made of it, over and yet over again, a shambles.

In brief, the strange shape of the St. Johns River affected continually—in one or another degree, but continually—the shaping of American history throughout two centuries. If but for this more or less important reason, the main course of the St. Johns may be thought worthy of record.

To start with, the source waters of the St. Johns arise only twenty feet above sea level, and but a trifle more than that many miles north of Lake Okeechobee—which is the second largest body of fresh water lying within the confines of the United States, and a marked example of those pre-historic depressions in the floor of the ocean that once covered all Florida. Beginning its northward course, from out of the large and uncharted quagmires already mentioned, the St. Johns passes through what, to all appearances, is the remnant of an aforetime coastal lagoon—a small stretch of water bearing the odd name of Lake Helen Blazes; after which the St. Johns alike enters and leaves the less captivatingly christened Lake Sawgrass.

In the seeming of a rather modest canal, the St. Johns

first woos public attention where the adolescent river is spanned by the highway between Kissimmee and Melbourne. Here the stream widens into Lake Washington, that immemorial nesting place of the white ibis; and later, loiters through Lake Winder and Lake Poinsett. About twenty-five miles west of Cape Canaveral lighthouse, the St. Johns re-encounters human doings, where it is crossed yet again by a main thoroughfare, the Cheney highway, which connects Orlando with the Atlantic coast. After touching a chain of small lakes near Titusville, the river begins to turn, very gradually, toward the west in its still northbound course; and so drifts through Lake Harney. It here makes contact with history, inasmuch as upon the western bank of this lake one finds the former site of Fort Lane, which, in the 1830's, headed a string of fortifications builded along the upper part of the river so as to serve as checks against the rash tendency of Seminole Indians to indulge in treachery and carnage unauthorized by the United States of America.

As the St. Johns leaves Lake Harney, the river is bridged by a railroad, at the mill town of Osceola; where, turning almost due west, with a flavor of irresolution, the St. Johns wanders past the head of Lake Jessup, dividing and subdividing itself into bewildered and shallow, circuitous channels enmeshed by palmetto hammocks. It thus straggles, from the east, into Lake Monroe, upon the southern shore of which the human palate has caused to flourish Sanford, an agricultural center producing a large part of the world's celery. After thrusting through the west bank of this lake, the St. Johns, as though putting aside indecision, meanders no more; but sets forth sturdily with the North Star as guide. From this point, also, the St. Johns assumes the unarguable appearance

and proportions of a river, with a channel eight feet deep
and with an average width of one hundred yards.

A few miles beyond Lake Monroe, the Wekiwa—which
is the river's first large tributary—enters the St. Johns, after
a twelve-mile run from a spring that emits (it has been
calculated by persons whom, for some unexplained reason,
such figures interest) about forty-two million gallons a day.
The river's west shore, from the mouth of the Wekiwa,
for more than ten miles northward, as the crow flies in the
cliché, is low, swampy, and most opulently ornamented with
ancient moss-draped cypresses, water maples, sweet gums, and
large bay trees, which flourish like the wicked in King David's
moralizing. One settlement alone remains hereabouts as a
relic of the busy traffic which once kept all this part of the
river no less noisy than important. This village is Astor;
from which, in the 1880's, a railroad was builded toward the
southwest; and so led to the increase of Eustis and Leesburg.
Near-by stood the early Indian trading post of Volusia,
as well as the plantation of Moses Levy, who, in the early part
of the nineteenth century, laid plans to found an American
refuge in which the persecuted Jews of Europe might regain
the lost ease of Zion; and at this same broad bend in the
river, John Cabell Breckinridge, Confederate secretary of war,
after having eluded his pursuers during the six fevered weeks
that followed Appomattox, embarked on a four-oared cutter,
so as to ascend the St. Johns under an united onslaught of
hunger and mosquitoes, and after a short overland journey,
to escape from that habitual enemy of unrestraint which we
still call "the federal government," toward Cuba and comfort.
The east bank of the river, from Lake Monroe northward, although but a trifle less swampy and tenantless than is

the west bank, displays at least its uncountable gaunt cows.
These, wading out into the river so far that only their heads
are visible, feed pensively all day long upon water hyacinths;
and thus demonstrate the bulbs of the water hyacinth to be
the most efficient reducing diet which nature affords.

One here confronts a noteworthy product of altruism;
for the water hyacinth was not known in the St. Johns, nor
elsewhere in the United States, until 1884, when some specimens of it were imported from Venezuela and exhibited at
the New Orleans Cotton Exposition. It was there seen floating
lightly about clear pools of water aglitter with robust gold-
fish. It bloomed lavishly, with a delicate purple blossom which
resembled an orchid. It was admired vastly. People clamored
to obtain this very beautiful, exotic plant.

So a few samples of it were presented to the more influential patrons of the Exposition, including Mrs. W. F. Fuller
of Brooklyn, in New York, who then owned a winter home
called "Edgewater" near San Mateo. Mrs. Fuller placed fondly
her fair souvenir of the great Exposition in her private fish-
pond, at "Edgewater," where it thrived, and where it ex-
panded daily into more and yet more buoyant, brightly
flowering bulbs with their roots interlaced. It thrived so
creditably that by-and-by she began to put small sections of
these lovely floating mats into the St. Johns, so that they
might adorn the river. There too—as Mrs. W. F. Fuller of
Brooklyn noted, with a benefactor's heart-glowing—her
prized plant thrived, and it gave, to the broad St. Johns, new
beauty.

Her water hyacinth so thrived, indeed, that within ten
years it had covered some fifty million acres of the river and
of the many tributaries to the St. Johns; for cattlemen, who

noted that their herds fed with complacence upon the water hyacinth, had distributed it among lakes and streams everywhere in the neighborhood. The fact was discovered far too late that these plants contain so few solids as to afford, practically, no value as food.

Meanwhile, the floating bulbs of the water hyacinth increased always in numbers; and they continued to enlace their strong thick roots with the roots of one another, in the form of larger and yet larger rafts, which began now to hinder the progress of boats. The navigation of the St. Johns, in brief, became threatened by the frail-seeming water hyacinth. Since there was not any known way to get rid of the lovely plague, an appeal was made to the scientific destructiveness of the United States government; and Washington showed its compassion so far that during the next forty years a total of $598,170.69 from the nation's money was spent upon a continuing attempt to destroy the water hyacinth.

Yet Mrs. Fuller's water hyacinth still thrives.

The United States Engineer Office at Jacksonville devotes nowadays an annual average of about $75,000 to a partial control of this pest, with the aid of especially designed 15-foot boats equipped fore and aft with circular saws which slash through the floating rafts of bulbs at the rate of ten acres a day; for without this constant labor, it is certain, the St. Johns within ten years would become unpassable; but the water hyacinth still thrives, as an ever-living memorial to the good intentions of a gentlewoman who is now safely interred, near Brooklyn, and can do no further hurt.

Returning to the east bank of the St. Johns, one finds that beyond Lake Monroe the dark peacefulness of the river is momentarily shattered, where the waters of Blue Springs enter the St. Johns with abandon. Somewhat beyond this commotion, yet two more lakes vary the monotonous shore line. Of these, the first is Lake Beresford; and the second is Lake Dexter, a notable plantation site of the last century, during which, in the early 1830's, it restored good humor to a snarling John James Audubon, and caused him to write, with that customary immoderation which seems to beguile every student of life's more simple aspects, in praise of its birds and wild oranges.

Twenty-five miles west of Daytona Beach, the St. Johns expands into the largest and, as it were, the superb pendant of its chain of lakes, Lake George, which reveals, throughout every winter, to the gaze of properly assessed tourists, a length of eleven miles. Here, to the north end of the lake, stands Drayton Island, the two thousand acres of which once formed the southern boundary of Zephaniah Kingsley's large seraglio and patriarchal 90-mile-long slave kingdom, both of which he attempted to keep fertile and contented with Biblical piety.

Beyond Lake George, the river is joined by its main tributary, the Oklawaha, which Sidney Lanier—not inexcusably, but even so, with a lushness of diction such as one has learned more ordinarily to associate with the prattling elder poets of New England—declared to be "the sweetest water-lane in the world." This confluent parallels the St. Johns for a distance of some fifty miles before turning eastward, near Orange Springs, so as to enter the larger stream; and if with equilibrium you can endure yet further statistics, about four hundred thousand acres, or more, between the Oklawaha and the St. Johns have been incorporated, by the divergent activities of democracy which daily constrict human living, into the Ocala National Forest for the preservation of unhampered plant- and animal-life.

The east bank of the St. Johns is next broken by Dunn's Creek, in which the U.S.S. *Darlington,* while on a scouting trip up the river, ran upon a scuttled Confederate blockade runner, the historic yacht *America*—whose unequaled record, in having extricated a silver cup from England's not unadvertised fondness for good sportsmanship served afterward, through a dreary series of yacht races about Long Island, to assist Sir Thomas Lipton in advertising Lipton's Unequalled Tea. The bluff a bit farther north of Dunn's Creek, where once stood Charlotta, recalls the benevolence as a reformer and the intolerability as an acquaintance of Denys Rolle, Esquire. This not unfamiliar alliance of traits in a philanthropist led to his founding here a colony for the penitent prostitutes of England, as well as to its disruption after their repentance, under the rejuvenating effect of Florida's climate, turned out not to be nocturnal.

At Palatka, the St. Johns makes an elbow turn such as pushes its banks a full mile apart. Rafts of huge cypress logs towed down the river are here cut (it is instructive to reflect) into forty million feet of lumber annually, in what is reported to be the largest cypress mill in the world. (Nothing in Florida, let it be explained, is ever described, by the peace-loving, without a suitable coalescence of superlatives.) As the river completes this elbow turn, it passes by an orange grove, the former property of Colonel R. G. Cole, at Orange Mills, where in the April of 1870, General Robert E. Lee passed an entire night during the triumphal four-day tour of the St. Johns made by the unhappy president of Washington College.

Opposite St. Augustine is the site of the old town of Tocoi, terminus of the St. Johns Railway, which in the 1870's defied human credulity by conveying the more heavy freight and all the passenger traffic of the river steamers overland, to St. Augustine, upon wooden tracks not less than eighteen miles long. Beyond Tocoi, the eye of appreciation can still repose with delight upon the edges of the once very extensive Fatio plantation, at New Switzerland, as well as of William Bartram's indigo plantation (which recolored the literature of western Europe); and at Mandarin, may avert with embarrassment from the copulatory-looking huge oak tree about which Harriet Beecher Stowe erected and infested a winter residence.

As for the west bank, the St. Johns flows, darkly and equably, past Green Cove Springs, and Magnolia, and Hibernia. Beyond them is the mouth of Black Creek, the second largest tributary of the St. Johns. Then appears Orange Park, where, yet again, Zephaniah Kingsley contrived a negotiated peace between God and his bank account, and where Mrs. Stowe puzzled over the remarkable conduct of her own son; and where nowadays the Yerkes Laboratory would seem to commemorate the mental strivings of both these Pharisees, through its study of primate biology. Still farther along is a creek distinguished, if but ambiguously, by bearing the name of Daniel McGirth, that stanch colonial patriot during the first years of the American Revolution, whom of a sudden a horse turned into a Loyalist, and whom afterward the dictates of self-protection transformed into an outlaw.

At the head of this 70-mile-long broad stretch of the St. Johns, which after passing Palatka ranges in width from one mile to more than three miles, the river suddenly varies where now sprawls, and exports a vast deal of lumber, the modern city of Jacksonville. It is here that, with an afore-mentioned abruptness which colored blood red two hundred years of American history, the river turns at an angle from its previous course; and flowing eastward, thus makes of itself a complete natural barrier between some half of Florida and the north parts of the United States. When once the English had come to Jamestown, this irrational-seeming about-face of the St. Johns toward the Atlantic proved to be rather less important as a freak of nature than as a factor in North America's development; and perhaps nowhere in geography has the excursiveness of any river's flowing been attended by results more turbulent.

—Whereafter the St. Johns becomes a tidal outlet, some twenty-three miles long, pursuing, among very broad salt marshes, a tortuous course to the ocean. Upon its northern bank appears a fringe of sea islands, which terminate in Little Talbot Island and in Fort George Island, just inside the mouth of the river; and to the south side, the fishing village of Mayport still commemorates the name of that day upon which the first Europeans to discover the St. Johns first reached its banks, to begin with delight a tragedy.

3

The River of May

Seventy years after Columbus had inadvertently discovered a new world, two high-masted royal *roberges* and a large sloop, sailing from the French seaport of Dieppe, completed a tedious voyage as bare of incident as it was of legality. They cast anchor, in what custom decreed to be Spanish waters, just off the Atlantic coast of North America.

The patron of this quiet enterprise was Gaspard de Coligny, head of the French Protestant party; and since his noble if necessarily furtive object was to usurp, in the

Western Hemisphere, a safe refuge for the Reformed Religion, his deputy had been chosen with care. Admiral Jean Ribaut, reputedly the best seaman not merely of France but of his era, and in very many battles an attested defender of that rigid Huguenot faith which he esteemed far too highly to coarsen through private practice, commanded this small expedition, of 150 Protestant marauders, which had now paused about twenty-three miles east of the present city of Jacksonville in Florida.

"Then perceiving toward the north a leaping and breaking of the water, as of a stream falling out of the land into the sea,"—runs Ribaut's account of the first incursion of the St. Johns into Aryan history,—"forthwith we again set up sail . . . And as we had done so . . . there appeared to us . . . a great river." At its mouth the French spent the night in perturbed anticipation of what the morrow might hold for them, in lands to which rumor ascribed no less of opulence than of evil. When the rising sun had caused the dew on the dense foliage ashore to glisten, Ribaut with a small party of adventurers entered this river, a slight distance, in rowboats; and landed on the north bank.

They found awaiting them some scores of smooth-faced, hawk-nosed and tawny-colored Timucuan Indians, who, says Ribaut, were "all naked and of good stature, mighty, fair and as well shaped and proportioned of body as any people in all the world; very gentle, curious and of a good nature." Their bodies were most handsomely painted with figures of blue, of red, and of black—all executed as well, the admiring French declared, as any European artist could have done. Either decorum or sartorial elegance led many of these Timucuan warriors to screen their "reins and privy parts" with breechclouts of gaily colored deerskin; and had caused the women to bedrape the middle of their otherwise bare persons with a brief festooning of gray Spanish moss. Yet these pagan women, "although well-favored," as Ribaut records, were well-behaved also, to an un-Protestant extent: for he adds, with a stray flavor of aggrieved remembrance, that they would not allow any French Lutheran to approach too near to them with dishonest intentions.

Inasmuch as all this occurred upon the May Day of 1562, Ribaut christened his new-found stream the River of May. He then bestowed upon the Indians' leader, and a half dozen or so of the foremost warriors, gowns of blue cloth garnished with · yellow fleurs-de-lis. Crossing to the south side, the adventurers received an equally heart-whole welcome from equally naked and equally friendly savages. At the conclusion of these amenities, which involved the exchange of "gifts of haberdashery wares" and glass beads for tropic fruits and "much loving entertainment," the white men entered and viewed the country.

This land was, said the French admiral afterward, in the best vein of Floridian advertisement, "the fairest, fruit-fullest and pleasantest" he had seen anywhere. It abounded in honey, venison, wild fowl, forests, woods of all sorts, palm trees, cypress, cedars, and bay trees, as well as "the highest and greatest and fairest vines in all the world with grapes accordingly." Strange birds of many colors and sizes and some equally unfamiliar beasts the French observed also in these incomparable domains. A fact of more grave importance was that the natives appeared to possess an "abundance of gold and silver, precious stones and other great riches"; their arrowheads were of sharp-pointed turquoises; and these Indians had pearls as large as acorns which they were well willing to exchange for a looking glass or a penknife. When

the Frenchmen returned to their ships for the night, it was
with a complacent reassurance as to the veracity of many
wonders about which they had heard through the reports of
Columbus.

The next day, Ribaut set up, to the south side of the
river, near the modern site of Mayport, a stone pillar bearing
the coat of arms of his sovereign; and he claimed for France
the surrounding lands which a pope previously had declared
to belong to Spain by right of discovery. The French then
sailed up the coast; not far from the present city of Charleston, in South Carolina, they left a small military force, which
soon perished after an attritionary indulgence in cannibalism;
and Ribaut went back to Europe prosperously.

In the mean time, a religious conflict had roused the
magnanimity of all France, and the seaport of Dieppe, to
which the River of May expedition returned, had become
the center of such enormities as customarily attend human
zeal. A nominally Protestant England, lying just across the
channel from the high chalk cliffs under which Dieppe
nestled, offered to Ribaut a more tranquil refuge, and to
England he went.

There his accounts of the semifabulous fairyland surrounding his newly discovered huge river so cordially aroused
the concern of English empire builders that by-and-by his
fervent descriptions were printed (as *The Whole and True
Discouerye of Terra Florida*) and were thus made available
for such highly cultured persons as could read. Among these
was Queen Elizabeth, to whom an offchance of securing, for
her small and weak but ambitious country, a foothold in
these lands claimed by her former brother-in-law, Philip II
of Spain, was not averse. So Ribaut was summoned to Hamp-

ton Court. His recital, in a private audience which was
granted to him after the queen's happy convalescence from
smallpox, as to the tribal customs and large wealth of the
aborigines, excited alike her curiosity as a spinster and her
greed as a Tudor; and evoked the conclusion that an alliance
with these opulent heathen would serve nicely the English
exchequer.

Accordingly, the French admiral was called more and
more often to the side and service of the 29-year-old monarch of England. He was awarded an income of 300 ducats
and a fine home in return for such personal and official services as a hardy and widely traveled mariner, in the prime of
his forties, was well able to render to an unmarried queen
of easy conscience and debatable virtue. People whispered
smilingly; and yet difficulties ensued. Among the men named
to organize with Ribaut an English expedition to the river
which France had discovered and Spain claimed, was found
much unmistakable dishonor and disloyalty. Ribaut's own
part in the matter stays uncertain; but charged with some
obscure design to betray his Protestant comrades in the proposed voyage, to the Protestants of his native land, he was
lodged, with precarious safety, in the Tower of London.

During the two years which Ribaut spent in prison,
before having his liberty restored as unexplainedly as it had
been curtailed, the religious wars in France subsided; and
Coligny's attention was again directed to the development
of a French colonial empire in the American lands of his
Catholic Majesty, King Philip of Spain, under the commodious cloak of Huguenot ardor. Another expedition to the
River of May was prepared; and since Ribaut as yet remained the unwilling guest of England's rate-payers, in the
strong Tower of London, his lieutenant during the first voy-

age, René Goulaine de Laudonnière, was appointed to take charge.

Now, the opportunities of this American venture were not wholly restricted to the conqueror and the colonizer: for did there not exist, in this faraway land of beauty and of friendly inhabitants, who in an earthly paradise clung to the old ways of Arcadia, a most favorable field of exercise for the talents of an artist? Jacques Le Moyne de Morgues, a young painter, who, like Ribaut, was a native of Dieppe, thought so.

One's burly, bearded townsman might influence the future of kingdoms, for a decade or more, through the covetousness and the international larcenies aroused by his printed panegyrics as to the fair land called Florida: but could not a highly gifted artist—such as was Jacques Le Moyne de Morgues, meditation suggested—perform a task just as noble, and in the long run even more useful, by drawing from life the leading figures of Florida's unique and prehistoric culture? and by thus recording for all time—*ære perennius,* meditation cited hereabouts—wild institutions which differed so utterly from the trite customs of western Europe? Young Jacques Le Moyne took fire at the thought of his rendezvous with a duty so beneficent.

He applied to Laudonnière; by whom he was engaged forthwith, "when we should reach the Indies . . . to map the seacoast, and lay down the position of towns, the depth and course of rivers, and the harbors; and to represent also the dwellings of the natives, and whatever in the province might seem worthy of observation."

So, when the second French expedition, of some three hundred male adventurers and of four remarkably vigorous young spinsters, anchored at the mouth of the River of May, in the June of 1564, Le Moyne the painter was among those who peered at the lovely land wherein most of his fellows were to find death, and he, the materials to interpret for Europeans a new mode of life. Guarded by twenty-five soldiers and with Le Moyne at his heels, Laudonnière landed, as Ribaut had done, on the south bank; and the white men were warmly welcomed, just as before, by an affable assemblage of the aborigines. Their leader, who was called Athore, Le Moyne describes as "very handsome, prudent, honorable, strong, and of very great stature, being more than half a foot taller than the strongest of our men; and his bearing was marked by a modest gravity which had a strikingly majestic effect."

It reminds one—does it not?—of Swift: "The Emperor of Lilliput is taller, by almost the breadth of my nail, than any of his court, which alone is enough to strike an awe into his beholders. His features are strong and masculine . . . his body and limbs well proportioned . . . and his deportment majestic . . . His sword was almost three inches long."

Athore exhibited to his guests, with frank pride, the several sons and the two daughters whom he had begotten, after his father had secured a divorce, upon the still buxom person of Athore's mother. Athore showed also, to the white men, how the stone column ornamented with the arms of France continued to be worshiped by his tribesmen; for the Timucuans, through a pardonable error, had assumed this column to represent the same emblem of fertility which they themselves honored. It followed that about this symbol of French sovereignty in a Spanish land lay many devout pagan offerings of fruit and of game, along with vessels of perfumed oil, and bows and arrows; and wreathed around the supposedly phallic column were those garlands of fresh, gaily colored flowers with which the Indians were accustomed to decorate their own idols of this genus.

Here was a droll confusion before which Laudonnière paused to stroke his small chestnut-colored mustache; he cleared his throat; yet after all, he reflected, his own object in this country was to seek unrestrained freedom in religious matters. So he said only:

"This tribute to the upright manhood of the great Admiral Jean Ribaut and of all France is not incongruous. It reveals that which we call *l'esprit gaulois*."

With the friendly aid of the natives, the French explored the near-by country; and according to Le Moyne, they selected as the locale of their settlement "a certain mountain," but, in reality, a bluff some ninety feet high, which rose impressively on the south bank of the river, about six miles inland from its mouth. Here they prepared for divine worship; and thus discovered that because of their extreme haste to reach a land in which every church rite of the Reformed Religion could be performed without let or hindrance, they had failed to include among their necessaries a pastor. Nevertheless, they thanked God, extempore, for a safe passage into North America. They then set about lustily, with spade, saw and ax, to erect homes. Palm fronds were used to roof the wooden huts builded by these settlers about a small fortress, which they named Fort Caroline, in honor of their young King Charles IX; and Le Moyne's drawing of this fort, when supplemented by contemporaneous descriptions, gives, it is thought, a fairly accurate idea of this the first Christian settlement within the borders of the present United States of America. The log fort is described as triangular in form, and as protected upon one side by the river, and on the other two sides by a moat and a wall of sod nine feet high.

Throughout the course of a year after the founding of this colony, Le Moyne observed many forms of early American life, and all these he depicted with a delighted wonder. Concerned, in chief, with his interpretation of native manners and customs, as being "worthy of observation," he did not record, so far as extends our knowledge, the activities of his comrades. But it is known that they were, for the most part, devoid of the resourcefulness of colonists and empire builders. They borrowed, bought, or they stole food, from their friendly Indian neighbors, nor when resentment arose among the latter did the white settlers hesitate to enforce their demands through violence. Moreover, the French quarreled among themselves, and so far put by the standards of law and honesty as, for a while, to imprison their leader Laudonnière while his rebel followers engaged in piracy, among vessels of the Spanish West Indian Fleet. Finally, upon the verge of starvation, and disillusioned over the river site which Ribaut had declared to possess possibilities beyond any rhetoric, they decided to abandon America; and began to prepare a couple of but dubiously seaworthy ships against their return to France.

While the French Huguenots were so employed, came to the mouth of the River of May four ships belonging to England. One of these, the *Jesus of Lubeck,* was from the royal navy of Queen Elizabeth. The others were owned by Captain John Hawkins. Consummate seaman, ruthless slave trader, successful smuggler, and a diplomat of parts, he was now returning home after having sold to many traders along the Spanish Main, illicitly but with a clear profit of sixty per cent, the Negroes whom with an equal lawlessness he had captured in Guinea. It was a business venture in which Queen Elizabeth owned a fourth interest.

So, the present mission of Captain Hawkins, to the lower east coast of North America, was to investigate for the benefit of his royal partner in theft those unforgotten reports of Jean Ribaut as to Florida's fabulous riches; and putting aside for a while the role of pirate, Hawkins, who very much needed some reliable information from the forlorn French colony, purchased it through courtesy and generosity.

In all likelihood, Captain John Hawkins was really moved, to a British extent, by the troubles of the French. Such was the distress of the colonists, his reports declared afterward, that they were reduced to eating acorns and roots; yet they were too improvident, it is added, to "take the pains so much as to fish in the river before their doors, but would have all things put in their mouths." Their incompetence, indeed, so deeply touched the piratic heart that Captain Hawkins made a free gift, to these shiftless foreign wretches, of some twenty barrels of meal, in addition to fifty pairs of shoes, and four pipes of beans, along with "divers other victuals" such as he could spare without any personal inconvenience. He then, casually, questioned his debtors as to the lands over which his queen meant to extend English rule.

He confirmed Ribaut's statement about "the highest and greatest and fairest vines in the world" so far as to observe that the French had made from them twenty hogsheads of excellent wine. He became enthusiastic about the fertility of the soil, and foresaw a rich trade in lumber and naval stores. Fish grown to the length of a man appeared to be commonplace phenomena; and everywhere one saw deer and yet other edible animals. The English were impressed, in particular, by three strange birds: the flamingo "having all red feathers and long red legs"; the "Egript," as they called the egret, "white as a swan"; and the pelican, which even though it were "feigned to be the lovingest bird . . . and rather than her young should suffer want, will spare her heart's blood out of her belly," they found to be uncommonly ugly.

In fine, this country, which belonged perhaps to Spain, and was held insecurely by France, would afford just that opportunity which was needed, by Captain Hawkins' partner and sovereign, Elizabeth Tudor, for the colonial expansion of England. The uncertainty as to the land's legal ownership appeared, in the eyes of both buccaneers, a trifle.

So urgent became the loving-kindness of Captain Hawkins, in the light of these thrifty considerations, that he offered to the colonists a free passage home. The French declined; but instead, bought from the Englishman one of his smaller ships, on which to make the voyage unaided. Convinced that they would soon leave America or starve, Hawkins then bade them farewell—foreknowing the Atlantic seaboard would be made available in no long while for the English, now that the French had been evicted from this wonderland, called Terra Florida, by their own improvidence.

4

The River of Blood

THE Huguenots did not leave the banks of the River of May in quite the manner they planned. Everything had been made ready for their departure, when, in the late August of 1565, seven unfamiliar ships cast anchor near the French column, and a small sloop brought to Fort Caroline, of all unexpected persons, Admiral Jean Ribaut, freed from the Tower of London and once more in Coligny's pay. Surprise became optimism when the inhabitants of the river bluff learned that on board these galleons were six hundred more or less Huguenot settlers, sent over by Coligny, comprising soldiers, and carpenters, and farmers, and laborers, and a number of liberal-minded young women. The orders brought by Ribaut were explicit. The French were to remain; the Spanish claim was to be ignored; and the English, should they come again, were to be repelled.

Yet the Spanish were more active in reclaiming these lands than the French had expected. Ribaut had been at the little river settlement scarcely a week when five Spanish ships appeared near the mouth of the river and challenged the larger French fleet. Taken by surprise, the French sailors cut their cables, and escaped to sea, leaving at Fort Caroline, in perturbed uncertainty, Ribaut and all the newly arrived colonists. The less speedy Spanish caravels then went southward; and Ribaut, upon the return of his truant fleet to the river's mouth, made ready to engage the enemy. Sailing south some twenty-five miles, he sighted the Spanish expeditionary force near what was later to be the city of St. Augustine.

Philip II of Spain was determined to rid Florida of all Lutheran marauders. His Catholic Majesty had observed, with a hostile concern, the depravity of the French heretics in attempting to found a settlement upon the banks of a river which, by not merely human law but through a pope's special bull, belonged to Spain; and in response to his angry protests, tendered with grieved etiquette through an ambassador, the French replies had seemed to be no less deficient in a right reverence for Rome than for veraciousness.

"—For indeed, Don Francisco," declared Burdin, the French king's head secretary, "the river upon which our oversea colony has been established, through the right of discovery, is in lands which, very long before the absurd intrusions of the Jew called, to the best of my recollection,

Christofero Columbus, were visited, over and yet over again, by Breton fishermen."

"Why do you force me to discuss such nonsense?" returned Don Francisco de Alava. "Whether you assert this river to be in the Land of the Bretons or among the Mountains of the Moon, the province which is being invaded by the Huguenot vassals of your king is that same Florida which our Mother Church granted to Spain a full seventy years ago."

Burdin answered: "For more than a hundred years, monsieur, France has possessed her just claim to this river in the Land of the Bretons, that claim which today she is exercising. And before his accession, that good Pope Alexander VI, who made this unreasonably illegal grant, was called, you must permit me to remind you, Rodrigo Borgia. The Borgias were subject, at times, to frailties, both human and criminal."

"You speak of sacred matters, señor," remarked shocked Alava, "with the depraved levity of a Huguenot."

"Monsieur," Burdin protested, "I speak merely as a mathematician when I make bold to confess that a hundred years appears to me a longer period than is seventy years."

"That is not the point," said Don Francisco; and he flung off in a huff.

Indeed, neither gentleman had mentioned the main point involved, which, as they both well knew, was the dangerous, or if you so preferred it, the uncommonly convenient nearness of Fort Caroline to the Bahama Channel; through which waterway, in coming from Mexico or from South America, passed the West Indian treasure fleets of King Philip when they transferred American gold to Spanish coffers. And with these Catholic fleets the French Lutherans at Fort Caroline had begun to deal religiously, in the capacity of pirates.

Although Spain and France remained at peace, King Philip reasoned that this tortuous question—where his own subjects and the subjects of his brother-in-law were entitled to settle in America?—could be decided, without straining the ties of kinship, through an oversea war kept unofficial. To conduct it Don Pedro Menéndez de Avilés was pardoned (for his irregular behavior, when captain of the West Indian Fleet, in refusing to accept bribes) and was let out of jail. One of the most able mariners of his day—in which he was ranked second only to Jean Ribaut—and a stanch Catholic as well as a high-minded patriot, the unchained zealot was more than eager to punish the French and to eliminate the Huguenots, those "thieving pirates and perturbers of the public peace," as he termed them with a hint of reproof.

Thwarted in his first attempt, at the mouth of the River of May, to engage these criminals, he now sailed southward; and began vigorously to found the city of St. Augustine. He had little time for the maturing of his plans before Ribaut and the larger French fleet hove into sight. Menéndez, at this instant, it so happened, lay becalmed, upon his flagship, outside the harbor bars; and by all human standards was helpless. Yet when the French heretics made ready to capture him, a sudden and most violent storm swept southward the entire French fleet, in the same moment that the ship of Menéndez was lifted over the sand bars into the safe harborage of Matanzas; and by this hurricane, which dispersed the French, the Spaniards were saved from destruction. Menéndez very properly thanked God for the miracle; and proceeded to take of it full advantage.

Menéndcz guessed that when the French fleet sailed to attack the Spaniards, the French fort upon the River of May must have been left virtually defenseless. Without hesitating, he deserted his own fort, and led his army, of some five hundred soldiers, through the storm's continuing fury, across almost impassable swamps, toward Fort Caroline; and found that his inspired guess was correct. Taken by surprise, the two hundred French who had remained at the settlement were attacked before breakfast with implacability.

It is recorded that most of the garrison were yet in bed. Since the powder of the Spaniards was wet, from the storm through which they had traveled, and the cords of their arquebuses had become water-soaked, they could use only their swords and pikes to kill the French, some few of whom expired with decorum in their nightshirts where the majority, who had slept naked, perished nakedly. Yet of the French garrison not all were put out of living, because forty-odd of them escaped in the darkness, and reached by-and-by the mouth of the river. Nor, inasmuch as Menéndez had given orders to spare the women as well as all the boys who were under fifteen, were very many of these killed during the tumult intentionally. Moreover, Don Pedro was at pains to rescue and to preserve the French drummers and trumpeters, so that they might be added to his military band. Like all narrow-minded persons, he delighted in music.

His first act, after the last throat had been slit, the few prisoners hanged, and the resultant corpses added up to a gratifying total of 132 dead Lutherans, was to remove the French arms from over the main entrance to the fort, and to replace these abhorrent symbols of theft and heresy with the golden castles and the blood-colored lions of Spain, surmounted by a cross and two angels. With his own hands, Governor Menéndez burned nineteen packs of playing cards, which were found in the fort. He disapproved of the vice of gambling. He burned also at this time six large boxes of religious books, so called, exceedingly well bound and handsomely gilded, but pertaining to the abominations of the Protestants' wicked faith.

With these moral duties discharged, Menéndez burst open the fort's arsenal, and he discovered it to be well filled with dry powder and new arquebuses. He then collected his soldiers, and addressed to them the ensuing exhortation:

"My dear and very valiant brothers in Christ, it is not we but Our Great God Himself Who has performed these wonders, miraculously, in behalf of Spain and of His Own holy cause. He has revealed to us of late His exceeding tenderness, which in this arsenal He perpetuates. I consider that without delay we ought to make plain our gratitude to the sublime Father of all mankind, inasmuch as, in this moment of need, His ever-loving care has provided us with firearms."

Having uttered these inspiring words, Menéndez knelt, and he entreated a continuance of Heaven's charity, before leading his men into the woods south of the fort. His prayers were answered, at once, with a benignant generosity, since in these woods they found thirty-eight naked Frenchmen, whom the Spaniards shot down, laughingly and at leisure, with the French guns. It was excellent, said the Spaniards, to wind up a hard day's work with this half hour of sportsmanship.

Menéndez then gave way to the frailties of human flesh so far as to sleep, they record, for almost four hours, so extreme was his exhaustion. Upon awakening, he appointed a lieutenant governor to take charge of the fort, where Menéndez left all the Spaniards except thirty-five soldiers, with whom he returned down the seacoast, toward St. Augustine and the missing French fleet.

Fewer than fifty Frenchmen, including Laudonnière and Le Moyne, under cover of darkness, escaped the swift ruin which annihilated their fellows. Never before had Le Moyne come so close to despair (with his fine paintings ablaze behind him) as during the nightmare-while that these refugees —who at best had fled in their nightclothes, but most of whom went in complete nakedness—limped through deep forests, and swam across snake-infested swamps, on their way to the ocean. Reaching there, they equipped one seagoing vessel, the *Greyhound*, with the necessaries provided by some smaller ships anchored in or about the mouth of the River of May; and at once left America.

Meanwhile, their fellow Frenchmen who, under Ribaut's leadership, had sailed out against the Spanish only to encounter a hurricane, had been swept down the coast of Florida, from St. Augustine to somewhere near the present city of Daytona Beach. Their ships were wrecked thereabouts, and the survivors were thrown upon the lean mercy of the delighted Indians of Seloy, who sportively scalped about fifty of them. Bedraggled, without food, and desperate, the remainder trudged northward, in an attempt to reach the river settlement at Fort Caroline, which they believed still to be theirs. About fifteen miles below St. Augustine, they were met by Menéndez, at the head of a small force, and to him they surrendered. He fed all his enemies—rather bountifully, to grant him justice—and he then killed them, ten at a time, amongst the grass-grown sand dunes and the gleaming coquina ledges of Anastasia Island.

Jean Ribaut was so far spared as to be the last Frenchman murdered. He adorned his final moments with a suitable Latin quotation; he spoke condoningly as to life's necessary briefness; and of the handsome red felt hat which he was wearing he disposed with a no less affable good breeding.

"—For since, quite plainly, I shall have no more need of it, now that you are going to remove my head, Monsieur Vicente," he remarked, to his executioner, "I would be honored should you consent to retain this hat, as a souvenir of our meeting."

So bravely, and with such complete fitness, died Jean Ribaut, within a few miles of that great River of May which he had been the first of Europeans to discover.

—Whereupon Menéndez, with all his more sanguinary and pressing duties attended to, proceeded in the furtherance of his king's scheme, for the colonizing, by loyal Spaniards, of the lands from which the French Lutherans had been evicted in a fashion so satisfactory and thorough. He re-named the river settlement in honor of St. Matthew, upon whose feast day it had been captured; and he likewise rechristened the River of May the River of San Mateo.

Thus more or less edifyingly, in the present United States of America, closed the first episode of European influence upon the first river to which Europe brought its civilization and the benefits of modern warfare.

5

Afternoon of an Artist

Laudonnière and Le Moyne, with some fifty other survivors of the Fort Caroline massacre, let it be remembered, had escaped to sea in the *Greyhound*; and "God . . . gave us so fortunate a voyage, although attended with a great deal of suffering," Le Moyne said, later, "that we made the land in that arm of the sea bordering on England which is called St. George's Channel."

With the aid of M. de Foix, the French ambassador to England, Laudonnière then proceeded toward Paris; and Le Moyne, it seems likely, accompanied him, inasmuch as the painter, in subsequent writings, refers to a personal interview with the French king, Charles IX, "when, after having escaped from the remarkable perfidies and atrocious cruelties of the Spaniards, I returned to France." Yet for a Huguenot, with the large Massacre of St. Bartholomew in the making, upon a scale qualified, in even its more casual murders, to bedwarf into insignificance the Massacre of Fort Caroline, France very rapidly became Florida's rival, as a desirable place from which to be absent; so that Jacques Le Moyne de Morgues removed into England with haste and discretion.

He reached London eventually; and there, as "the skillful painter James Morgues," his alias combined with his art to support the refugee in fair comfort. To the one side, he gave drawing lessons; to the other, Sir Walter Raleigh, who was then planning to found a colony in North America, paid liberally for James Morgues' knowledge of that continent. James Morgues, for the rest, married—upon terms so conventional, it would seem, that at no time did his wife ever bother about his wishes—and in due course, he averted from the pensive sympathy of a physician to the brisk attention of gravediggers, during the year of grace 1587, after having become as well thought of by his British neighbors, in Blackfriars, as a foreign painting fellow, who in private perhaps ate frogs, could ever hope to be.

Toward the end of his life he occupied himself in reproducing from memory those long-lost paintings which he had first made in America, beside the huge brown River of May, when Jacques Le Moyne was young. He remembered all that starved wild time so very clearly, it seemed, now that, to James Morgues, life had become a fairly safe and a rather humdrum affair. He wrote out, too, with an old brown-splotched hand, which became rheumatic also, nowadays, the full story of his stay in Florida; and to each painting he added an account of its subject matter. He got together, in this haphazard fashion, a strange small masterpiece which has not anywhere in humane letters its peer.

Le Moyne refused steadfastly, none knows just why, to sell either his manuscript or his paintings of such matters as, to him, had seemed "worthy of observation" in Florida. He may have weighed them as a sort of memorial to Jacques Le Moyne, from out of which James Morgues ought not to wring profit. His widow shared in this sort of romantic nonsense not at all, inasmuch as after her husband's decease she disposed of this book, to a publisher, at once. It thus happened that Le Moyne's story, along with forty-two engravings made from his spirited and intricate, naïve paintings of the natives of Florida, of their wars and their tribal customs and religious observances, and of aboriginal pursuits in general along the River of May, appeared in 1591, in the *Great Voyages,* as published by Theodore de Bry at Frankfort-on-the-Main; and that, in Germany, with the aid of a Latin text, pictorial art gave to Europeans its first great autochthonous interpretation of North American mores as composed by a Frenchman in London.

Great, let it be repeated! for it is hardly possible to exaggerate the historic and ethnological value of the unique engravings which at this time were made from the paintings of Jacques Le Moyne, and which nowadays survive, one notes regretfully, in the illiterate isolation and the special bindings of "a collector's item" alone. These reproductions have suffered, somewhat clamantly, from the editorial freedom which was then allowed to an engraver in his copying of a picture—so that, for example, the Indians do not always have the features of an Indian, the very features which Le

Moyne himself describes in the accompanying text; nor does
the trim brick-and-stone building which, in these engravings,
represents Fort Caroline, very strikingly resemble Le Moyne's
account, in the text, of that crude assemblage of turf-sods
and logs and faggots which was the actual fort. One grants
furthermore that, in hypercritical bosoms, stags which are
taller than palm trees, or ships more diminutive than their
seamen, may strike a frank note of incredulity; for Le Moyne
honored strange laws of perspective.

There is, in the English version, yet another sort of
discrepancy to be noted, by the curious, in the fifteenth
engraving, which depicts—nominally—how the victorious
Indians "never left the field of battle without shooting as
deep as they could an arrow into the armes of each corpse."
The engraving affords proof that, to the extent of a mono-
syllable, the text has here been altered, in the interests of
decorum.

But in the main, Le Moyne has set down a very nearly
complete social history of the Timucuan Indians, in an inspired mélange which, despite some incoherent or droll
touches, remains none the less invaluable and unique. —For
Le Moyne omits little. His pictures show to us, for instance,
the simple and drastic ways of the Timucuans in healing all
such of the ill as stayed vigorous enough to survive tribal
remedies, along with the Timucuans' far milder methods of
killing deer, and of cultivating land, and of securing for
their crops the required sort of weather by worshiping a
stuffed stag. His art is equally explicit as to how these Indians
dried fish and cured meat, and builded towns (or burned
the towns of an enemy) and indulged in tobacco as well as
in blood-drinking, and punished criminals, and fought

against alligators—which reptiles, under the influence of Le Moyne's imagination, display dimensions they have not retained. His pictures record also how the comely but sullen-seeming hermaphrodites with whom Florida at this time abounded, to a degree not since then equaled, were made useful; with what elaborate rites the marriage of a Timucuan chief, to each one of his numerous wives, was celebrated; the pomp with which a first-born child, among the better classes, was clubbed to death by the local clergyman; and just how all self-respecting Indian widows mourned, beside the brown River of May, for those husbands whom war or disease had removed from their exuberant bosoms, even in the same instant that (for this ritual was very comprehensive) each desolate widow asked for another husband.

Nor was Jacques Le Moyne one whit more interested in the domestic annals than in the sports of the red race. With what fervor they delighted in archery contests his pictures show—and in foot races, as well as in the depressing pastime of eating lukewarm food out-of-doors, in unsuitable places, such as people yet call a picnic. They played a crude sort of basketball; and they especially liked to display their skill as swimmers in the placid waters of the River of May.

The Timucuans, in brief, set an admirable example for all Europe, through the temperate hue of their recreations; so that many notable Christians, "who both shorten and disfigure their lives through an immoderate indulgence"—the text of the French painter here philosophizes, with it may have been a side glance at the insane Hapsburgs, the homosexual Valois, and the syphilis-racked Tudors—"very richly deserve to be put under the authority of these savages . . . to be taught sobriety."

The enthusiasms of Timucuan warfare, also, Le Moyne has depicted, with a perhaps somewhat morbid insistence upon the more ugly details of scalping, of dissection, and of murdering without hurry. Yet he does not neglect the more statesmanlike aspects of Floridian carnage; but instead, shows to us how Holata Outina (who was called rather more generally the King of Kings), after having consulted in due form with his privy council of sorcerers, was accustomed to paint himself all over, with bright crimson, before beginning any campaign against the unprovoked aggressions of warmongers. On account of these diplomatic precautions, Outina was never conquered.

The strategy of Chief Saturioua (father of the handsome Athore, and the overlord of some thirty villages) was of a different school, it would appear from another engraving, inasmuch as the foreign policy of this monarch, in times of dissension, was to exalt toward the sun a consecrated wooden vessel well filled with spring water, which was then spilled out upon the ground with the prodigality of a native-born American executive who is dealing with taxpayers. This precautionary measure ensured that the blood of all foreign enemies would be spilled in exactly the same way, by-and-by, at least possibly; and in fact, with a more civilized substitution of wealth for water, this ancient and generous Timucuan custom has been observed even nowadays to retain its practitioners.

6

"Not Peace but a Sword"

IN THIS MANNER did it happen that a river in Florida became, in Europe, much talked about. So was it that, from Le Moyne's fine pictures, and from the writings of Jean Ribaut and of René de Laudonnière—as well as, nowadays, from the official reports of the new governor of Florida, Don Pedro Menéndez—the peoples of Europe acquired a large deal of more or less accurate information as to the aborigines who lived on or about the remote stream which Spaniards called the River of San Mateo. And the native Indians were beginning to observe, with an interest not any whit less lively, the ways of their white neighbors.

In 1562, the Timucuans, all whose own boats were hollowed-out logs in which you rowed laboriously, had viewed with surprise, and some disquiet, the strange and huge and high-masted, white-sailed ships of Jean Ribaut's expedition. Their knowledge as to the tribal customs of the East-people broadened during the fifteen months when, at Fort Caroline, Laudonnière and his three hundred shiftless settlers starved rather than work. And then, in 1565, the Indians had seen, briefly, a more brisk and quite different tribe, who were led by the chief called Hawkins. After that, the East-people came yet more numerously, through the return of Ribaut, along with his six hundred colonists. All these were followed by a still different tribe, under the chief called Menéndez.

Menéndez had gratified, as was wholly proper, the need of a brave warrior to kill as many of his tribal enemies as he found possible. He had murdered all the Frenchmen except only the few that were able to escape with Laudonnière and Le Moyne. Here was conduct such as even Saturioua, who had maintained always a firm alliance with the French, could regard with respect and with comprehension.

Evidently, said the Indians, these white men, although insufficiently civilized to scalp or to dismember their defeated enemies, might be sane and companionable enough, when you once got to know them. In one matter alone did the white men remain obtuse beyond argument. They could not understand that all such precious metals and gems as the Timucuans possessed had been obtained either in barter or in warfare with tribes from the far south, or else had been salvaged from the wrecks of these East-peoples' own ships. You could not ever convince any one of them that your country did not abound with gold mines and silver mines and enormous pearl fisheries. That seemed to be with these East-people a fixed delusion, before which you had to be patient.

While the Timucuans thus reasoned with philosophy, Menéndez had begun with vigor to explore the former River of May, which he, the more piously, had christened the San Mateo. Accompanied by a hundred soldiers and sailors, in three brigantines, he ascended some distance beyond the island of Edelando, in the present Lake George. His ways were benevolent during all this trip, and his bleak smile unfailing. Menéndez quite honestly wished to make friends with the neighboring Indian tribes, and thus to discover economically if the San Mateo would not afford to him a most useful short cut toward Mexico and the riches of the Far East. And his reputation yet again was served by the elements, to such an extent that at one point along the river he was hailed as a rain-god—perhaps even Tlaloc of the Nine Ocelots himself —when upon his advent, rain, which had been withheld for nine months, poured down in torrents. After that, however, the Indians honored this no doubt divine personage with an inconvenient respect, which, by causing them to run away from him as fast as they could, checked freedom in conversation.

When Menéndez had ascended the San Mateo far enough to observe that before him the river narrowed and seemed undecided in its course, he returned to its mouth, after having spent in this exploration trip twelve days. He learned, at least, as he wrote to his king, that the great river extended seventy leagues inland, and "turns southeast, emptying into the bay of Juan Ponce, and from there to New Spain"—as the Spaniards then called Mexico. He gave, in short, as to the San Mateo River, a profound and well-balanced official report, which displayed an unusual knowledge of geography, as well as the not infrequent official failing of being incorrect.

Foremost among the matters about which the Indians had to learn from the lean Spanish governor, Don Pedro Menéndez, were the true facts of religion. They were told bluntly that their present mode of adjusting their lives to the supernatural, through adoring any special member of the masculine body, was inadequate, and would have to be changed. Not every one of the Indians stood ready to accept this pronouncement, at once, forasmuch as the white men themselves appeared to be divided as to what they called the Christian faith. This had been proved, rather strikingly, by Menéndez' massacre of the entire French colony, not simply as enemies, but as heretics. And besides, it was Jean Ribaut, after all, who had first introduced into Florida the religion of the East-people by setting up a fine phallic image. The discrepancy seemed puzzling.

These Indians were destined yet further to notice incongruities in the religion of the white men as this religion was interpreted to the Indians by the strangely robed persons, those Christian priests, who corresponded to, and who behaved not unlike, their own sorcerers.

To begin with, one finds in Spain, a few years earlier, the primal and miraculous link, in a long chain of happenings, to connect the perplexed Timucuan Indians with their first missionary. —Which means that in 1533 Pedro Martínez was born, in Teruel, in the kingdom of Aragon, of which his uncle was regent. Upon nearing manhood, Pedro Martínez received the usual training given to young Spaniards of the upper classes, in loose living and literary graces, at the University of Valencia. While achieving honors in philosophy, music, the globes, and rhetoric, he thus made for himself a high name among noble ladies through his vivacity—which was seasoned by discretion—and among gentlemen, through his aptness at homicide. "A youth of quick wit, but quicker hand," it was said of him, "there was rarely a duel in the city in which Martínez was not principal, second, or promoter": and in fact it was through this foible for swordsmanship that he attained sanctity.

—For it so happened that, very early one morning, young Martínez had an appointment to fight against an adversary who failed to appear. Since he had not any other engagement in hand before breakfast, and disliked time-wasting, Don Pedro Martínez, on his way home, went, out of curiosity, into the newly established home of the Jesuits in Valencia, to sit through a mass; and he there suffered a change of heart.

He set about obtaining his admission into the Society of Jesus through the forthright expedient of declining, upon any other terms, to leave the chapel. Inasmuch as tact combined with charity to prevent the well-bred Jesuit fathers from overharshness, in getting rid of the regent of Aragon's nephew, it thus came about that Don Pedro Martínez, after a probationary period of serving as their cook, was accepted by the religious.

The energy which, before his conversion to correct behavior, he had devoted to his opponents, either in bed or upon the field of honor, was now applied to the demands of his brotherhood. So complete became his addiction to holiness that his too constant scourging of himself, and his rash indulgence in hair shirts, had to be limited, by his superiors, to a half hour daily. With the zeal of a crusader, Father Martínez served as chaplain in an expedition against the infidel Moslems—through which he developed "a special gift for assisting the dying." He completed his theological studies at the University of Salamanca; and in Gandia, it is said, he once stopped a bull fight singlehanded. For some years he was rector of the universities of Valladolid and Monterey; he preached fluently, but with tact, in nine languages; and this never idle prelate was overjoyed, in 1566, to receive, as one of Spain's pre-eminent clergymen, that appointment to the mission field, in faraway Florida, for which he had been begging ever since he relinquished cooking to assume holy orders.

At Puerto Rico the ship upon which Father Martínez sailed toward his evangelistic labors in the New World separated from the main fleet. Pilots unfamiliar with the Florida coast became confused; and when land was sighted, the captain ordered a small boat to put ashore, so that the persons in it might determine the nature of the aborigines and the degree of their predilection toward Spaniards. Not overconfident as to a friendly reception, the sailors in this skiff refused to go forward without the protective company of their spiritual leader, who had become deeply endeared to them during the voyage from Spain; and with a disregard of mere carnal dangers, such as was characteristic of the good priests of that day, Father Martínez entered the boat without hesitation. He, with two Spanish and six Flemish seamen, then made for the shore; and so reached the present Cumberland Island, off the south coast of Georgia, in the September of 1566, in a rising storm which during that same night blew the larger ship out to sea, not to return.

The eight sailors, who were rain-drenched, and hungry, and without any hope of saving their lives except through the infirm possibility of reaching St. Augustine, very much needed the comfort and inspiration which Father Martínez at once gave to them. He spoke, at refreshing length, as to the high privilege which they now enjoyed, of suffering discomfort, and it might be death also, in their service of the True Faith—addressing the two Spaniards in their native tongue, and then repeating his remarks, to the six Flemings, in Flemish. They all prayed together; and properly encouraged, the party turned southward, toward St. Augustine. No native showed himself, but as if in answer to their prayers, they came to a cluster of five wigwams, away from which before the approach of white men the owners had departed in so great haste as to leave behind them a half-grown barbecued alligator.

At first, Father Martínez said it would not be right for his people to partake of this food without its owner's consent, but he at last permitted them to eat half of it. In return, he cut out of his Bible the two pictures most prized by his little flock—which represented, by one account, The Seduction of Lot and The Rape of Tamar—and he left both these sacred engravings, beside an exact half of the alligator, in payment for what they had taken.

Refreshed by this sturdy meal, which they assumed, gratefully, to have been catered through divine intervention, the castaways then proceeded, in their tiny boat, down the inland waterway; and thus reached Alamacani (as the Spaniards called the present Fort George Island) in the mouth of the San Mateo River. There they unknowingly came into lands which were tributary to Chief Saturioua, friend of the French.

Being yet again in need of food, Father Martínez landed near the present Mount Cornelia. Against the advice of their leader, seven of the sailors went ashore in the belief that a second miracle would now aid them to satisfy their hunger in yet another deserted wigwam. No sooner had they passed into the thicket than twelve Indian warriors appeared of a sudden, each armed with a club, and they came toward the boat in which remained one sailor and Father Martínez.

"These savages intend mischief," said the sailor, who was called Flores. "So let us row out into deep water, beyond reach of their horrid clubs."

"No, my son," replied Father Martínez: "for it would not be right to desert our comrades. Let us go to them."

Thus speaking, he stepped out of the boat with that same dislike of time-wasting which, indirectly, had led him to become a Jesuit; and was seized at once. The natives dragged the unprotesting priest ashore. He was last observed, by the less mettlesome Flores, to be holding up a crucifix, and composedly addressing toward Heaven his final supplications, while twelve pleased Indians clubbed him to death. In this way, upon an island at the mouth of the San Mateo, did these impulsive savages bestow upon Pedro Martínez the supreme honor of primacy in martyrdom, among the not numerous persons who, upon the eastern seacoast of the present United States of America, any where between Miami and Bar Harbor, have thus merited sainthood.

"Surely the good father went straight to heaven," Flores remarked, as the sailor rowed away—"where, please God, at some more convenient season, I shall meet him again."

Indeed, a great many others were grieved by the tragic death of the once famous duelist. "Both noble and virtuous," declared Governor Menéndez, "Father Martínez alone would have accomplished more good than can now be achieved by all the soldiers of Florida."

"He would have accomplished more good," said Menéndez; for "to accomplish good" was the declared object of

all the white men who invaded the San Mateo River: yet
their standards, as to just what was, or was not, "good,"
may very well have seemed to the neighboring Indians a
bit multifarious.

In Rome, at all events, the Holy Father considered it
was good to turn the American aborigines from their idola-
trous manners; to convert them to the True Faith; to uphold
in all parts of the New World that same faith, with sword
and rope, against the evil influence of Protestants; and by
thus protecting the Indians from license of thought, to allure
them into the mental quietudes of Catholic civilization.
Since the country through which flowed the San Mateo had
been pre-empted, along with almost all the Americas, in the
name of the kings of Spain, it was to them that Pope Pius V
allotted secular control of this program; and in the New
World the Roman cross became inseparable from the Spanish flag.

It was thus the duty of Governor Menéndez, as the
representative of Spain in Florida, to direct such missionary
work; and he began his religious labors, with flawless zeal,
by removing from the banks of the San Mateo, as well as
from mortal existence, all Huguenots. He had established St.
Augustine in the same year of grace 1565, and during the
following year he planted a small fort near the present city
of Charleston. He made friends with the Indians so far as
he was able, although Saturioua remained unreconciled. And
then, in 1567, Menéndez went back to Spain to report
progress, to receive the Holy Cross of la Çarça, and to collect
a well-earned reward of 200,000 ducats, in addition to yet
more missionaries and settlers, along with a store of adequate
provisions, for his American colony. During his absence the
French returned to the San Mateo, calamitously.

7

Concerning Patriotism and Piety

THE head of the French party which of a sudden invaded the San Mateo was nobly born young Dominique de Gourgues, a former galley slave; and he brought with him, from the gutters of Bordeaux, upon one large caravel and two smaller ships, about 150 gallant rascals. The party landed a little distance north of the river's mouth, in Saturioua's land, and formed with him an alliance. The combined armies of the French and the Timucuans then attacked the former Fort Caroline (which was now called, it may be remembered, Fort San Mateo) just as its garrison, of some 250 Spaniards, were rising from dinner; and took the place

by surprise. During this onslaught the French were remarkably merciful, and killed no one of the Spaniards who was
willing to surrender. It thus happened that almost all these
Spanish soldiers—barring, of course, those whom the Indians
scalped and mutilated—were made prisoners, and had their
hands tied safely.

In the forest beside the river, De Gourgues addressed
them, and proclaimed himself to be a stanch Catholic, who
regarded them, one and all, with much loving-kindness, as
being his brothers in Christ. For that reason, he (we refer
to Dominique de Gourgues) must ask his fellow communicants, in mere fairness, to believe that with the heresies of
the depraved Huguenots who, as the representatives of
France, had preceded him here in Florida, he had not any
sympathy. The most illustrious Don Pedro Menéndez de
Avilés (whom, with a sincerity no less fervent, de Gourgues
regretted not to observe among the many valiant Catholics
now present with their hands tied) had acted with a com-
mendable piety in eliminating these Huguenots.

And yet, to the other side, messieurs—

De Gourgues coughed. He sighed. He asked for a cup
of water. It was brought to him. He sipped slowly.

—To the other side (he continued) in this world it
was demanded of every gentleman to be a good patriot as
well as a good Christian: and as best one might, to recon-
cile the two not infrequently discordant roles. The task was
not always easy. The task might sometimes develop an
aspect such as, from the private point of view of both victor
and vanquished, might appear repellent. De Gourgues preferred, however, not to dwell upon these subtle considerations, such as the less patient among his hearers might find
tedious. He would turn, instead, to plain matter-of-fact. He

desired merely to remind his audience that the quite properly rebuked heretics had all been Frenchmen. Don Pedro, after having made prisoners of about two hundred Frenchmen, and after tying safely their hands, had killed two hundred Frenchmen, in batches of ten. He had fed them first. That was true. That point should be weighed. Yet of food, it so happened, no one of the present company could have any pressing need, inasmuch as everybody had dined, at undisturbed leisure, hardly an hour earlier.

"—So that, in brief, messieurs," de Gourgues concluded, "what now detains me from the performing of my plain, if somewhat painful, duty as a French patriot?"

Since nobody replied to him with coherent logic, he then hanged his two hundred or so prisoners, ten by ten. So careful was he to avoid miscomprehension, however, that to each corpse he affixed a placard stating that these Spaniards had been killed, not upon religious grounds, but merely as murderers. He burned their fort afterward; and with the honor of his native land scrubbed clean through blood and destruction, young Dominique de Gourgues returned homeward, pausing but once, so as to capture, to rob, and to sink along with their crews, three rather large Spanish galleons.

Here yet again was conduct such as dark Saturioua could regard with respect and with comprehension. Hah, but even so, the chief reasoned, as he wiped clean and put back into its deerskin sheath his scalping knife, in what special feature did the behavior of a Christian patriot, whether Spanish or French, differ from that of a well-reared Timucuan Indian?

After the departure of de Gourgues, and the furious but impotent return of Pedro Menéndez, Spanish fortifications along the Atlantic coasts were so very vigorously strengthened that the Floridian Indians did not hear any more about French incursions, nor even about the outrageous attempt of Captain Hawkins' people to steal land from King Philip III, in the north parts of Florida, at a place they called Jamestown. But in compensation, these Indians heard more and yet more as to the good motives of the padres who had journeyed out of the sunrise to make tangible the goals outlined by the Holy Father at Rome, and who came attended by soldiers. The savages soon learned that, if they did not save their souls according to Roman methods, their bodies would be enslaved; so that, bending before the loving-kindness and the firearms of the white man, a majority of Timucuan Indians embraced the Christian faith with a temperate affection; and began, upon the whole, to obey, without any too frank criticism, the orders of the missionaries.

Many sites upon the San Mateo figured handsomely in the progress of Christian improvement. One of the larger missions stood near Picolata, just west of St. Augustine: from which point, divers crusaders for the Catholic faith crossed the river so as to establish military and missionary posts as far west as now stands Tallahassee, and later at St. Marks, on the Gulf of Mexico. Steadily, at more and more stations along the river, now more and more priests taught Christian doctrine to the uncomprehending Indian; and initiated him, day by day, into Christian methods of warfare, of building cabins and barns and chapels, of herding cattle, and of raising crops; while during the evening they supervised with discretion the activities of their pupils in games and dances and liaisons. That these forerunners of a new sort of restraint for Americans met with at least a modicum of success is proved by a letter written at this period, to the queen of Spain, by his Grace the bishop of Cuba—who had found the lately acquired skill as carpenters of these Christian Indians to be edifyingly displayed in the construction of some large churches. With a tinge of discontinuity, the bishop adds that the fare of these industrious converts comprised pumpkins, hominy, beans, and deer meat.

The best known of all these cultural and religious centers upon the San Mateo was the Franciscan mission of San Juan del Puerto, near the mouth of the river, in sight of the Atlantic. Here, over temporal affairs, presided shrewdly a feminine ruler, the Cacica Maria, who, by a personage no less nominally sonorous than his Very Reverend Lordship Bishop Juan de las Cabezas y de Altamirano, had been converted and baptized and married, to a Spanish soldier called Clemente Vernal, all during the one calendar month of May, 1606. The later, not inillustrious lectual exploits of her prince consort need not here detain us; but in tribute to his accomplishments, his wife's panegyric survives, as to most explicitly just what an Indian woman who did not marry a Spaniard was missing. One regrets it cannot be quoted. And at San Juan del Puerto, also, Father Francisco Pareja advised the Indians as to matters which, if of no less interest to both sexes, were more habitual to the pulpit.

Father Pareja, a Castilian, who had entered the mission field in Florida in 1594, and who until 1610 passed most of his time at San Juan del Puerto, on the present Fort George Island (from which Father Martínez had departed toward Heaven), combined with the more noble generalities of religion the patient and plodding particularity of a scholar. He mastered the Timucuan dialect, and he set about preserving this language by translating it into Spanish, in addition to describing many customs and peculiarities of the Timucuans. He made numerous expeditions to the interior, there gathering information which he recorded with care. When not ministering to the spiritual needs of his copper-colored children in the spirit, he devoted his hours of leisure to writing, in both Spanish and Timucuan, on the fifteen Mysteries of the Rosary, the pains of Hell, the joys of Heaven, the governance of Purgatory, and a brief exposition of Christian doctrine in general.

It is therefore to Father Pareja, next only to Jacques Le Moyne, that the world stands indebted for what today is known of the speech and manners of these Indians, who have been extinct since the 1820's; for in Mexico, early in the seventeenth century, were published the works which Pareja composed in the little mission on the St. Johns. They include a bilingual catechism, in Timucuan and Spanish, as well as a *Confessionario*, which presents (with that accurate knowledge such as the consecrate appear always to have acquired, somehow, with the more intimate details of viciousness) an important account of Timucuan beliefs and abnormalities, in addition to a treatise on the syntax and pronunciation of their heathen dialect.

At about this time, as has been stated earlier, the San Mateo began, gradually, to be called, in honor of the Christian stronghold at its mouth, the River of San Juan—or in brief, the St. Johns—and so, to this fourth and continuing name for the river we may with profit adhere henceforward.

So far-reaching, for that matter, was the influence of Father Pareja and his colleagues at the mission of San Juan del Puerto that in the practice of Christian rites all the aborigines who lived near the rechristened Welaka became passably adroit: and for their further betterment a choirmaster was imported, in the person of Father Pedro de Chozas. He proved an excellent and sympathetic teacher.

Even so, the advance of his choral instruction was hindered, unforeseeably, by a long-established Timucuan custom that to the winner in a ceremonial foot race should be presented a freshly culled human scalp. This he was afterward privileged to wear about his leg like a garter. The cazique of Tama, having laid a wager with the cazique of Quaque for the two of them to participate in a friendly contest of this nature, in which the prize would be furnished by Father Chozas, entered the classroom of the last-named tumultuously; and set about removing the top of the choirmaster's tonsured head.

With an undiminished dignity, Father Chozas dismissed his pupils. He knelt then beneath the obtrusive knife; and addressing God the All-Father, requested that, if such were the will of Heaven, he should now be afforded the grace to suffer martyrdom. His organist, however, prevented any immediate increase to the ranks of the blessed, for this Gaspar de Salas fetched an arquebus and put to flight the cazique.

Upon the following day, it is recorded, Father Chozas prayed for a much-needed rain, which fell promptly; and the cazique accepted this utilitarian sort of wonder-working, in place of a scalp, with resigned cheerfulness. Amicable relations were resumed henceforward, along with choir practice.

Chozas gave to these Indians two lessons a day; and they soon became able to chant both high mass and vespers. During the last week of Lent, indeed, and especially upon

Maundy Thursday, "they gave up all to piety, spending the entire night in religious revels"; and the fact was noted that, as if to reward their devotion, the birth rate among these Christian Indians became little short of miraculous toward the holy season of Christmas.

8

Friends in Need

Now, while the Timucuan Indians upon both banks of the St. Johns were making more or less progress with that particular type of worship taught to them by the Spaniards, still another Christian sect caught the notice of these river Indians so as to arouse wonder.

This sect was the Society of Friends. The Quaker faith was introduced into Florida, informally, by the September storms of 1696, when the barkentine *Reformation*, bound from Jamaica to the city of Philadelphia, was wrecked near

Jupiter Inlet, a bit north of the present site of Palm Beach. From out of this disaster twenty-four survivors reached land alive. They included nine sailors, some Negro slaves, and several Quaker passengers of unblemished integrity—of whom one, to be sure, was but "a sucking child of six months old," the son and namesake of Master Jonathan Dickinson, himself among the preserved Friends. It was the elder Dickinson who no great while later recorded, and either published or allowed to be published, in Philadelphia, in 1699, an account of the party's misadventures.

His tale tells, first, how the entire company were captured by Indians, each one of them foaming at the mouth, who "looked on us with a wild, furious Countenance"; and how, after being stripped of clothing, the Quakers were made ready for execution, as being "Nickaleer." By this name did the Indians now call the English, from killing whom (since the founding of South Carolina) the Spaniards did not at all violently discourage their red allies. In these touch-and-go circumstances, Dickinson reports, "A notion arose from one of us, that if we should put ourselves under the denomination of Spaniards . . . this might be a means of our delivery."

It is a most dignified way of stating that the sailors and the Quakers decided they would all lie as to their nationality and religion; and profess themselves to be Spanish Catholics. One or two of the sailors, by good luck, had a sufficient smattering of the Spanish language to color with possibility the impromptu fraud; and so the doubting but cautious Indians allowed the black-and-white party to proceed, in the general direction of South Carolina, along the east bank of the St. Johns.

Since presently they overtook the survivors of yet another wrecked English vessel, says Dickinson,—"the *Nant-*

wich of Bristol, which came out of Jamaica with us,"—six sailors and "a woman passenger named Penelope" were thus added to the masquerade. Thenceforward the self-styled Spaniards traveled, between the St. Johns River and the Atlantic, "through the thicketty woods," very slowly, with large discomfort, and feeding as they best might upon palmetto berries, coco plums and sea grapes; yet the main cause of their suffering had now become the unfortunate conduct of Master Robert Barrow, who, most inconveniently, had fallen a victim to high moral principles.

Of this Quaker elder's past it is recorded that he had been "a resident of one of the northern counties of England" (said to be Lancashire) until 1694, when "the Spirit of God . . . requiring him to come over into these parts . . . he was not disobedient to the Heavenly call." Yet now a revered elder among the Society of Friends—whose duty it was "to advise others, as he, in the wisdom of God, may find occasion"—had fallen, through the insidious counsels of cowardice, into the most monstrous if not uncommon malpractice of lying, by misrepresenting himself to be, not merely a Spaniard, but a misled practitioner of Rome's errors. Here was a degradation before which no conceivable breed of Quaker conscience could be asked, in common reason, to lower its dreadful head. It was a sin before which the conscience of Master Barrow, at all events, and with aggrieved scorn of his fellow apostates, ramped. He would lie no more, he stated.

Nor did he. Henceforward, while his comrades were "some . . . asserting what was wrong, others concealing the Truth . . . this honest-hearted Man, being directly asked the Question, 'Nickaleer, Nickaleer?' . . . could do neither; but in Simplicity answered, 'Yes.' " Yet worse, when "a barbarous People, such as were generally accounted Men-Eaters," asked of him if his fellow Friends were not English, he again answered, "Yes."

It seemed to the other Quakers an excess of virtue, because almost daily did groups, gangs, or squads of the river Indians attack the castaways with drawn scalping knives and with loud hoots of "Nickaleer! Nickaleer!" And placidly Master Barrow agreed with the savages. He stated that his entire party was "Nickaleer" in the same instant that, like Father Chozas, he bowed toward the flashed knives his patient head. To his more tactful companions in religious faith, the obtrusions of any such relentless candor became distressing, and highly blameworthy; for this implacable Robert Barrow, just for his own soul's sake, was exposing their bodies to danger. They could but convey to the Indians, by discreet signs and whispers, the fact that their padre was a bit touched in the head; for they were all Spaniards; nor did earth anywhere afford more stanch adherents to the Holy Father in Rome, the twelfth Innocent.

The Indians doubted, sometimes; they may well have questioned, in any case, the desirability of a spiritual guide whom his own followers knew to be demented: yet the ways of the East-people, declared the Indians condoningly, are not our ways. The customs of the white man are very far beyond comprehension. So they still let the Quakers and the sailors and the slaves trudge forward unscalped, through never so many "thicketty woods," even unto St. Augustine.

In that city the Spaniards received them with a slightly disappointing lack of brutality; and although—as either Dickinson or his editor is at pains to remark—of a religion such "as doth not teach its Votaries . . . Compassion towards those they count Hereticks . . . clothed these naked People, fed their hungry Stomachs, and caused them to be conducted safely to Carolina." Thence, all but two of them were returned by the governor of South Carolina to the city of Philadelphia; they were made much of, as miraculously preserved martyrs; and Dickinson's account of their journey was at once put into print so that (of all unimaginable purposes) "it might testify to an unsympathetic and even hostile world," records Dr. Charles M. Andrews, without any apparent intention of levity, "that God was guiding those who accepted the truth."

For the persecuted Quakers this was a happy outcome, marred by but two mishaps. The woman named Penelope proved somehow to have become "big with child" during her stay among Friends; so that her grieved associates were compelled to leave her behind, in St. Augustine, to endure, among loose-living papists, the just punishment for her wantonness. Moreover, Master Robert Barrow, who alone amongst them had not rationally compromised with his conscience, "was taken very ill of the belly-ache and flux"—between which brace of disorders he soon died, in considerable agony. From the circumstance that those who had lived with a larger freedom survived and prospered, one hesitates to evoke a moral.

It, instead, appears sufficient to remark that, when Dickinson's account of his Floridian sufferings and apostasy was published, either he or his editors bestowed upon it the edifying and compendious title:

God's Protecting Providence, Man's Surest Help and Defence, in Times of greatest Difficulty, and most eminent Danger, evidenced in the remarkable Deliverance of Robert Barrow, with divers other Persons, from the devouring Waves of the Sea, amongst which they suffered Shipwrack; and also from the cruel devouring Jaws of the inhuman Canibals of Florida, Faithfully related by one of the Persons concern'd therein, Jonathan Dickenson.

—To which, one grants, the acerbity of hypercriticism might reply that Providence would seem to have defended the Persons concern'd rather less frequently than did perjury; that Robert Barrow was delivered from the devouring Waves of the Sea but to fall prey to the more lethal spasms of bellyache; and that no "inhuman Canibals" (with jaws of whatsoever nature) happen to traverse the text in its published form.

Yet the point here is, rather, that the observations of Master Jonathan Dickinson—when the Quakers paused to inspect the Timucuan town at the mouth of what Dickinson calls the "St. Wans" river—reveal in general the results obtained by the Spaniards during so many and, upon the whole, unselfish years of missionary work. The converted Indians were industrious; they lived in commodious cabins; and they possessed a fair number of fowls and hogs and wide fields of corn. They attended, at the prescribed seasons, a house of worship, over which presided an ever-busy and kindly Catholic priest. The native tribes of Florida, in brief, were, for the most part, up to 1700, allies of the Spaniards; and aided them with willingness in the establishment of military mission posts as far west as the present-day site of Tallahassee.

The aggressions of English colonists, marked boldly in 1670 by the founding of Charleston, weakened both the political and the spiritual influence of the Spaniards. Now came about increasingly frequent revolts of the Indians against the more chilling rigors of Christian routine and against the imposition of enforced labor. A degree of progress was still made, in some quarters, from time to time, but new difficulties seemed always to prevent a permanent foundation of missions and settlements along the St. Johns River such as the Spaniards were making in most other parts of their American colonial empire.

This lack of progress in the expansion of the Spanish system of worship and colonization appears to have been due partly to the but human nature of the Indians and partly to constant bickerings between church and state officials. In 1668, for instance, the curate of the church at St. Augustine reported to the king that the governor of Florida "lived without fear of God." It was a gubernatorial omission which yet other, more worldly-wise, clerical critics, who appreciated the value of some sexual interest as a sauce to mere atheism, amended forthwith into living "without fear of God, and as openly in sin as if his life were entirely moral with a legitimate wife in his house." This was not any sort of example, it was humbly submitted to King Charles II, for Governor Francisco de la Guerra y de la Vega to be flaunting before Timucuan Indians, who stayed always loth to put aside their lustful régime of polygamy.

Countercharges were at once laid, by the governor, against the friars, that they loitered in the plazas of the towns instead of instructing their flocks in the True Faith. Other supposedly holy fathers of the church maltreated the Indians, Don Francisco pointed out with grieved horror; for indeed, it was common knowledge that of the 400 Indians at one of the St. Johns River missions, 350 had fled from Christian instruction on account of their padres' too vigorous whips. Conveniently omniscient witnesses then testified that the shoulders of all these enforced backsliders into heathen error showed marks of the most cruel punishment inflicted by clergymen "who should be called Moors rather than Christians."

The perplexed Council of the Indies, when confronted by so very many inconsistent affidavits, could but vaguely recommend to everybody involved a little more "suavity and sweetness."

This period, in fact, was unmistakably marred by a lessening in gentle ardor by the Franciscans, who had succeeded the early Jesuits. Yet there were now other and even more serious dangers which leaders of the church were called on to overcome, because of the political rivalry between Spain and England, a great part of which was fought out within eyeshot of what both nations now called the St. Johns River. It was a contest very well designed yet further to confuse the understanding of the Timucuans concerning ethics, as they had observed European ethics to be practiced by the lax Huguenots and the relentless Catholics of France, by the bloodthirsty Spanish Catholics, or by the piratic Episcopalians and the perjured Quakers of England.

9

"The Odious Stranger"

NOMINALLY allied with the Spanish Catholic
St. John, who without protest had shared with their river
his good name, the Timucuans who lived on or about this
stream were permitted, none the less, as time went by, to learn
a vast deal more than proved pleasant about another saint.
This was St. George of Cappadocia, who represented a different form of worship; a quaint habit of not taking naps
during the daytime; another and a more briskly ejaculated
language; and, in short, the English nation.

Here is for hagiology no place. Otherwise, one might pause here to remark that St. George, like most of us, has been aspersed by detractors; and that these assert this duly canonized if unamply authenticated personage to have been a dishonest army contractor, who, in Nicomedia, at about the beginning of the fourth century, met with disaster, less on account of his pre-eminence in virtue than through the inferiority of his bacon. At all events, the caress of legend did—somehow—enrich his repute with a patina of holiness: so that (in Gibbon's agreeable phrase) "the odious stranger, disguising every circumstance of time and place, assumed the mask of a martyr, a saint, and a Christian hero; and the infamous George of Cappadocia has been transformed into the renowned St. George of England."

The first disciple of this Anglicized Cilician Arian to reach the banks of the St. Johns was that Captain John Hawkins, whose behavior in bringing his beans and some fifty pairs of shoes to the destitute French colony at Fort Caroline, in 1565, was entirely exemplary. His behavior upon other occasions—which involved the slave trade, the abduction of the tribes of Guinea, the robbing of Spanish ships, the rifling and burning of several towns, and the general activities of a sixteenth century buccaneer—was per- haps more open to question. Hawkins was, in brief, a fair representative of those dauntless admirals who established for Britannia an at least choric rule of the waves. The Eng- lish called them heroes; and the queen of England knighted them: but the rest of the world called them pirates and, when the chance offered, hanged them.

Twenty-one years after Captain Hawkins had displayed to the Floridian settlement at Fort Caroline the underlying warm benevolence of a forthright, bluff British tar, a near kinsman, Sir Francis Drake, without any depressive warning as to his intentions, attacked and demolished the Floridian settlement of St. Augustine. Such inhabitants as outlived their surprise fled toward the present St. Johns River; and the English completed their ruin of the infant city by hacking down the small orange groves, imported from out of Asia by way of Spain, such as already signalized in Florida the tiny beginnings of a vast industry. They then burned alive the captain of the near-by fortress of San Juan de Pinos; they burned what remained of St. Augustine; and after burning out, with hot irons, the tongues of a few dozen women, who —as Drake reported later, with the necessarily reserved judgment of a bachelor—"were ungracious, perchance from their husbands' having been killed before their eyes," these bluff, forthright British tars sailed toward England, to bask in all England's approval.

Some two years later, the chivalry of England—aided, it is true, very much as Menéndez had been aided, by an unusually high wind—succeeded in crippling the hitherto invincible Armada of Spain. It was this disaster in the English Channel which heralded the decline of Spain's sea power; and which brought about the disintegration of its colonial holdings beyond the Atlantic: for the English at once began to take over not merely all which was portable, but large provinces likewise, in the north parts of America.

By 1607 a handful of Englishmen had managed to settle Jamestown, in the land which was called Ajacan by the Indians, and Florida by the Spaniards, but by the English, Virginia; and with Jamestown began the inexorable, sturdy, and resistless southward march of many Englishmen, who had helped loyally to raise the moral standards of England by leaving it, toward the Spanish St. Johns. In the same instant that any hostility toward Spain was denied, the kings of England proceeded to parcel out, either to their personal friends or to colonizing agencies, large parts of Spain's territorial possessions in America. No English patriot asked, untactfully, the question, how or just when these lands had become English property? So, by 1630, land grants for many regions between Albemarle Sound and the St. Johns had been distributed among British magnates. The Earl of Clarendon and his seven associates received, in 1663, an especially large grant, upon which was settled the name of Carolina and a small colony of Englishmen. Two years later—and again, without any tedious bothering over the affair's lawfulness— this patent was so far increased as to include, in theory at any rate, all the north half of the peninsula of Florida; so that by 1670, Spain had been compelled, through the settlement of Charleston, to recognize the undeniable if illegal English ownership of lands within 120 miles of the St. Johns River.

Yet the Spaniards held on. Through the channels of diplomacy, and by military attacks, they disputed each inch of aggression, even though they were forced, always, in the end, to release vast tracts which they had not yet been able to colonize. They regarded, now, the St. Johns River, to the north and to the west of their chief outpost, St. Augustine, as a natural, and even as a perhaps tenable, barrier against the invaders; and so, in 1672, between St. Augustine and the St. Johns River, Spain began the construction of a fort. This was the Castillo de San Marcos, of which the iron-gray walls, sixteen feet thick, rose some thirty feet above the shore line; and of which the enclosure was capable to maintain fifteen hundred soldiers.

Reminiscent and symbolic of the grandeur of Spain's

once all-powerful empire, and in design a superb example
of the finest seventeenth century architecture, this majestic
last lair in North America of harsh despotism, as opposed to
the more oily imbecilities of an electoral government, was
builded, by Indian labor, out of coquina, or shell rock,
hewn from the quarries upon Anastasia Island just across the
inlet which human unreason has elected to call the Matanzas
River. Inasmuch as it had been here, precisely, upon Anastasia
Island, that Menéndez made complete his grasp upon Florida
by murdering all the French Lutherans, so now the same
blood-stained slabs of conglomerated small seashells upon
which Spain in her prime had conquered the entire peninsula
of Florida without mercy were digged up without delay; and
were put together so as to form a shelter for Spain in her
decrepitude. One scents here, as in the unexplainedly atrocious decease of Master Robert Barrow, an intended moral,
without being able, quite, to divine its nature.

Within the Castillo de San Marcos, at any rate, despotism
could hope to die in the grand manner, among suitable surroundings, for this place was regal. England, in common with
all other petty brabbling enemies, this place defied with an
exceeding, grandiose, cold strength. The view, both of the
bay and of the ocean, from the terreplein of San Marcos was
unexcelled; its interior was furnished with complete comfort,
even sumptuously; and its drawbridge spanned a 40-foot-
wide moat surrounding deep-set, snug dungeons, in which
a vast number of Englishmen were to have the tedium of their
imprisonment varied by refinements of torture. Indeed, upon
the construction of this fortress was expended so much
money, not a little of which went into the pockets of dishonest officials, that a king of Spain once voiced his regret

that he had not ever seen the most splendid castle which belonged to him.

"—For to judge by my accountants," his Majesty remarked, "its doors must be made of gold, and its walls builded of silver pesos."

Yet even while the hard-pressed Spaniards were stirring up, with cowhide whips, the industry of their Indian peons toward a more early completion of this castle, many representatives of England's uncompromising pursuit of cash and empire were percolating, unostentatiously, through the woods between the city of Charleston and the St. Johns. Their quadruple mission was: to trade for fur with the Indians; whenever possible, to capture Indians whom they might sell as slaves; at all seasons to foment among the Indians enmity against the Spaniards, those blackhearted papists who were scheming to make slaves of free-born Indians; and to secure among the Indians, as allies, such strong heathen tribes as by-and-by could abet England in a Protestant kingdom's moral and remunerative duty to conduct bandit raids against Florida. One of the most efficient leaders in this English commerce, in fine furs and in double-dealing and in his fellow creatures, was Henry Woodward, that dashing South Carolinian, who time and again but narrowly escaped capture by the troops of the governor of Florida; yet who did not ever fail to leave behind him a courteous letter expressing his regret that, for the present, necessity should have debarred him from the delights of any personal acquaintance with Governor Cabrera.

Thus futilely, if with superficial politeness—and aided upon both sides by the Indians, who, despite their lack of sound Christian training, remained fond of bloodshed—proceeded an intermittent but unending warfare which resulted in the destruction of a great many far-outlying Spanish fortifications, and which virtually disrupted the Catholic mission system. By the beginning of the 1700's, the Spaniards were being continually harassed, and had been fretted back into a defensive condition, of which the frontier was nominally the Savannah River, but in reality the St. Johns. Meanwhile, the Castillo de San Marcos had been completed, no whit too soon for the Spaniards.

The Castillo de San Marcos sustained its first attack in 1702, when for the not instantly apparent reason that a grandson of the king of France had been crowned in Madrid, the province of Florida was invaded by an English army, to which fate had granted the distinction of being led by the current governor of South Carolina, Colonel James Moore. So very feebly opposed, and in consequence so wholly complete, was Colonel Moore's destructiveness throughout the unguarded country north of the St. Johns, that when he crossed the river, near the present site of Jacksonville, in order to attack St. Augustine, the Spaniards had reached a state of gray hopelessness, which seemed justified by his prompt capture of the city. The victorious if unengaging vicar of "the odious stranger," St. George of Cappadocia and England, then turned with an Olympian calm, such as many persons called stupidity, to destroy the Spanish fort. The conqueror thus gained—it was stated, with a shade of unkindness—"a foolscap rather than a laurel wreath," inasmuch as the fort proved to be blandly impregnable. San Marcos, in brief, withstood an ardent two months' siege by the English army without appearing to be at all impressed; and compelled Governor James Moore to retreat northward in supreme disgust, in but scantily controlled anger, and in open bafflement.

He seasoned his inadequacy, however, with a fair deal of ingenuity, by at once attending to the publication, in London, of a volume entitled, *The Successes of the English in America, by the March of Colonel Moore, Governor of South Carolina, and his taking the Spanish Town of St. Augustine near the Gulph of Florida.* The text, it was remarked, did not dwell tediously upon the Castillo de San Marcos.

During the following year, Colonel Moore, who had been removed from his office as governor, yet further assuaged his hurt pride, and he refurbished his out-at-elbows reputation as a soldier, by returning into the St. Johns area with a far stronger English force, attended by some thousand Indian allies. Inasmuch as he had over-well learned that San Marcos was best left alone, he ignored St. Augustine with British hauteur; and addressed toward places of a more susceptible nature the full ardor of his martial attention, persuasively.

When Colonel Moore had ended this second campaign, as begun by Protestants with artillery, and rounded off by the scalping knives of Creek Indians, only one village (at the cost of giving him its church silver) remained undemolished; an encouraging total of twelve papist mission houses had been destroyed; and almost fifteen hundred of their Indian converts to the religion of Rome had become the captives of Colonel James Moore. These deluded Indians were at once conveyed into South Carolina, where they were disposed of at auction to right-thinking Episcopalians: whereafter for a reasonable while, no harsh sign of the tyrannic Spaniards remained anywhere visible along the banks of the St. Johns save only the ashes of their burned homes, their hacked-down orange groves, and a rotting corpse or so which the English lacked time to bury.

10

What Mr. Castell Caused

WITH the Spaniards pushed back, southeast of the
St. Johns River, and protected only by the obstinate Castillo
de San Marcos, the northern banks of this river, in common
with the entire wild country between St. Augustine and
Charleston, which belonged in theory to Spain and in point
of fact to nobody, remained for some while a precarious trading ground for the English; a rich source of declamation

among Spaniards; and the facile prey of an occasional Caribbean pirate who had shiproom for a dozen or two Indian slaves. Then the future ownership of the north bank of the St. Johns was settled by Mr. Robert Castell, an empire builder whom a rather large number of historians have neglected.

Mr. Castell—"an ingenious gentleman well skilled in architecture"—accomplished forever notable results, in contradistinction to any special notoriety, when, in 1728, he published, at his own expense, *The Villas of the Ancients Illustrated (Large Folio)*. The book failed to find purchasers; the author, in consequence, was imprisoned for debt; and he so died, of the smallpox, during the following year, among the indescribable horrors of Fleet Prison, where during his incarceration he was visited, upon divers occasions, by his friend and admirer, General James Oglethorpe, the M.P. for Haslemere in Surrey.

The last-named philanthropist was approaching hoarseness at this time, on account of his daily demands that the House of Commons should take instant action in behalf of the oppressed Moravians of Bohemia. In Fleet Prison (thitherto an unfamiliar habitat) General Oglethorpe found rather more than enough oppression, along with yet other bloodchilling miseries, all which had the additional charm of being more tractably near at hand, to provoke an about-face such as was characteristic of this largehearted but unpredictable person—concerning whom Alexander Pope was to remark, a bit later, that "one driven by strong benevolence of soul, shall fly, like Oglethorpe, from pole to pole." Just so impetuously did James Oglethorpe at once throw overboard the oppressed Moravians, in order to salvage the oppressed of his own race and faith in Fleet Prison. To these unlucky followers of unthrift in business matters and of King Henry VIII in religion, rather than to the downtrodden adherents of Cyrillus and Methodius, General Oglethorpe determined henceforward to give over all his excesses in philanthropy; and to find, not for Bohemian, but for British wretches a more endurable refuge, in America.

—For in America, he now began to remind Parliament daily, there was still a great deal of Spanish land as yet unpre-empted by the English, between the Carolinas and the river called (he believed) the St. Johns. What person present (he made bold to inquire) could regard without unbounded enthusiasm the prospect of founding, in these half-savage and half-papist lands, a stanch Protestant colony, in which the more worthy of British bankrupts, instead of acquiring small-pox among highly unpleasant surroundings, could occupy themselves, far more commendably, by raising cotton, or hemp, or medicinal herbs, or, better still, by producing silk?

Silkworms, it was objected, had never been, and perhaps could not be, reared with success in North America. —Whereupon General Oglethorpe became eruptive with oratory and rebuke and memoranda and pamphlets, all which, in his best parliamentary manner, dwelled upon the circumstance that in the lands between South Carolina and the St. Johns River grew mulberry trees—the leaves of which tree, as any schoolboy could inform his honorable if misguided opponent, were the natural food of silkworms. What more could one ask?

None did, apparently, ask more, now that opposition was overshadowed by mulberry trees. The circumstance was weighed also that a buffer colony, between the Carolinas and Florida, if settled by paupers, such as in the long run were an expense rather than an asset to England, would absorb nicely the ruthless papist fury of Spain over being robbed daily, upon the best moral principles. So, in 1732, Parliament granted to "the American project of General Oglethorpe" £10,000; the gentry of England subscribed £26,000; about seven hundred debtors were released from jail to become pioneers; and General James Edward Oglethorpe was named governor of Georgia. He accepted the title upon condition that alcoholic liquors (barring only beer) should be declared contraband in the new colony; and that its official seal should represent a happy circle of well-nourished silkworms.

Such, in statecraft, was the unintended outcome of *The Villas of the Ancients Illustrated* (*Large Folio*), but for which weighty volume General Oglethorpe would not ever have visited Fleet Prison.

So then did it happen—under the far-reaching influence of *The Villas of the Ancients Illustrated* (*Large Folio*)—that a half dozen Indian scouts from above the St. Johns River reported to Spanish officials at St. Augustine, in the February of 1733, that General James Oglethorpe, with his seven hundred ex-prisoners, had landed early that month, in Spanish territory, some 155 miles to the north; and that these new invaders from England had already laid out a town, which they called Savannah. Liberal, not here to say licentious, in his interpretation of the charter of his colony, General Oglethorpe then dismissed as a triviality that special item which fixed the Altamaha River as the south boundary line of Georgia.

He remembered it may be, with a pang of remorse, his put-by Moravians, who still languished in Bohemia. He sent back for large detachments of them, as well as for some silkworms, some Highlanders, a sprinkling of Swiss, an assortment of Jews, and some Salzburg Protestants from out of

Bavaria; and he occupied more and yet more land beyond the Altamaha, so as to afford, for these unfortunates, each and all, homes. It was an extension of good works which presently caused General Oglethorpe—without any least shadow of authority from his own government, or from any other government upon earth—to erect an English fort on the same island, at the mouth of the St. Johns, upon which the Spaniards had maintained the mission of San Juan del Puerto until James Moore destroyed it. By Oglethorpe this fort was loyally named Fort George, not in honor of the Cappadocian swindler, but of the more honest, if somewhat less intelligent, second English monarch of the house of Hanover.

The establishment of an English fortress, even though it were prompted by strong benevolence of soul, within less than forty miles from St. Augustine, was an affront too high-handed to be tolerated by the Spaniards, howsoever accustomed they had become to regard theft as a vice which the British pursued as a virtue. Between English and Spanish officials arose controversies distinctly torrid, such as resulted by-and-by in a reluctant abandonment of the illegal English fort; but the name of George still hovered over that part of the river, no less tenaciously than did English aspirations.

Meanwhile, these persistent encroachments on the part of England had stirred up the harried Spaniards also into an outburst of fortifications. Antonio Arredondo, an able engineer who acted as chief of staff for the Spanish governor, now worked out a plan for holding safe the valley of the St. Johns against the valor and unfaith of the British. He like-wise perfected a system of small forts to defend St. Augustine. These fortalices were constructed at the mouth of the river and upon each bank of it directly west of St. Augustine—

namely, at Picolata on the east bank, and at St. Francis de Pupa on the west bank—now that the perturbed Spaniards made ready to preserve, at any reasonable cost, what little was left to them today of Spain's former formidable possessions in the present United States of America.

Nor to the north of them did philanthropy fail in precaution. Foreseeing the time when a formal declaration of war between England and Spain would enable him legally to attack St. Augustine and all Florida, General Oglethorpe now diverted his attention from the sad stubbornness with which every one of his silkworms (through a purely pedantic distinction between the *Morus rubra* and the *Morus alba* as its natural diet) died almost instantly after reaching Georgia; and he strengthened his military forces. He contracted an alliance with all three of the leading potentates in his neighborhood—who, at this period, were Raven, war chief of the Cherokees, and Malachee, king of the Creeks, and Tooanhowi, Mico of the Yamacraws—now that under cover of the first colorable pretext, all Georgia had made ready to defend the miscellany of its religion and the quiet of its hearthstones against the insolent aggressions of the retreating Spaniards. Yet the final and the most potent ally of General Oglethorpe proved to be Captain Robert Jenkins.

When Robert Jenkins, late master mariner of the brig *Rebecca,* was examined before the House of Parliament, in 1738, his grievance, to the light glance of casual sympathy, might well have appeared to be no less personal than remote. A good seven years ago, in fact, by his own account, had his ship, when about to return from Jamaica, been held and ransacked by a body of Spanish coast guards whom a more violent malignity alone distinguished from demons; and whose

fury, after they could discover nothing of a contraband
nature in a cargo of unique and, indeed, of improbable innocence, had treated Captain Jenkins with a brutality so extensive as to remove one of his ears. In proof of this tale's
veracity, Captain Jenkins now produced, from out of his
left-hand pocket, wrapped with white cotton wool, the ear
involved in his tragic experience; and he begged leave to
submit this relic, to the right honorable House, as his evidence.

"I commend," he then stated, "my conscience to God
and my cause to my countrymen."

So neat was the alliteration that all Westminster (that
home of stylists) rang with applause; Captain Jenkins was
at once named supervisor of the East India Company's office
at St. Helena; and war was declared against Spain.

The unpleasing facts transpired, a while later, that
Jenkins had lost his undeniably missing ear in a pillory, and
that the mummified object which he exhibited to Parliament
was a dried bit of rabbit skin; but inasmuch as by that time
an heroic crusade against Spain's infamous treatment of
Captain Jenkins was in full progress, to have weighed either
fact would have been highly dangerous for the Englishman
concerned in any such hairsplitting. Captain Jenkins could
well afford, in the remote southern part of the Atlantic, and
sustained by his present large salary, to repel all detraction
with dignified silence; and upon the northern bank of the
St. Johns River, General James Oglethorpe had got, at long
last, his opportunity.

Oglethorpe had at his disposal some nine hundred soldiers
and as many more Indian allies. After crying (it is to be
presumed) "Havoc!" the general let slip all these dogs of

war, rather late in the spring of 1740; and yet another English invasion of Florida had begun. First, Oglethorpe seized the lower St. Johns River forts of Pupa and Picolata; and he thus managed to separate St. Augustine from Pensacola and still other Spanish settlements to the west. Yet the strong benevolence of General James Oglethorpe's soul was not destined at once to triumph where the hurt pride of Colonel James Moore had averted from failure into fiction writing. Oglethorpe's reinforcements did not arrive while he was besieging St. Augustine; and abetted by mosquitoes, disease reduced toward impotence his none too numerous forces encamped upon the hot sands surrounding the little Spanish city. The great Castillo de San Marcos meanwhile held firm; it defied surprise; and it stoutly deflected the most vigorous assaults of the British batteries. Very bitterly disappointed, Oglethorpe was compelled to withdraw, rebuffed, toward Savannah, "where the most illiberal reflections were cast upon his conduct during the entire enterprise," and where the Reverend George Whitefield—who was yet another unpredictable philanthropist, not ever to be curbed—ascribed the disjection of Georgia to the fact that a rival clergyman played both whist and a fiddle.

Next, it was the Spaniards who attacked. They passed by the mouth of the St. Johns in full force, led by Don Manuel de Montiano; and more than three thousand Floridian and Cuban troops invaded English territory with élan. Yet the leadership of this army was far out of proportion to its bravery; and the battle of Bloody Marsh, during the July of 1742, resulted in an overwhelming Spanish defeat which could not easily be distinguished from destruction.

—Whereupon the Reverend George Whitefield remarked that "the deliverance of Georgia from the Spaniards is such as cannot be paralleled but by some instances out of the Old Testament." General Oglethorpe assured the secretary of state that he had returned all proper thanks to God Almighty, for His infinite mercy in restoring to Georgia the enduring ways of peace, before raising another battalion, and laying in a fresh supply of shot, powder, and cannon. And in epistolary form, the governors of New York, New Jersey, Pennsylvania, North Carolina, Virginia, and Maryland united, not merely to congratulate the governor of Georgia upon his superb victory, but to express the renewed confidence of all these governors "in the Supreme Governor of Nations, for placing the destiny of the southern colonies under the direction of a General so well qualified."

Spain was, in brief, beaten; and both sides knew it. Yet nobody, to the best of our knowledge, remembered to give any proper credit, for this British triumph, to *The Villas of the Ancients Illustrated* (*Large Folio*).

Thus, in reality, ended the struggle between Spain and England for the north bank of the St. Johns. After the official close of war between the two nations, in 1748, the enmity between Georgia and Florida degenerated into casual border raids, wherein theft, murder, and arson all figured with an equal frequency and a shared inconsequence; both sides maltreated, where they did not abolish, the perplexed Indian; and the St. Johns River began to lose the only permanent population which it had ever possessed, the aboriginal.

Conditions grew steadily more chaotic until 1761, when yet again Spain allowed herself to be drawn into an English war, through the hope of regaining Minorca. She lost, instead, Havana, in addition to the Philippines; and was thus forced to give up her claim to Florida in order to buy back Cuba.

So in 1763 the flag of St. George and of George III fluttered above the dark waters of the St. Johns; and a new era had opened in this river's history, the more thanks to Mr. Robert Castell.

I I

A Scot Intervenes

ENGLAND'S inexpensive but statesmanlike triumph, in securing Florida in exchange for an island which happened not to belong to England, gave to the St. Johns, as being the main waterway, and, in effect, the north boundary line of England's thus purchased colony, a special significance; and appeared likely to bring to this river an unfamiliar visitation in the form of peace. Georgia and Florida, now that both were English, would desist from interchanging, across its sluggish dark waters, interminable raids against each other; the outlaws who, with a generous impartiality, had begun to pillage both its banks, would be eliminated by due process of law and lynching; and in place of continual guerrilla warfare would now flourish, beside the huge St. Johns, just as continually, huge crops of cotton and sugar and indigo. Thus roseate became the English program, which looked forward, also, to a commensurate Elysian development of the river's upper stretches.

Nevertheless, most of the Spanish inhabitants had left Florida, after its surrender to England, so as to establish yet other homes, unharried by democratic principles, in Cuba or in other colonies belonging to Spain; of the 5,000 residents of St. Augustine, for example, remained only 288 householders bold enough to confront the freedom which an electoral government grants to the irresponsible; and so, the main problem now set for British profiteers was how to re-populate these fertile and lovely, but, except for stray Indian tribes, now virtually deserted riverbanks. It was a task undertaken, and in large part achieved, by James Grant, who, in common with divers English benefactors, was not English.

Concerning the first British governor of East Florida—Colonel James Grant of Ballindalloch, by birth a Scotsman—it is recorded, discreetly, that he did not cherish feminine friendships; but that, to the more normal side of his characteristics, inasmuch as "he loved both good company and a bottle . . . he kept a good table"—at which same table, after his coming into Florida, he developed a special fondness for the baked flesh of rattlesnakes.

This foible may, or may not, account for the chronic indigestion which incessantly troubled Colonel Grant; and which of a sudden, when he was but eighty-six, killed him. He maintained, however, along with his biliousness a sound head for business, such as during his governorship proved no less beneficial to Florida at large than—as remains recorded

also, with the same benign flavor of tact—to his private bank-
ing account. Colonel Grant, in brief, made money in Florida,
as befitted a Scotsman, in the while that, as befitted a statesman, he made progress.

He saw to it that grants of rich river lands were allotted
to former British soldiers by proclamation; and that handsome bounties were provided for the growing of cotton and
sugar and indigo; inasmuch as James Grant, he remembered
always, had been sent into Florida to increase the new colony's
production of cotton and sugar and indigo. To speculative
noblemen, who fostered a vague notion of acquiring unbounded wealth by founding small settlements, he assigned
suitable tracts along the St. Johns; for this splendid tranquil
river (James Grant reminded his clients) afforded the most
convenient and a wholly safe transportation for the nobility's
remunerative, if as yet unraised, crops of cotton or of sugar
or of indigo. Moreover, across its broad brown expanse, near
the present city of Jacksonville, Governor Grant caused to
be builded the Kings Road, which extended southward parallel to the St. Johns as far as New Smyrna; and which, northward, led from the river toward Savannah, and thus to an
eager market, in the untropical upper provinces, for such
necessaries of life as cotton and sugar and indigo.

Of the natural wealth of the St. Johns, and of all Florida,
divers printed accounts, no one of which appears to have
been disfigured by understatement, were now vended, inex-
pensively, at the suggestion of Governor Grant, among the
other American colonies and throughout England. So lively
was the curiosity aroused, and so permanent is human faith in
the existence of not inaccessible fairylands, that Englishmen
bought with avidity edition after edition of William Roberts'
Account of the First Discovery and Natural History of

Florida, which was now published in London. Inasmuch as Roberts, a highly talented Munchausen, was receiving (at the suggestion of Governor Grant) a commission upon all the lands he sold, and since his fancy stayed unhampered by any personal knowledge of Florida, he spoke as one with authority; and in an Arcadian depiction of life along the St. Johns vied handsomely with St. John's own depiction of life in the New Jerusalem. Into this western paradise, however, were to be admitted both marriage and giving in marriage, forasmuch as Roberts, in particular, advocated that Englishmen who settled in Florida should intermarry as quickly as might be with the native Indians, so as to ensure harmony between the red race and the white race. The assumed improbability of any squabbling among relatives by marriage has been acclaimed as Roberts' highest reach in romanticism.

Trade, if not matrimony, with the Indians was increasing, to a gratifying if ungigantic extent, through posts founded along the St. Johns by Scots merchants. So pleased by this increase was the thrifty heart of Governor Grant, after he had visited the post of his fellow countryman, James Spalding, near the largest lake in the river—now called Lake George—that the Scotsman in office promised the more candidly mercantile Scotsman to make out of this post a town. The governor's official survey of the river, as published in 1767, declared that its banks were being populated rapidly by his Majesty's subjects; and that its valley was marked out by destiny to become the most flourishing part of his Majesty's new colony. By 1768, at least five hundred thousand acres along the St. Johns had been parceled out among patentees. "The principal river of this province in point of utility and beauty," the St. Johns, was not inferior to any watercourse in America, declared yet another report; and upon the banks of the St. Johns now flourished, if not huge crops, at least a quite respectable quantity, of cotton and sugar and indigo. The Scots have stamina.

With the aid of a good advertising bureau, in brief, abetted by thrift and mendacity, Governor James Grant, during the seven years that he held office, did more to promote the well-being of the St. Johns, and of all East Florida, than the Spaniards had accomplished in two centuries through piety and valor. His reward was commensurate, to a native degree: for in 1771 a dying nephew left to James Grant a snug fortune, along with a large estate. The colonel's chronic indigestion, that so efficiently disguised blessing, made it possible for him to ask for a year's leave of absence, upon the ground of ill-health; and to quit America, after having topped off, in the company of two handsome boys, at St. Augustine, with a bottle of sound Rüdesheimer, his final Floridian rattlesnake.

The Trouble about Altruism

"I HAVE the satisfaction to believe," Governor Grant remarked, in taking leave of his Council, "that my endeavors to serve and oblige every gentleman who has come to settle, or even to look at the country, have succeeded except in the case of Mr. Rolle, though I have been at more pains to please and accommodate him than all the rest."

His hearers murmured agreement. They too had found that to think with kindness about Denys Rolle was a mental exercise beyond human ability. And since it was altruism (as exemplified in theft and warfare by James Oglethorpe) which had got for Florida its first English governor, the fact did seem rather odd that so much of James Grant's stay in this colony should have been embittered by altruism as exemplified, in squabbling and in penny-pinching, by Denys Rolle.

He, like Oglethorpe, was an M.P. obsessed by that same strong benevolence of soul which the House of Commons, like all other legislative bodies, is so often forced to applaud in oratory and to restrict in action. Benevolence, in this special case, had "fired Mr. Rolle with the philanthropic desire" to establish a colony wherein the poor in virtue—but, in particular, those members of the sex which irony terms gentle, for whom either disease or middle age, or perhaps merely an unappreciative clientele, had made vice unremunerative—could dwell estranged from all forms of misdemeanor; and build up in this way "an Ideal society." So well-born, well-to-do, well-meaning, and yet, somehow, well-nigh insufferable Denys Rolle had set forth from his native Devon, in 1764, with papers which entitled him to twenty thousand acres near St. Marks in England's new province; and equipped also with a decisive letter, from the Earl of Shelburne (then secretary of the colonies) stating "it is His Majesty's Pleasure that all suitable Encouragement should be given to Denys Rolle, Esquire, in his useful undertakings in the Province of Florida." It followed that when he reached St. Augustine, like a petulant human sleet storm, Governor James Grant, bowing submissively before His Majesty's Pleasure, had made the best of the fanatic foisted upon him by royal ill-judgment.

"I could not command respect from other People to Mr. Rolle," James Grant recorded despairingly, "but I treated him with great attention myself; had him every day at my Table; and asked the favor of a Gentleman to invite him . . . to lodge at his house . . . but he disliked his Guest so much that he would not give Mr. Rolle a bed when he returned to Town a second time."

It really does seem to have been instinctive, the way in which the average sensual man recoiled before this high-nosed and pale-eyed altruist, who was bent upon making his fellow creatures more virtuous and more happy, whether they liked, it or not.

Rolle's patent, let it be repeated, was for land near St. Marks; but after reaching Florida, he exhibited toward his patent the same philanthropic disdain which Oglethorpe had shown for his charter. Denys Rolle decided that, patent or no patent, the better site for his Ideal society would be upon the banks of the St. Johns River. "My answers," Governor Grant records, "were as Civil and as much to the purpose as I could contrive to make them to a man who for the most part I did not understand . . . but wished to get off my hands upon any Terms. . . . Therefore, tho' Mr. Rolle's Conduct was unprecedented in an established Government, as it was not attended with serious bad consequences to the Publick, I thought the best way was to overlook his Behavior" —and in brief, through dismissing legality, to get rid "upon any Terms" of this toplofty but well-connected utopian, who "hates, and, indeed, never forgives a man who differs in opinion with him."

In this fashion Denys Rolle obtained, through the combined virtues of illogic and altruism and obnoxiousness, a superb tract of about twenty thousand acres situated upon the east bank of the St. Johns, a few miles north of the present town of San Mateo; where, for the benefit of some forty bankrupt practitioners of womankind's oldest profession, he established Charlotta. He thus named his colony as a compliment (perhaps not shaped beyond criticism) to the wife of King George III—of which Queen Charlotte it stays recorded that "she purified the British Court by admitting to it no lady who did not bear a spotless character." This was a quaint innovation, which disturbed half the peerage of England, among whom since the Norman conquest morals had remained largely a matter of expediency; and a high-minded achievement which, in the opinion of high-nosed Denys Rolle, had, somehow, made Queen Charlotte the right patroness for retired prostitutes, as well as for the yet other English riffraff whom, as a collector of the contrite, he now began to assemble, beside the St. Johns, to compose his Ideal society.

Rolle stated the climate of this part of the lower St. Johns to be "extremely fine, perhaps not to be surpassed; its greater fruitfulness exceeding that of the Carolinas and Georgia." He declared that to each side of him "everything in nature seems to correspond towards the cultivation of the productions of the whole world, in some part or other of this happy province." Florida was, in short, "the most precious jewel of His Majesty's American dominions"; and the rich grant of Denys Rolle, as assigned to him by an all-seeing Providence which overlooked the laws of mankind, lay in the "heart of the province, on a river"—howsoever inconceivable might appear this extravagancy of nature—"bigger than the Thames." The enthusiast, in brief, babbled with rapture now that for his Ideal society he had found (at the not excessive annual rental of one halfpenny an acre) an earthly paradise—whereinto very soon had entered the serpent of human nature. His colonists were wholly willing to repent verbally all day long, in exchange for board and lodgings, but not eager to labor; and Denys Rolle, if pious, was penurious.

You have, indeed, the man's measure in the fact that he

directed his wards to erect a church first of all, and to put by the carnal thought of building homes for themselves until after the house of God was completed. His converts, in a semitropical jungle, demurred; and one, upon the whole, sympathizes. He sighed then over their worldliness; and yet compromised with these Laodiceans by setting them to clear his twenty thousand acres of palmetto stumps, so as to make way for Charlotta's Ideal society—"and when they enquired what advantage they could reap from such Labour, his answer was that they could sell half the palmetto roots for their own profit. They saw that they never would be able to buy a pound of Bread at that rate"—and so refused to work. He stopped their food supplies; and at that, the entire colony ran away, to St. Augustine, with their patron pursuing them. Perplexed Governor Grant had thus upon his hands, once more, the petulance and the highly un-Caledonian altruism of Denys Rolle, in addition to "the Discontent . . . as increased by bad living, and by Acts of Injustice and oppression . . . of a parcel of troublesome lazy people."

—Whereafter the affair became a dark and immoral muddle. Governor Grant agreed with the fugitives in principle, since he thought it but rational for human beings to avoid the society of Denys Rolle, Esquire, by any means they found feasible. Yet the duty of a statesman is less often candor than compromise: he may need, for example, to appraise the crops of his province as set against the temperate compassion of a Presbyterian. So Grant made his choice; and he stuck to it, unflinchingly.

"If I had not underhand interposed"—James Grant records, with the cool amenity of a Scots politician—"the greatest part, if not the whole, of these unfortunate persons would have been discharged from their indentures; but I represented that . . . servants' getting the better of their Masters would be . . . hurtful to the future Settlement of the Province . . . In any other County in America every man of them would have been set at Liberty."

—For he saw to it they were not set at liberty. Through urging "underhand" every justice of the peace in St. Augustine to disregard the laws of England, James Grant compelled the unhappy, half-starved mob of as yet but imperfectly reformed prostitutes and pickpockets and professional beggars to return, chaperoned by their pale-eyed patron, toward the St. Johns, so that upon its fertile banks they might resume their decreed raising of cotton and sugar and indigo. Through malfeasance in office, and through still another "Act for which I have no Authority"—so Grant confesses, with that naked amoralness which one both abhors and admires—the governor of East Florida had got rid, yet again, of Denys Rolle, Esquire, without any possible offense to the Earl of Shelburne or His Majesty's Pleasure.

The philanthropist, after having thus recaptured his virtue's prey, proceeded now with renewed ambition, which parsimony alone kept in check, to enlarge his Ideal society. Despite what he regarded as "every obstruction given by the jealousy or designs of the evil-minded," he provided his indentured wards with the necessaries of life, along with a not sybaritic supply of conveniences. He entrusted to their keeping a large flock of cattle, and divers herds of hogs and sheep, as well as a more limited supply of poultry—since for the not utterly regenerated, to steal, in no less flat opposition to Exodus 20:15 than to Mark 10:19, and thereafter to devour, an entire fowl, nay, even two fowls, was a performance, howsoever reprehensible, yet facile. Then Denys Rolle, in his own prim, sleety and all-disapproving person, superintended their planting of his newly cleared fields, with cotton and sugar and indigo.

Thus far at least did James Grant score, at outset, in putting up with this pale prig—to whom, it was true, the sun of East Florida had begun now to lend an apoplectic brick color—and in allotting to Denys Rolle, at the groaning gubernatorial Table, an appropriate portion of baked rattlesnake.

As the fruitage of several trips to and fro across the ocean in pursuit of philanthropy's sirenlike anthems, Rolle assembled about two hundred destitute and by-and-by desperate protégés upon the east bank of the St. Johns: yet the results, even in the gnashed teeth of altruism, were discouraging. Always, it seemed, the more plainly and the more variously a pauper needed reformation, the less brilliant adornment he proved to an Ideal society; nor did even the repentance of Charlotta's most voluble prostitutes, when tampered with by the well-to-do, gay blades of St. Augustine, appear hale enough to survive night air. In brief, the philanthropist observed ruefully that everywhere alongside "a river bigger than the Thames" the perfection of humankind was being rather seriously retarded by diseases of a not genteel nature, as well as by laziness, by obstinacy, and by a dissatisfaction so widespread and so wanton as to embrace even Denys Rolle. His own beneficiaries could not abide him; the more righteously he scolded them, the slighter, to all appearance, became their affection: and desertion—not here to mention such distressing byplays as theft, fornication, late hours, drunkenness, cutting scrapes, or lax attendance at divine worship—had begun steadily to make thin and wavering the ranks of his Ideal society.

So often as even the most tiny of these mishaps occurred, then Denys Rolle, with the pertinacity of a homing dove of unpeace, sped straight toward the stalwart but unsympathizing bosom of Governor James Grant, to demand the affair's adjustment. "Because of a thousand mean, low, trifling Litigious Disputes with his Neighbours," the harassed Governor fumed, "and in short, with every Body he deals with. Mr. Rolle thinks it is in my power to make his servants work and to settle every Dispute he has . . . 'Tis to no purpose to point out a Chief Justice, Assistant Judges, Justices of the Peace, King's Attorney, &c. All that costs money: and he will have recourse to me only."

In brief, this pale-eyed philanthropist—who, for all his troublemaking, yet came attended by tall wraiths of the Earl of Shelburne and of His Majesty's Pleasure, like admonitory specters—pestered James Grant to distraction, but not ever into any injudiciousness. —For the man did, at least, raise cotton and sugar and indigo. The man had wealth. The man had influential connections. So you could but regret, year after year, fruitlessly and without fidgeting (you hoped) beyond decorum, that there was no possible way of pleasing, and far less of keeping silent, this high-nosed Denys Rolle; that there was no method known to you, free from un-Scots-like imprudence, in which to get rid of his complainings, his whines, his threats, his stinginess, his all-embracing futility, or his depressingly high moral tone; and that even when, at long last, the jackass had put by philanthropy, his disposition still failed to mellow any more appreciably than did his brayings dwindle.

—For Denys Rolle did finally give up, in a glacial disgust with recalcitrant human nature, his Ideal society; he replaced his truant sneak-thieves and strumpets with Negro slaves;

and he increased his land holdings from twenty thousand to eighty thousand acres. Then, for a while, Charlotta prospered (after having become Charlotia, and later, Rollestown) under the tonic of expenditures which by-and-by had amounted to $125,000. In an especially favorable year, Mr. Rolle succeeded in producing for export as much as a thousand gallons of orange juice; he reared poultry, hogs, goats, and sheep, with profit; he shipped to England the turpentine drawn from fifteen hundred pine trees; he boasted of possessing for his thousand head of cattle the finest range in all North America; and Denys Rolle raised, annually, huge crops of cotton and sugar and indigo.

The main point in six years of contention was thus won by James Grant, without ever upsetting the Earl of Shelburne or troubling His Majesty's Pleasure.

13

Introducing the Romantic

AMONG blunt and uncountable commentators upon the "extreme parsimony" of Denys Rolle at Charlotta, his "bad choice of citizens," and his "ill-concerted plan," it is pleasing to find an established and unarguable expert as to the unpractical, in William Bartram—that heartbroken lover who came to the St. Johns, in 1766, to forget about Mary.

He was, at this time, the ne'er-do-well son of a fairly famous botanist, that same John Bartram who, in 1728, had founded, at Kingsessing, near Philadelphia, in his Majesty's colony of Pennsylvania, the first botanic garden to adorn North America; and, at twenty-six, lean, handsome mild-mannered William Bartram, who had failed as an artist (though for his own diversion, he still sketched), and after that as a surveyor, had but now rounded off, at his uncle's mansion near Cape Fear, in the colony of North Carolina, his third financial collapse, as a merchant. His uncle William Bartram, in addition to Uncle William's rather ugly, dark daughter (the touch of whose thin hands woke every sense to ecstasy, the sound of whose compassionate, wise tender voice made you heroic) had been sympathetic as to this final evidence of ordinary people's incomprehension. Mary, in particular, had been dear beyond any poet's rhyming; but for first cousins, of course, when a young man had not any trade or any money, and when both of you were Friends, there remained for William Bartram only the life of a hermit, and for Mary, a man named Robeson.

So you came, with your ever-careful, staid, and rather old-smelling father, into Florida, in order to assist him in his grubby, dexterous fussy fiddling with plants and flowers, because he had told you to do this, and because he paid for the food that you were incapable to earn, and because nothing whatever mattered, in particular, anyhow. You came thus to the St. Johns River; and you found, upon its east bank, near Picolata, just the right place for a hermitage. You decided to live there, quite alone, forever; and to fill in the necessarily vacant moments, between addressing poems to Mary, by raising indigo.

John Bartram, with a dour beneficence—because no middle-aged person, as you granted condoningly, had ever become the noble victim of an undying love—agreed to supply the funds needed for this disappointing, so vague son's fourth start in life; and with the punctiliousness of a Quaker, this ever-careful, staid, and rather old-smelling father of a sublime poet-to-be kept his promise. The planned existence of a cenobite, however, beside the slothful and dark river (which had reminded William Bartram, at first sight, of the Styx as it so elegantly figured in Mr. Pope's *Iliad*) began by-and-by to develop such unepic flaws as left, to its antisocial contriver, but infirm grounds upon which to criticize the plans of a philanthropist as being "ill-contrived." William Bartram, in brief, like every other adolescent poet, appeared doomed to flounder, from out of the most pleasant sort of high-minded misery, into gross physical discomforts such as stop versemaking.

This fact is well borne out by a letter from the celebrated South Carolinian, Henry Laurens, whose unusual success as a merchant was about to make of him, inevitably, a leading American statesman. To his friend, John Bartram, Laurens wrote, in the August of 1766, an account of how Laurens had "thrice visited the River St. Johns"; and added:

"I did not carelessly pass by your son's habitation. . . . His situation on the river is the least agreeable of all the places that I have seen—on a low sheet of sandy pine-barren, verging on the swamp. . . . He assured me that he had but two, among the six negroes you gave him, that could handle an axe tolerably; and one of these two had been exceedingly insolent . . . The house, or rather hovel, that he lives in, is extremely confined, and not proof against the weather . . . No colouring can do justice to the forlorn state of poor Billy Bartram. A gentle, mild young man, no wife, no friend, no companion, no neighbor, no human inhabitant within nine miles of him"—for to a well-bred South Carolinian, of course, six Negroes did not add up to the full amount of a human being—"seated upon a beggarly spot of land, scant

of the bare necessities, and totally void of all the comforts
of life."

The picture, in fact, is more graphic than engaging. One
does not marvel that after a while "poor Billy Bartram"
should have abandoned, in common with versemaking, his
indigo plantation upon the St. Johns; and returned to his
father's home, at Kingsessing, a confessed failure, now quad-
ruply. He began yet a fifth career before long, as a day
laborer, upon a neighboring farm; and what between outdoor
manual toil all day and, at night, the sound, stupid dreamless
sleep begotten by bodily fatigue, he found less and less
chance to think about Mary.

Then Dr. John Fothergill, with whom your father corresponded, wrote from London. William Bartram found that,
somehow, he had become engaged, at the ornate salary of
£50 a year, not any longer to clean out privies or to clip
privet hedges, but to travel about the south parts of his
British Majesty's dominions in America, so as to collect rare
plants and seeds for this Dr. Fothergill, "and to draw birds,
reptiles, insects and plants, on the spot, at a further payment." William Bartram set forth docilely; and after many
years of such not unpleasant, highly-colored errand running,
about the Carolinas and Georgia and Florida, he wrote, in
chief for his own diversion, a book as to his travels.

None who knows writers will suppose, for one half
second, that William Bartram ever confessed his incentive.
The sketching botanist, instead, masked his auctorial hedon-
ism, upon a happy middle ground between the theologic and
the utilitarian, by stating, with meek diffidence, that always,
during his pursuit of the "productions of nature, my chief
happiness consisted in tracing and admiring the infinite

power, majesty, and perfection of the great Almighty Creator, and in the contemplation that, through Divine aid and permission, I might be instrumental in discovering, and introducing into my native country, some original productions of nature which might become useful to society."

That is phrased profitably; it displays indeed, in William Bartram, an unlooked-for amount of tact; for this Heaven-directed need of the talented, to serve nobly the ungifted, is a duty which in every era the ungifted have viewed with approval, and which the talented have customarily avowed and avoided. It followed that William Bartram's *Travels through North and South Carolina, Georgia, East and West Florida* enjoyed popularity for an appreciable while before the book reached a sort of world-wide famousness. Published at Philadelphia in 1791, it was republished within, as people say, the twinkling of a bedpost, at London, Dublin, Berlin, Haarlem, and Paris; and William Bartram found himself to have become, somehow, a distinguished scientist, a universally admired writer, and even, in his tiny way, a capitalist. Such fates do occur, though but now and then, to mild-mannered experts in the unpractical.

William Bartram by this time was—just somehow—more than fifty years old. He took charge, since no other particular choice offered itself, of his dead father's botanic garden at Kingsessing; and there, for the next thirty-two years, "William Bartram led a simple, quiet life, occupied with his scientific observations, his diary, and his correspondence." Many very famous Americans, such as James Madison and Alexander Hamilton and William Dunlap and Charles Brockden Brown, visited William Bartram with respect; for he now ranked as a Philosopher, or as some journals put it, a

Sage; and each month's post appeared to be making him a member of yet another learned society. Nothing of any special importance, though (he sometimes thought), seemed ever to happen; nor did anybody (he noted wonderingly) seem to detect how really inadequate he was, at bottom.

He never married. He had loved one woman only.

Yet Mrs. Robeson, with that tactlessness which one's first love appears always to acquire along with her second chin, did write to him, of course, after the success of his book; and the fact that she was now a widow she mentioned, with just the right shade of desolate optimism, before signing herself, "Your Mary."

—Whereupon the perturbed Philosopher replied at once to his life's one love; and tore up the letter. He wrote then a second letter to assure Mrs. Robeson "that time, the vicissitudes of fortune, tribulation, and the decrepitude of old age, are not sufficient to erase from my mind the impressions which it received during my residence in my Uncle's family in No. Carolina." In all his dreams by night, or serious reveries by day, he remarked yet furthermore, "thou, my cousin, art the foremost pleasing object." —For something of this sort (the distinguished scientist reflected) was the civil thing for a well-bred person to be saying, in view of all the circumstances; and besides, it had once been quite true. He then remained, with every sentiment of regard and esteem, her much obliged Friend and Relation, Wm. Bartram.

He would not ever again be bothered by this Robeson woman, he hoped, as the snuffy, staid, and rather old-smelling fellow sealed, and sent out to be posted, his second letter. Then he got back to his grubby and dexterous fiddling with a new lot of tulips.

Here to attempt an appraisal of William Bartram's *Travels* would be foolish, if but because human intelligence has not, as yet, found the subject matter of his book to be quite definable. The man, just somehow, had been born with that talent for noticing sharply, and for remembering sharply what he had noticed, which, in a world of mostly muggy-minded persons, is a born writer's uncompromising chief assistant and tyrant; and with this gift as his sole support, he had strayed about half-savage and unfamiliar lands rather less in the capacity of a scientist than of curiosity embodied. "William Bartram observed trees and shrubs, geological formations and Indian mounds, land and aquatic animals, man and woman, human institutions and Divine emanations," it has been remarked—appraising all with the same benign but reserved judgment. Toward each of these phenomena he directed the same mild-mannered but alert acute inquisitiveness; and he recorded his unbiased verdict, in a style which, if abundant, as his first London reviewer put it, "in somewhat too luxuriant and poetical language," yet stays, in his every sentence, very ardently and actually, communicative. William Bartram does, in brief, transmit to his readers his own impressions, unadulterated, entire, and undimmed: he obeys the gnomic injunction of a more modern writer, "to make you see." No style can have any other merit more serviceable.

What here concerns us, however, is, first, the fact that Dr. Fothergill was not at all interested in Florida; his need was of hardy plants such as would withstand an English winter's abominable rigors; yet, patron or no patron, mild William Bartram—for this once all iron—was intent to go back to the river beside which he had spent the most bleak period of his life fruitlessly. He therefore returned to the

St. Johns again and yet again. From his *Travels* he omitted, perhaps wincingly, any least reference to the fact that— none nowadays knows in the company of what black grief, what callow despair—he had once lived upon the east bank of the St. Johns; of Picolata he speaks, indeed, as if it were a place unfamiliar to him; yet he wrote about the St. Johns at pronounced length, even with a special gusto, one might think; and he thus brought the St. Johns into literature, in a fashion which William Bartram, it is certain, did not anticipate.

—For his book was published, one must remember, in 1791, just when that which was labeled, some while after-ward, "the romantic movement" in European creative in-sularity had made fashionable its intense, not here to say ill-balanced, concern with Nature (that paramount abstrac-tion, which in print wore always, like a diadem, the largest capital N in your printer's fonts) and with Humanity, among conveniently remote and exotic surroundings, from out of whose native customs your wife had not any right to deduce anything personal. Here, then, in this curious uncul-tured book come out of the wild parts of America, were mingled, pell-mell and with God's own profusion, every one of the ingredients which a romantic writer most needed. So the romantics all dipped into Bartram's *Travels* prehen-silely; and the flora, the fauna, and the landscapes of the St. Johns River system began to make their surprising débuts, in verse, in fiction, and in alleged memoirs, under a fine variety of aliases.

Coleridge was, it is thought, the first verbal engineer thus to divert the St. Johns from out of its normal course into a number of poems—including *The Ancient Mariner, Kubla Khan,* and *Christabel,* through all which the St. Johns, as William Bartram wrote of it, glides intermittently. Then Wordsworth began to adapt Bartram; Southey joined in; and Thomas Campbell likewise entered the band of poetic shoplifters—to the somewhat startling extent, indeed, when he came to write his *Gertrude of Wyoming,* of transporting the river's alligators as far north as Central Pennsylvania. Felicia Hemans abducted from Bartram's account of the St. Johns a tribe of Indians, whom rhythmically she disguised as exiled Greeks; William Lisle Bowles abstracted a whippoorwill; and Shelley borrowed a flock of cranes. Then Alfred Tennyson blandly immersed in the fluent backwash of his *In Memoriam's* rancid anguish a rattlesnake pilfered from William Bartram; whereas the petty larcenies of Chateaubriand, in the way of landscapes and of vegetation peculiar to all the present counties between Nassau and Brevard, became so many as to stagger one's faith in Nature, when Human.

It would be wholly pleasing here to enter at length into this matter of the enormous contributions which, by way of William Bartram, the St. Johns River thus made incognito to the nineteenth century literature of Great Britain and of western Europe at large; but, by the professorial, a sufficing number of such embezzlements from the *Travels* of William Bartram as the refined, in assassinatory parallel quotings, call "likenesses," have been hunted down and impaled in the proper theses.

We confront, though, an enigma without any known solution in that surprising record of the Seminole Indians which—since the phrase needs be fitly orotund—was composed and indited by William Bartram, Esquire (in addition to being Embellished with Copper-Plates), after his travels up and about the St. Johns River.

These aborigines had broken away from the Creek nation, in Georgia; and had lived in Florida, at the time of Bartram's visit, rather less than a half century. He duly notes their nine towns, and the general contents of these nine towns, which had an average population of two hundred, and so afforded for the entire tribe a membership of scarcely two thousand. He records also how the Seminoles derived their sustenance, in the main, from deer, bear, wolves, and yet other wild animals, the skins of which, along with fruit, honey and wax, they bartered, with their white neighbors, for clothing, guns, ammunition, household utensils, and cheap, shiny trinkets—for all which the Seminoles paid dearly but with contentment.

This interchange of commodities was supervised, in chief, by Spalding & Kelfall, who during the time of Bartram's observations maintained in Florida five trading posts, of which the most important stood on the west bank of the St. Johns, a few miles to the north of Lake George. It was hereabouts that Governor James Grant, but a little while before his ascension to opulence and to the concomitant privilege of thumbing his nose at the Earl of Shelburne, had promised to establish a town. Two other posts graced the river, south of Lake George, one thirty miles distant, and the other, sixty. Bartram, on his way to the St. Johns, had visited the senior member of the firm, James Spalding, at Frederica in Georgia; and was entertained afterward by Charles McLatchie, the company's head agent in Florida. From these white traders, "as well as from the general and impartial report of ancient respectable men," Bartram supplemented his own observations as to the Seminoles, Muscogulges,

Chickasaws, and yet other Creek tribes; and in his *Travels* he published his "description of the character, customs and persons of the American aborigines."

This account of the Floridian Indians becomes an enigma, one repeats, in view of the quite certain fact that William Bartram, whatsoever his defects, was not ever a liar. He had spent, not months, but years, among these Indians; and he reports them to have been, by nature, "as blithe and free as the birds of the air, and like them as volatile and active, tuneful and vociferous. The visage, action and deportment of a Seminole are the most striking picture of happiness in this life; joy, contentment, love and friendship, without guile or affectation, seem inherent in them, or prediminant in their vital principle, for it leaves them but with the last breath of life."

It follows that "as moral men they certainly stand in no need of European civilization. . . . It is . . . a sharp reproof to the white people . . . and, I must own, elevates these people"—which means, the aboriginal Floridians—"to the first rank amongst mankind, that they have been able to resist the continual efforts of the complicated host of vices that have for ages overrun the nations of the old world." The confederate tribes of the Creeks were also, it develops, absolute teetotalers, even to the extent of tomahawking hogsheads so as to spill forth their pernicious contents untasted. And to conclude, "their excellent policy in civil government cannot derive its influence from coercive laws, for they have no such artificial system. Divine wisdom dictates, and they obey."

Yet even under the burden of so many and weighty virtues, it appears, the tribes of the Creek Confederation so

managed their own halcyon estate as to sustain a sound sense
of social criticism; for Bartram assures his readers that, at an
unnamed English settlement, "I saw a young Indian in the
Nation, who when present, and beholding the scenes of mad
intemperance and folly by white men, in the town, clapt
his hand to his breast; and with a smile aloft, and as if struck
with astonishment, and wrapt in love and admiration to the
Deity, as who should say: 'O Thou Great and Good Spirit,
we are indeed sensible of Thy benignity and favour to us
red men, in denying us the understanding of white men.
We did not know, before they came amongst us, that mankind could become so base, and fall so below the dignity of
their nature. Defend us from their manners, laws, and
power!'"

That a doxology quite so extensive could have been
compressed into just one "smile aloft," appears unlikely.
Yet here is an apostrophe which, as one strives rather des-
perately to believe, was printed a good while before the birth
of Anatole France; France would have liked that thanks-
giving for being denied "the understanding of white men";
nor, indeed, was this apostrophe, as a whole, unsuited to the
"reddish-brown barbarians" so far blessed as to live alongside
the St. Johns River, in any wigwam standing between the
present sites of Georgetown and Bishopsville, as Bartram describes this special part of Florida, about "the little ocean" of
Lake George, by saying:

"What an Elysium it is! where the wandering Seminole,
the naked red warrior, roams at large, and after the vigorous
chase, retires from the scorching heat of the meridian sun.
Here he reclines, and reposes under the odoriferous shades
of Zanthoxilon, his verdant couch guarded by the Deity;

Liberty and the Muses inspiring him with wisdom and valor, whilst the balmy zephyrs fan him to sleep."

Now, to sneer at this sort of writing is, for almost any sort of fool, facile. One almost irresistibly is tempted to remark, with a superior languor, that since 1791 the neighborhood has so far changed that many of these phenomena are now uncommon in Crescent City; or that in Pierson the sight of a naked red warrior asleep upon a verdant couch, under the immediate supervision of any species of deity, would be appraised today, it is possible, without calm; and one inclines, in short, to shrug off the whole matter, as a high-flown invention of the "noble savage" school of romance.

Yet one would thus miss the main, the perplexing point of these rhapsodies about the Indians of Florida—which is, that William Bartram was not ever a liar.

The man was, instead, painstakingly truthful. In his exact, unbiased, and his microscopic faculty for observation he was excelled by no person then living. He was writing down—quite soberly, it is to be presumed, in view of his lifelong, almost rabid abhorrence of alcohol—a plain natural history of such plant- and animal-life as he himself had studied, at Dr. Fothergill's suggestion, "on the spot"; and was describing the toad, the live oak, the yellow bream, the alligator, the Muscogulges, the highland turtle, and the laurel magnolia, let us say, all with the same mild-mannered and most careful particularity, as being more or less noteworthy products of the St. Johns valley.

One is thus forced to conclude that almost anywhere alongside the present U.S. Main Highways Nos. 3 and 17, Bartram's naked red Seminole reposing under Zanthoxilon and lulled by Liberty (in addition to all nine Muses) was, during the last years of the eighteenth century, a familiar spectacle; and yet, one is certain—just somehow—that no flesh-and-blood persons were ever in the least bit like Bartram's Seminole Indians.

One confronts here, in brief, an enigma which, it can but be repeated, has not any known solution.

14

The Almost Loyal Colony

IN THE mean time, while, at Kingsessing, William
Bartram compiled his *Travels*, had occurred the American
Revolution; and reverberations of the shot fired by embattled
farmers near Lexington, although reputedly heard round
the world at once, had failed at all to annoy the peacefulness
of the St. Johns valley for some four months.

Florida, it must be remembered, had been under English
control a mere dozen years; and so had not acquired that
resolute distrust of England such as colored the judgment
of Samuel Adams and of Thomas Jefferson and of Benjamin
Franklin, and of still other apostates to England, who at
this instant were about to deprive a large part of North
America of its colonial status for more than a century.
Florida's population—of approximately 1,000 white persons,

2,000 Indians, and 3,000 Negroes—had not yet, in fine, been seriously exposed to that gradual pandemic of representative government which had now driven their northern neighbors to declare war rather than drink tea at its current market price. Moreover, a not inconsiderable number of Florida's white citizens were either on or else hopefully near the payrolls of Great Britain; and governmental salaries do not often beget a radical tendency. The few unpensioned, who did of course believe in a change for the better, effected their departure, with haste and secrecy, across the St. Johns River and so to Georgia.

Early in the August of 1775, official Florida was averted from disapproval into consternation, by news that the sloop *Commerce,* coming unperceived into Matanzas Harbor at St. Augustine, had nefariously eased herself, under cover of darkness, alongside the British brigantine *Betsy;* that South Carolinian rebels had thus obscuredly contrived to board the *Betsy,* and to seize the 111 barrels of gunpowder destined to defend the garrison and merchants of Florida's capital city; whereafter, speeding their sloop past the mouth of the St. Johns, these pirates had fled northward, to commence fighting against the mother country, at a safe distance beyond the reach of Florida's police force.

Henry Laurens, whose wide knowledge of the peninsula had been acquired by sundry mercantile trips up and down the St. Johns—during which alert journeys, it may be remembered, he had visited "poor Billy Bartram"—was reputed to be the serpentlike, coiled mainspring of this exploit. Nor did anyone at the instant drawing a salary paid by the English government fail to rebuke the performance.

"Remember Matanzas Harbor!" became henceforward the war cry of every officeholder in Florida; and the entire

colony entered the war to help England, with the unanimity
of a single man who regrets his lack of dependents.

Apart from such merely noble sentiments as everybody
needs to express in wartime, the implications of this raid had
annoyed Floridians because they so very largely depended
upon the country north of them for provisions; and so, when
the royal governor, Sir James Wright, was driven out of
Georgia, then Florida's upset inhabitants began at once to
conduct bold raids across the border, against lonely plantations and undefended small settlements, in the hope of seiz-
ing, from their rebel neighbors, supplies of corn, of rice, and
of yet other foodstuffs, for the maintenance of a loyal people.

At this time, the Earl of Dartmouth, through an official
saraband of "whereas," "inasmuch," "be it known," and
"therefore," communicated the desire of his regrettably
unregal Majesty, King George III, that the area through
which flows the St. Johns should be converted into a "secure
Asylum" for such of the staid Farmer of Windsor's subjects,
in the refractory colonies, as might have impaired their
fortunes virtuously, through opposing the crime of rebellion
against increased taxes, and as did not care to submit any
longer to the abuse and tyranny of misled neighbors who
(on account of the odd theory that in an ideal republic there
would be no taxes) "ranted about liberty." Restrictions upon
the sale of lands along the St. Johns were removed; and by
means of a special proclamation all proper-minded loyalists
were incited at once to enter into this paradise upon earth, in
the same astounding high terms which, if worn thin by
Jean Ribaut, and reiterated by James Grant, are still customary to advertisements of Florida.

Within what stylists have epitomized as a trice, some

thousands of Tories—from Georgia, from the Carolinas, and from yet more remote colonies—had swelled the peninsula's people; and of these, a great many settled swarmingly upon the rich river lands. St. Augustine in this way became the main bulwark of British orthodoxy, now that suitable heathen alliances had been formed, with the Seminoles and with the Creek Indians of Georgia, in a crusade against the Christians a bit farther north; and small garrisons were stationed at Cowford and Picolata, as well at yet other points along the river, whose quaint shaping had once more made of it the natural borderline between two nations at war.

High in the Governor's Council at St. Augustine, and exceedingly active in these preparations to defend the St. Johns, moved the ambiguous figure of Captain Frederick George Mulcaster—whose birth was ascribed by ordinary to an extramatrimonial excursion upon the part of King George III's deplorably vivacious father. With no less generosity had rumor granted to England's plump prime minister, Lord North, the same royal genesis; for Griff, as the unrevering called the late Prince Frederick of Wales, had resembled Joseph, that early Prince of Israel, rather more strikingly in a taste for coats of many colors than for continence; and had thus (so people said) kept the American Revolution, as far as it touched Florida, a snug family affair.

Having succeeded Gerard de Brahm as surveyor general of East Florida, Captain Mulcaster was at praiseworthy pains to acquire complete knowledge as to his territory; and he thriftily averted the fruits of official experience toward the increase of his private fortune. From time to time he took up the more desirable land grants, which eventually reached a respectable total of five thousand acres. His fraternal zeal, at the outbreak of the American Revolution, became vigorous and vivid, alike in preparing Florida for armed resistance and in providing to the representatives of his two reputed half brothers in London a vast deal of information as to Georgia and South Carolina, for military use. Later, he joined the English army, in New York; and at this point he—who was perhaps the one scion of the pigheaded house of Hanover not resolutely to assist England toward defeat in the Revolution—would seem of a sudden to have vanished.

Meanwhile, Frederick George Mulcaster had seen to it that, in Florida, local troops were mustered to serve with the regular military forces of England which, upon the stanch, age-old principle that the best way to conduct your wars is to let other peoples fight them, the English were now importing from out of Germany. A combination of native volunteers with young Tories, who had escaped from the north into Florida, resulted in creating the East Florida Rangers. Foremost in this prenatal attack upon the as yet but imperfectly United States of America was Daniel McGirth, who had deserted from the American army when his superior officer—to whom McGirth had demurred in presenting his fine mare, Gray Goose—began, quite affably, to incite a more liberal nature by having McGirth flogged in public. McGirth's fellow apostate was Thomas Browne, an unappreciative young planter from beside the Savannah River, who, after having been honored with a coat of tar and feathers by the Liberty Boys, had been accorded, when thus equipped, the distinction of a public parade also, in a dung cart. Applauding spectators had then entertained themselves, yet further, by burning off a few of Browne's toes with hot irons.

Unamused by these patriotic pleasantries, this couple

escaped to Florida; and McGirth, it is of interest to note, still rode upon Gray Goose. Henceforward these two traitors to the larger principles of democracy devoted their most lively energies to requiting their own ill-treatment; and among the followers of these unhumor-loving refugees were enlisted fifty-three volunteers from the St. Johns River district.

When all-loyal St. Augustine was first horrified by hearing about the adoption of the Declaration of Independence, by a lewd mob of rebels, then popular opinion, as is customary, inclined to express its more noble sentiments through maltreating somebody; so that only by the skulking remoteness of Samuel Adams and John Hancock, who were then fulminating in the City of Brotherly Love, was the loyalty of Florida prevented from attesting its firmness through the public ceremonials of a lynching. To the grieved glance of loyalty, the straw-stuffed effigies of both these persons, which were at once burned in the plaza, could not but appear an inadequate substitute for their flesh-and-blood bodies.

High sentiments of this nature ascended to yet more lofty, volcanic peaks when news came as to the destruction of lonely plantations upon the wrong side of the Georgian border, such as the home of William Chapman, who had removed therefrom, to a tract near Picolata—but temporarily, and so as to aid England, through the production of naval stores and lumber for the king's navy. It was felt that an unfair advantage had been taken of his absence on an exalted errand. Defection to the rebel cause by a number of self-seeking Floridians, who preferred liberty to the strong pure glory of serving Great Britain, then resulted in the issuance of a proclamation to prohibit the keeping of boats or canoes on the Georgian side of the St. Johns after sunset;

and likewise forbidding anybody to cross over this river without having a signed permission from his Excellency the new governor, Patrick Tonyn.

These martial preparations in Florida aroused many Georgians, who had become perturbed by the boldness with which the English now made ready for battle their allies, from among the Seminoles, the Creeks, the Cherokees, and the Choctaws, to safeguard the pretensions of England. These Georgians appealed for aid to Major General Charles Lee, then second in rank to General Washington. With permission of the Continental Congress, Lee moved, from his headquarters in Charleston, to Savannah, as the first step toward invasion of the—at any rate, rhetorically—loyal fourteenth colony, and the despoiling of its plantations along and about the St. Johns River. Providence, however, at this instant, afforded to Great Britain unbribed allies, in the form of malarial germs which haunted the Ogeechee swamps and of the summer's unusual heat. Such morbid factors united against the American troops, whose valor proved to be an inadequate defense against chills and fever; so that these champions of human brotherhood were not able to advance their program of rapine and arson any farther south than to the seaport of Sunbury, about twenty-five miles below Savannah.

In the mean time, the English forces in Florida had become yet more active, alike in strengthening their defenses and in emitting destructiveness. The schooners *Rebecca* and *Tuncastle* and *St. John* lay in guard over the river; and precautionary dissuasions against treason took form as several arrests by the police, so as to avert rebellion at New Smyrna. Following the nonarrival of General Lee's proposed invasion of the St. Johns country, Governor Patrick Tonyn (who was Irish) proposed a retaliatory expedition; and this was carried out during the following year. Some five hundred regular troops and one hundred Florida Rangers, attended by a miscellaneous retinue of Indians, then destroyed, at the dictates of loyalty, a vast deal of personal property and of real estate in southern Georgia; and under the influence of the same praiseworthy abstraction, nearly two thousand head of cattle were driven southward, across the St. Johns River, into St. Augustine, where they were butchered and distributed to the local lower classes.

At this point the St. Johns River shaped an important part of the American Revolution, now that, incensed and with their pocketbooks hurt by the damage done upon the north bank of the St. Johns by East Florida Rangers, the indignant Georgians launched forth to convert General Lee's proposed invasion into an actuality. The leader of this retributory movement was that Button Gwinnett who, to the disgust of autograph hunters, appears, in his brief lifetime, to have signed hardly any other document except the Declaration of Independence; and who now got southward a combined horde of Continental troops and of Georgia militia. So pessimistic became the Floridians as to the risk of having a rhetorical desire to die for the sake of England involved crudely with the ugly and irretrievable process of dying that many of the colony's most stentorian loyalists proposed an informal agreement with the invaders that, as an offset to their withdrawal, Florida should promise to remain neutral throughout the remainder of the Revolution. This plan was at once overruled by the English governor, who (still being Irish) argued that the loyal fourteenth colony might be able to attest its devotion, a bit more efficiently, during wartime, by fighting.

The Georgian forces, in the spring of 1777, then penetrated as far south as Sawpit Bluff, about eight miles above the river's mouth; while the English, enforced by Florida Rangers and Indians, crossed the St. Johns and encamped at Rolfe's Saw Mill, eleven miles north of the present city of Jacksonville. St. Johns Bluff, overlooking the former site of Fort Caroline, was fortified; two warships were set to guard the mouth of the river; and obtuse circumstances, yet again, appeared likely to contaminate with gore the academic desire of Florida to risk all for righteousness' sake upon paper only. Yet, when the English advanced against the invaders, near where the Atlantic Coastal Highway now crosses the Nassau River, the colonial army at once ran away, with a wholeheartedness so unarguable that Button Gwinnett's planned invasion of Florida collapsed before the will of the people of America. Thereafter yet more attention was given by the English to the St. Johns as a fortalice provided by nature; and almost all one group of 350 Tories, who had recently arrived from South Carolina, were stationed there on guard.

It was well for Florida that these defense measures along the river were made, for in the spring of 1778, the third invasion of northern Florida by American forces began. Their commander was Major General Robert Howe, whose expedition comprised some twenty-five hundred men, on board five galleys, two flats, and yet other small craft. Three ships of the East Florida navy were captured by the Americans, just above the present city of Brunswick. The English responded by taking, among other prizes, a number of French merchant vessels, on board which were the Chevalier de Brétigny, sixteen of his officers, and two hundred French soldiers, upon their way to join Washington's army. Wrangling among the English officers and the Floridian militia induced, however, among the British troops, far more lively dislike for one another than they could feel for Americans, and debarred the making of a firm stand against Howe's invaders. Yet, by assembling all the embroiled loyalist forces near the present city of Jacksonville and about St. Johns Bluff, the prospect of a stiff resistance was so delusively indicated as to beguile the colonial army, whose morale happened to be even inferior to that of their adversaries, and whose sick list was much longer. When their death toll through chills and fever and dysentery had reached five hundred, the Americans withdrew northward; and the welfare of Florida had been secured, yet again, by disease.

The governments of Georgia and of other colonies to the north began now, in default of military success, to conduct a legal campaign against those Americans who, in secret, remained loyal to England; and to rebuke, in the fashion customary to advocates of free principles, the convictions of an unpopular minority through confiscation of property, and through imprisonment, and through a few gay desultory lynchings, no one of which was viewed at all seriously by anybody except its main figure. Even so, these routine measures incited some thousands of loyalists to seek refuge in the St. Johns area. This exodus, from out of Savannah and Charleston in particular, was increased when both France and Spain joined the colonials, and so lifted the American-English conflict from the pettiness of a revolt into the splendors of international war. Pale and but barely escaped refugees from freedom now sought by the hundreds to find in Florida a subservience to fair dealing and common sense.

A large number of these Georgian and Carolinian émigrés builded, for themselves, log cabins, with roofs of palmetto leaves, on or about the banks of the St. Johns River, as far south as Doctor's Lake. But St. Johns Bluff rose rather nearer to the lands from which these loyalists had been driven; and since all this neighborhood remained more easy of access than was the harbor of St. Augustine, here Johns Town, or St. Johns Town, as people called the new settlement, became a sanctuary of impressive dimensions.

In 1779 its acreage was divided into building lots, each with an average frontage of 75 feet and a depth of 120 feet. So numerous frame dwellings then succeeded to log cabins prolifically that, by 1782, Johns Town could boast, not merely of two taverns, one public house, a livery stable, a dry goods store, a storehouse, and a hardware emporium, but of a Lodge for Freemasons also, overlooking the former site of Fort Caroline. A doctor stayed in attendance against any physical needs; whereas, so far as might go spiritual requirements, the Reverend James Seymour had been unloosed, by the Society for the Propagation of the Gospel, to rove eloquently about the riverbank upon which a more taciturn Menéndez had once inculcated his own gospel with swords and axes. Near-by were a half dozen large plantations active in the production of naval stores and of lumber, which muchneeded contributions toward a continuance of Britannia's somewhat wavering rule over the waves were then being exported, liberally, from Johns Town, of which the population, at this its heyday, exceeded fifteen hundred.

The prosperity of the new town and of the surrounding plantations died with extreme suddenness in the spring of

1783, when Britain made ready to give back all Florida to Spain, who had required this price for her but slight aid to the colonials; and who now received it through the terms of a peace treaty which, as the more pleasant alternative to dragging too many Englishmen into England's prolonged war against England's rebel colonists, conceded the existence of the United States of America.

Thus closed an episode in British colonization which, it was estimated by planters and other proprietors of land in the peninsula, had involved, as the price of open defeat, an expenditure of approximately $1,500,000. The human tragedy allied with this farce of transferring, from the German king who ruled over England, to the French king who ruled Spain, about fifty-nine thousand square miles of territory, for which neither nation now had any special use, was of more importance; for vast numbers of loyal English refugees, at Johns Town, along the river, and at St. Augustine, were thus checked in the process of securing, for their families and for themselves, homes and tranquillity.

These bewildered British Protestants had but the choice either to remain in Florida under the heels of Spain—whose heels were proverbially brutal in English oratory, besides being papist—or else, for pure faith's sake, in addition to the polite consideration which an Anglo-Saxon owes to his own safety, yet again to become emigrants. Virtually all these British subjects, whom Britain had abandoned, chose the latter course; and so found their ways, variously, toward Europe, Nova Scotia, the United States, Jamaica, or to the Bahama Islands.

Among those sailing for the Bahamas was Denys Rolle, who emerged from the Floridian disaster, if with but very little money left, yet, it is probable, without finding in his sudden downfall any special prompting to revise a lifelong opinion as to his fellow creatures' unworth. He chartered— with a sour sense of humor, perhaps—the *Peace and Plenty*, early in the October of 1783; and by means of two trips, he thus removed to Exuma his livestock, his household effects, his dismantled buildings, and all his slaves except only the fate-favored forty-five who died on shipboard. More than a thousand other Anglo-American refugees from the St. Johns valley, accompanied by twice that number of Negro slaves, sought out new homes in the Bahamas—where (so they were assured) from the ever-fertile farm lands of such quaintly named places as Harbor, New Providence, Cat, Eleuthera, Caicos, Watlings, Turks, Andros, and some twenty other fortunate far islands, prosperity beckoned; and where the lap of luxury awaited the pioneer's rump.

In brief, just as in 1763 the Spaniards had left Florida, so now the English abandoned it; and the St. Johns valley had lost, for the second time—and again, almost overnight— nearly every one of its white inhabitants.

15

Some Who Sinned Variously

To ANY troublesome demands by what an Englishman called honesty—such as, in part, had led the more respectable English to evacuate the St. Johns valley in 1783—Daniel McGirth had become immune. His belief in the free principles of America, it may be remembered, had been shattered by the would-be horse thief, in the buff-and-blue uniform of an American army officer who had ordered off this colonial scout to be imprisoned and whipped if in the cause of democracy he did not surrender, to his less well-mounted captain, McGirth's fine mare, Gray Goose. One notes here a deplorable touch of tenderness in the fact that a dissenter from the official turpitude customary during wartime should have elected to be flogged in public, with a familiar atrocious-ness very fully foreknown to him, rather than part with the dumb brute whom—it so happened—he loved. Thereafter, the no longer patriotic scout had escaped southward, still riding upon Gray Goose; and with a sort of logic which one is forced to admit, McGirth began life anew, upon the northern bank of the St. Johns, as a horse thief.

He stole only, it is true, from the rebel Georgians across the borderline, those horses and the supplies which were needed by an England that allowed him to retain Gray Goose and protected him from being flogged, yet again, unforgettably. Lieutenant Colonel McGirth of the East Florida Rangers served England in this fashion, with distinction, during a number of border raids, throughout the rest of the war. And by the English his intrepid Rangers were made much of, both for their daring and for their usefulness; the praise granted them was unlimited; nor any whit more limited was the well-worded sympathy with which, in preparing to give up Florida, Great Britain expressed to the East Florida Rangers the truism that the allies of a civilized nation, when of no further immediate use, are expected to protect themselves as they best may unaided. The services of the East Florida Rangers had been fully appreciated by his Majesty; it was hoped by his Majesty that these gallant men might, somehow, manage to adjust themselves to new conditions; for to hear of their destruction, either by brutal Spaniards or by no less reprehensible Americans, would be, to his Majesty, a source of considerable regret. In short, England abandoned the East Florida Rangers, with the adroit and resonant grace of a worldly-wise nation to whom rhetorical anguish was not a stranger; and McGirth's love for England expired.

Yet this stealing of horses and their equipment, of cattle

and provisions (he reflected) if not any longer to be conducted upon the high planes of moral duty, might, if it were but converted into a private enterprise—and if its practitioner should so far extend the business as to include all branches of larceny—why, but yes, his old trade might yet afford to Dan McGirth a pleasant living. So McGirth turned outlaw; from among the disbanded East Florida Rangers he selected as his recruits the more highly skilled thieves; and during the mischancy eighteen months that the English were leaving, and the Spaniards were entering Florida, McGirth at the head of his freebooters attacked the caravans of both nations impartially. Among the departing English, who carried with them all their portable possessions of any special value, his success was tremendous; and yet the Spaniards likewise, since they were fetching into Florida the materials to furnish their new homes, repaid his labors to an extent wholly praiseworthy.

Then after the English were gone, McGirth formed an alliance with the Indians; and with their aid, his men began to plunder both the Georgians to the north and the Spaniards southward. He made his headquarters in the deep forests between the St. Johns and the St. Marys rivers; and he so far increased the staff of his prehensile employees that, late in 1784, the Spanish commander at St. Marys reported the number of McGirth's outlaws to be "about sixty families." It is a phrase which lends to this woodland fortress of thieves an aspect rather pleasingly domestic.

Nor were the activities of Dan McGirth restricted to forests and highways, for he now began to attack, to strip, and to burn Spanish vessels in the St. Johns. With two nations embattled against him, he evaded capture, if at odd times but narrowly, yet with unfailing success. McGirt's Creek,

near Jacksonville, was so named in his honor after he escaped
from one party of pursuers there, by plunging into this large
stream on horseback. His steed swam across safely, with
McGirth on her back; and thus repaid equitably the flogging
which he had chosen rather than to part with Gray Goose.

So Dan McGirth fared merrily; he had always at his
disposal a superfluity of money and women and the best
wines; he robbed handsomely, in a very notable blue coat
with large flat silver buttons, and wearing about his neck a
fine frilled linen stock; his repute became that of a semifabulous ogre: and then—in a mere casual night surprise
attack upon an Indian village—a party of some twenty Spaniards found that, with an unintended intrepidity, they had
caught the all-dreaded McGirth sound asleep in bed. The
circumstance that it was not exactly his own bed has been
accounted for by the affectionate nature and the unusual
beauty of his companion.

The astounded Spaniards, at all events, conveyed Dan
McGirth, tied with strong ropes, to the Castillo de San Marcos. And there, instead of hanging him, Governor Manuel de
Zespedes—who did not believe in wasting, upon a malefactor
who had defied Spain with such boldness, the indulgence of
death—ordered Dan McGirth to be walled up in one of the
unlighted cells upon the river side of the castle.

The trapped outlaw passed five years in this little room,
some six feet underground, without any least sound to dis-
tract him from repentance except only, for the first month
or so, his own screaming, and without any ray of light except
when, every morning, an unseen jailer came with a lantern
and put dry bread and a pitcher of water through the barred
small hole in the wall. You could see then, beyond the rigid

iron bars, and back of the obscurely moving black hand, a vague, dull, yellow gleaming. You would not ever see anything else so long as your life lasted. You remembered your parents and their fond, constant, wasted care of you. You remembered a slim dark girl who—when you did not know quite enough about lechery—had said, "Oh, but I do!" You remembered this or the other sunrise when you were young. You remembered very bright moonlight upon one or another woman's face, uplifted toward your face. You remembered more than was at all endurable.

And at first you were not happy in this quiet damp darkness; then you knew you were going mad; and the thought frightened you, for a while; but by-and-by that did not matter either.

Another former colonial who cast in his lot with the common lot of the Spanish régime was William Panton; and his moral standards, though inferior to those of Dan McGirth, were reinforced so very properly by discretion as to enable William Panton, not simply to escape prison, but to extort a fair profit from out of each of the three governments the laws of which he, at one time or another, evaded.

Born in Aberdeenshire, Scotland, Panton emigrated to North America before the Revolution; and founded the trading firm of Panton, Leslie & Company, which maintained offices alike in London, Charleston, and Savannah. His quite temperate loyalty to England aroused by-and-by an incommensurate disfavor in the hotheaded colony of Georgia, so that, in 1778, Panton was declared an outlaw by the Georgian Provincial Congress, and his property confiscated. A Scot, however, was not easily to be overreached in financial matters by English-born legislators; for in anticipation of some such trouble, Panton had already extended his main operations into Florida.

His formal exile from Georgia thus simply transferred his headquarters, at first to St. Augustine, and later to Pensacola; and his post upon the St. Johns River, near Lake George, became forthwith for the English the main emporium of barter and bribery, and of malefaction in general, among their highhearted and credulous, and therefore not expensive, allies, the Indians. Here William Panton distributed the guns and ammunition with which the Indians had now begun to shoot down American rebels, from ambush, with a gratifying frequency. Swindling also thrived at this station, where, at a vast profit, cloth and coarse linens and sugar and salt and much strong whisky were exchanged with the Indians for fine furs; and considerable lumber was exported. Through so many and so well-paying misdemeanors did William Panton become a millionaire.

His master stroke in the way of finance, however, was to make with Alexander McGillivray, chief of the great Creek Confederation of some six thousand warriors, an alliance so mutually remunerative that William Panton was said, afterward, to have been the one ally with whom McGillivray never broke faith. So it came about that when the Spaniards took over Florida, the firm of Panton, Leslie & Company had its trading posts everywhere, as far west as Tennessee; that its commerce with the Indians had become to all intents a monopoly; and that William Panton, waiving for the moment his temperate loyalty to England, received, at his main trading post beside the St. Johns, the new governor, Don Manuel de Zespedes, with politeness.

He received, though, not at all the same august and granitelike personage who ordered off Dan McGirth to a prison cell, now that Don Manuel was dealing with quite another sort of rascal—a rascal who had very much money, in banks beyond your reach, and back of whom loomed the unscrupulous valor of almost every Indian cutthroat upon the east side of the Mississippi.

"My pleasure, señor, is beyond description—" the governor began.

William Panton said, "Yes?"

He then stated his terms. As a Presbyterian, he must ask that the religious conditions which were now being imposed by the Spaniards upon the English subjects who elected to remain in Florida should be dismissed, so far as Panton was concerned; as a loyal subject of the king of England, Panton was willing to take an oath of obedience to the king of Spain, but not any oath of allegiance. For the rest, Panton required merely of his Excellency that all business affairs of the firm of Panton, Leslie & Company should be left undisturbed.

He paused then, at much, superabundant ease; and he twirled negligently, between his stubby fingers, a bright blue pen.

Señor Panton (the enthusiastic governor answered) had spoken with that forthrightness which among gentlemen is always to be preferred, as well as with that nobility of soul for which, throughout the entire known world, Señor Panton had become famous. His conditions were wholly reasonable, alike as to religion, the sublime virtue of patriotism, and the great field of business matters—a field concerning which Don Manuel de Zespedes confessed, with candor, his own ignorance.

"Yes?" said William Panton.

For the governor of Florida, Don Manuel submitted, any such ignorance was a serious defect; and he sighed.

William Panton said, "Yes?"

—Because (Don Manuel continued) inasmuch as business matters had intruded, somehow, into this most pleasant conversation, Señor Panton must understand of course that, for some little while, the colony of·Florida would be hard pressed for money? Loans would be needed, perhaps, from the religious and patriotic, true friends of Florida.

His Excellency was answered dryly that, in any such case, and with proper securities provided, the firm of Panton, Leslie & Company would esteem it a privilege to act as bankers for the colony. Meanwhile, it might be that a draft upon London made out to his Excellency in person, and to be used by his Excellency at his own discretion, would serve as a stopgap. The nib of the bright blue pen was then dipped into a massive silver inkstand.

Everything was thus settled happily; and although, in the upshot, William Panton wrote yet several other personal drafts, and his firm advanced in all some $200,000 to finance for the Spaniards their regained hold upon Florida, William Panton did not lose, in the outcome of these broad-minded transactions, one halfpenny. He gained, instead, during the next eighteen years, about a million more dollars, now that his trading posts were left undisturbed. And then, in 1801, an uningratiating intruder, after a fashion such as no life-long faithful Presbyterian could reconcile at once with the doctrine of predestination, obliterated every trace of William Panton's power, and prestige, and opulence, and his self-complacency, with a gaunt hand.

It was not merely a wise move, but a necessary act of self-protection, by the Spanish opportunists who at this instant held office in Florida, to support Panton, at a reasonable price, so as to restrain those unlicensed aggressive traders who swarmed out of the United States of America with the ubiquitousness and the all-ruining pertinacity of termites.

To the Congress of the newborn Republic had been accorded, even at this remote era, the privilege of presidential instructions just how to vote. Congress had passed, therefore, at the dictates of President Washington, the demanded law which established, for the United States, a number of factories and trading posts appreciably beyond the legal southern limits of the United States.

"And so," remarked our first chief executive—who of necessity was a tyro as to the many painful duties laid upon his successors in the way of hypocrisy—"and so, señors, what are you going to do about it?"

He paused then, turning southward the sour and wide-jawed, omnivorous look, which Gilbert Stuart caught to perfection when his Excellency met face to face with a backward debtor; but out of Florida came not any reply. Very soon afterward, both Carolinian and Georgian fur traders were to be found unexplainedly pursuing their business along both banks of the St. Johns.

These interlopers were described by Prince Achille Murat as "intrepid hunters" and "shameless cheats," who undertook the "perilous trade of penetrating unexplored lands, through unknown dangers, so as to sell to the Indians powder, arms, coarse stuffs, but particularly whiskey, in exchange for skins"; and who traveled as a rule "in the company of Indian women, who serve them"—so the prince words it chastely—"as interpreters."

Beside these intrusive traders now arose yet another cause for trouble between the Anglo-Americans and the Spanish-Americans in the St. Johns area; for slaves who escaped from the Georgian plantations to the river swamps, where the Indians befriended and hid them, on account of an unlegalized native charity, were pursued by their owners irrespective of national boundaries; and this resulted in an almost continuous interchange of complaints and blustering between Spanish and American officials. War had become inevitable, said the judicious.

16

How the River Got a Commander

O F A SUDDEN, a new strange turn of affairs began in 1790, when Spain loosened her immigration requirements in order to populate more thickly the deserted British plantations which James Grant had founded alongside the St. Johns, those rich river lands at which now nibbled the jungle. Special privileges of land, exemption from taxes and military service, and gold in payment for agricultural products, were all promised to such Anglo-Americans as would become citizens of Florida and Spanish subjects.

Thomas Jefferson, who was then secretary of state, at

once wrote to President Washington that one needs hope at least a hundred thousand citizens of the United States would accept Spain's invitation; for in that case, Jefferson added, their apostasy might be made the instrument of "delivering to us peaceably what may otherwise cost us a war. In the mean time, we may complain of this seduction of our inhabitants just enough to make them [the Spaniards] believe we think it very wise policy for them, and confirm them in it."

Mr. Jefferson, it may be observed, did not often allow the integrity of his private life to interfere with his astuteness as a politician. He desired Florida for the United States; and to obtain it through subterfuge would be less expensive than to get it by fighting.

Pre-eminent among the Anglo-Americans who at once (for personal pecuniary reasons) succumbed to "this seduction of our inhabitants" was John McQueen, a native of Philadelphia. He had married, however, into a South Carolinian family of considerable wealth and distinction; and afterward settled in Georgia, on a plantation called "Colony," which graced a bluff near Savannah, upon which plantation, until the outbreak of the Revolution, John McQueen lived prosperously as a planter, and increased, every year, under the unqualified license of matrimony, the number of his children.

McQueen joined the patriotic forces in 1775, and was made by-and-by a captain in the American navy. General Washington, who in his marmoreal way approved of genial tall Captain McQueen, sent him abroad upon various confidential missions to Europe, which were continued for some while after the Revolution. McQueen was thus very often in France, where in diplomacy his more close associates were

Lafayette, Jefferson, and d'Estaing. Then, when at long last Captain John McQueen returned to his plantation near Savannah, he began to invest in real estate more and more widely. In addition to immoderately huge tracts on the mainland, he bought Sapelo and Little Cabretta islands, and very considerable parts of St. Catherines and Blackbeard islands, off the south coast of Georgia; and he thus found himself confronted with much, ever-growing trouble in the shape of real estate taxes. By 1789, he had been branded a tax defaulter; and entrusting his offspring to the ingenuity of Providence, tall genial John McQueen embraced, as an alternative to civil suits and bankruptcy, the resonant opportunities which Florida offered.

He prospered there to a wonder; for McQueen's experience as a captain in the American navy led almost instantly, when he had turned Spanish, to his appointment as commander of the River of St. John, as well as of the River of St. Mary. His uniforms, as designed by their wearer's unrestricted Celtic imagination, were commensurately impressive.

The former protégé of George Washington became a trusted adviser of the Spanish governor, Don Juan Quesada; and the erstwhile Episcopalian comrade of Thomas Jefferson in liberal thinking was converted to the Catholic faith, after a correct and convincing period of irresolution. As a former diplomat, McQueen cultivated a protective, devout friendship with Father O'Reilly, the parish priest of St. Augustine; a crucifix hung always above the bed of John McQueen, even when he did not sleep alone; nor did the tall commander's gay uniform very often fail to adorn the scented twilight of early mass. In short, the tact and the resolute joviality of John McQueen placed beyond dispute the wisdom of the Spaniards in attracting American settlers into Florida, about which the commander of the River of St. John was now moving flamboyantly, in scarlet and in an incredible amount of gold lace and gold-washed buttons.

The letters written by the commander, however—to his daughter, Eliza, between the years 1791 and 1807—reveal somewhat less gaudy glimpses of life alongside the St. Johns River, from which, during his reprieves from official splendor, McQueen shipped lumber; and upon the banks of which he raised cotton also, under the perennial impetus of hoping to pay off every one of his debts in Georgia, by-and-by.

These letters speak of but one visit paid by his family to the desolate, poor hermit and forsaken father (for so did the gold-embroidered, tall, jovial commander of the River of St. John see fit to describe himself) during some sixteen years of intending nobly, by-and-by, to pay off his debts in Georgia. He was cheered rather more frequently by the companionship of his son, the junior John McQueen, who, as an employee of William Panton, in the trading post at Pensacola, had learned how not to object, overstrenuously, to a swindler. John Jr. objected, instead—or at least, in chief—to Pensacola, the inhabitants of which city he disfavored. Fully half of them, it develops, were, of all un-American demerits, French. "So, altho' the society is but small, we generally, of a Sunday evening, have a kick-up at some of their houses; but they take great care, at the same time, that it should not lead them into expense. . . . They give you no kind of refreshment but cold water, to wash down the dirty talk; for they have totally banished delicacy from their conversation."

One makes no doubt that the genial, hollow, resplendent commander of the River of St. John sighed sympathizingly

over this lack of social polish. Meanwhile, the good-fellow-
ship in which Commander John McQueen basked daily in
Florida did not at all help to straighten out his bankruptcy
in Georgia. He wanted back his children, because he loved
his children; and paternal love was always urging the old
fellow to put aside his shrewd ceaseless blarney in favor of
some discreet branch of acquisitive lawbreaking.

"Pray, do you not think," he wrote, to one of his sons-
in-law in Savannah, "great Matters may be done in the African trade, from the Island of Amelia in this Province, when
the door shall be shut, next Year, by Congress, to the importation of slaves?"

He in reply was told that he was an aging reprobate
who, at his time of life, and with his unenviable past record
of bankruptcy, ought to be seeking out a more honest way
to earn his daily bread than by slave smuggling; and con-
forming humbly to the admonitions of virtue, John Mc-
Queen looked about for some better-thought-of, well-paying
form of misdemeanor, which he soon found.

It was the so-called profession of "wrecking," by which
the Bahaman "conchs"—as they were termed, for no ever
quite settled reason—now thrived, upon the lower east coast
of Florida. Sons of those English refugees who had been misled, by the combined counsels of loyalty and self-seeking, in
1783, to leave Florida for the Bahamas, and who had tried
without any success to wring nourishment from out of the
barren, coral-formed soil of the British West Indies, these
conchs had been bred, almost prenatally, to the rough give-
and-take of the sea. Than its grim turbulent takings they
liked better that which it gave when in a beneficent mood—
and when slightly assisted.

It followed, after the conchs observed that through salvaging ships wrecked upon the rocky isles which bordered the Straits of Florida they could acquire far more of luxury than through prosaic fishing, provided always that, by Heaven's will, a sufficiency of unhappy ships were smashed up often enough, they devoted their sloops and schooners to "wrecking"—which in its practical application did not, to an appreciable degree, differ from piracy. The crews and passengers of such vessels as struck a reef were robbed, and the ships plundered, by the conchs. Now and then their clients became so uncivil that an admonitory murder or so was found necessary; but at all times a healthful frequency of naval disasters was maintained through misleading buoys and signal lights placed so adroitly, among hidden shoals, as to guide ships safely toward destruction.

Observing with an appreciative disfavor the success of these British criminals, the neo-Spanish commander of the River of St. John decided to serve both his current fatherland and his own interest by imitating them; and the former diplomat obtained, diplomatically, the needful authority.

"I have the pleasure to inform you, my dear Mr. Mackay," Commander John McQueen wrote, with superb aplomb, to his reproving son-in-law, in Georgia, "that the King of Spain has been graciously pleased to grant me the exclusive privilege of fitting out vessels to 'wreck' on the Florida keys and all the Coast of Florida—for the purpose," he continued virtuously, "of supporting the Commerce & saving the Vessels & lives of the Unfortunate of any Nation that may, from time to time, be lost on the coast. This appointment will be not less honorable than profitable. . . . If I can—by any laudable means," he interpolated, with a benign rigor—"collect enough to pay my debts before I go to my long home, and leave something to my dear Children, I shall depart in peace."

The gaudy and indomitable, gray wastrel explained also, with a hint of pride, that his appointment to head the piratic flotilla, under the flag of philanthropy, "being directed from the King," neither the governor of Florida nor the captain general of Cuba would ever be able to displace him "unless for exceeding malpractice, & then not till the pleasure of the Sovereign shall be known." In brief, John McQueen had now got a free hand to plunder everybody right and left, so long as he paid to the king of Spain a rational share of his booty.

It followed that in all North America there was no pettifogger more free from care—barring only the shortness of breath and that ugly pain in your breast, which troubled you nowadays with an increasing frequency—than was the jaunty commander of the River of St. John. Through his knowledge of seamanship acquired as a captain in the American navy, and the flexibility of conscience which he had got as an American diplomat, he was equipped handsomely to beat the conchs at their own game. So he made ready some twenty small ships, knowing that there awaited him, in this new enterprise, wealth very nearly unlimited. The old Georgian debt, a mere $60,000, would be attended to out of hand; his children would be given back to him; and he would be no longer a discredited, forever wheedling, gray renegade, made gaudy with much gold and scarlet, but a well-thought-of nabob like William Panton.

Like William Panton, however, he encountered an obstacle. When all was in readiness for the future multimillionaire to begin his maiden venture at "wrecking," just then—a bit awkwardly—at one of his small mills beside the

St. Johns, that ugly and very sharp pain in his left breast annoyed John McQueen yet again. It lasted, though, at utmost, but for a few trapped, gasping, not wholly genial moments; and almost all St. Augustine went to his funeral, because you could not ever quite help liking the old rascal.

17

"Designed by Thomas Jefferson"

No MATTER how misleading may have been the diplomacies of Commander John McQueen, yet in the unpuritanic purlieus of the St. Johns River they were not unique. One needs to weigh, for example, the never quite explained doings of John Houstoun McIntosh.

Just why McIntosh should have been arrested remains an enigma. He was a Georgian, reared near Darien; he was a retired army officer who had served America throughout the

Revolution; and he, like Panton and McQueen, had removed to Florida to become—at any rate, nominally—Spanish. Rumor says that by the Cabinet of our most famous, first, and in some traits unique, chief executive, who could not tell a lie, the apostasy of John McIntosh was regarded with equilibrium; and that in Mr. Jefferson's Department of State, above all, the most charitable sort of broad-mindedness reigned untroubled.

The plantation of John McIntosh, called "Bellevue," upon the north bank of the St. Johns, was at Ortega Point, now within Jacksonville. There he raised cotton and, as became the climate, a slightly subtropical number of children, with discretion; and fared peacefully enough, until the morning when John McIntosh rode over to St. Augustine, to buy a cow; and when, at the city gates, he was arrested by the governor's order. That same day, a troop of Spanish soldiers entered Bellevue and searched throughout all the house, painstakingly. None nowadays knows just what they were looking for, or what they found, in the large pile of letters which John McIntosh had not committed, with a proper amount of forethought, to a considerably larger fireplace. Rumor alone asserts that he appeared to have been collecting, upon a somewhat excessive scale, the autographs of Th: Jefferson.

However this may have been, the governor of Florida, upon consideration, regarded the correspondence of John McIntosh with a disapproval so energetic as forthwith to remove John McIntosh into Havana, where he was locked up in Morro Castle. With no less of eloquence than of obliviousness that John McIntosh was now a Spanish subject, his wife appealed to the government of the United States, which would seem to have found her aphasia to be contagious; for

President Washington, dismissing curtly the consideration that neither over Florida nor over Cuba did he have any least jurisdiction, intervened with decision. McIntosh was released, without trial, and without having been accused of anything in particular—for indeed, at this naïve time, nobody had ever heard of a fifth columnist.

He returned to the St. Johns River with a broadened experience in dealing with Spanish officials, and with the painfully acquired knowledge that the letters of an employer may now and then be burned with immense profit. Acquiring Fort George Island—upon which had once thrived the mission of San Juan del Puerto, and where the strong benevolence of General Oglethorpe's soul had grappled with international fair dealing, and from the beach of which, yet earlier, Father Martínez had ascended toward bliss—John McIntosh henceforward made there his residence; and he installed in each room a convenient fireplace. He populated the island with his retainers, his relatives, and his slaves; he gave generous bribes to most Spaniards in authority; and he lived baronially, among his picked band of intending traitors.

McIntosh became bolder in his intrigues with the officials of the United States as his double-dealing advanced yet further along the muddied bypath which, somewhat later, rhetoric was to disinfect as "manifest destiny"; nor could his main correspondent in Washington be termed slothful. Peering westward of the Mississippi (after one last southward glance toward Florida), Thomas Jefferson now doubled the original size of the United States by purchasing, from the Emperor Napoleon, the Louisiana Territory, of about 828,000 square miles.

In dealing with Napoleon Bonaparte, it was remarked, our third president (apart from discarding all his former pronouncements as to the federal government's legal powers) went to the undiplomatic extreme of paying that which he had promised to pay—though only, it is true, at the rate of four cents an acre. Singularly, also, the acquisition of this inexpensive vast expanse did but whet the appetite of his people for still more expansion; since, as an honored historian has expressed it, "the hungry eyes of America looked always northward toward Canada, and at Florida to the south"— with some risk (one is tempted frivolously to object) of national strabismus.

The thorn-shaped peninsula of Florida, since its return in 1783 to Spain, had continued daily to justify its shape so far as went the side of Georgia. Border raids were conducted by Floridian outlaws, both white and red; escaping slaves found refuge in Floridian swamps alongside the St. Johns; and just south of the Georgian state line, Fernandina had become a lair of slave dealers, smugglers, and pirates. The abolition of slave trade in the United States made of this Spanish seaport a but too convenient depot for illicit importation; so that as many as three hundred square-rigged vessels, with cargoes from the African coast, or with contraband merchandise from South America, were, in the cosmopolitan harbor of Fernandina, an everyday spectacle.

Beside the improper nearness, to a proper-minded (but cotton-raising) Georgia, of this piratical trade in black cotton pickers, which Spain could not control, flourished the ever-present fear that England might seize the peninsula, and thus establish a new stronghold upon the continent of North America. So widespread became this apprehension that in 1811 Madison was empowered, by a secret act of Congress, to take such steps as would bring about the annexation of all

territory north of the St. Johns by the United States; and
with secrecy he sent south two commissioners. They found
that the unwillingness of Spanish officials to sign any definite
bargain was equaled only by the inability of Spain to ensure
that order would ever be maintained upon the north bank
of the St. Johns, or that the designs of England against
Florida would be rebuffed. The American commissioners then
entered into negotiations with some two hundred American-
born planters in the St. Johns-St. Marys territory, the leader
of whom, by an odd coincidence, was John Houstoun
McIntosh; and the scheme foreplanned by Thomas Jefferson,
about twenty-one years earlier, began palpably to take form.

McIntosh and his "Patriots" now formed a provisional
independent government; they adopted a flag; they drew up a
constitution; and they elected John McIntosh to be president
of the newborn Republic of East Florida. Flanked by nine
United States gunboats, the two hundred Patriots then
swarmed down intrepidly upon the fort at Fernandina—
which at this instant was occupied by ten Spanish privates
and one Spanish major. Major Lopez, not unjustifiably, surrendered.

Thereafter the affairs of this tiny Republic of East
Florida were administered, in large part, from Fort George
Island, upon which stood the home of President McIntosh.
An attempt was made to incorporate under his benevolent
assimilation the town of St. Augustine, but the Patriot
troops failed to capture the ever-impregnable Castillo de San
Marcos. Moreover, when too many protests, from both Spain
and England, as to America's part in abetting this pocket-
handkerchief free state became intrusively frequent, James
Madison virtuously denied knowing anything whatever

about the two commissioners whom he had sent into Florida; and ordered the immediate withdrawal of that part of the American military and naval forces which, to the president's intense, if histrionic, surprise, were found supporting the midget republic. It is true that the full strength of the United States was needed northward, now that in the warmth of maternal devotion the mother country was about to incinerate the Capitol of her misled children.

Although chiefly occupied by the Napoleonic Wars in Europe, England was able, without the expenditure of much lively effort, to defend Canada from invasion by Americans; and through demolishing the foreign trade of the United States, to trouble, with an unengaging vista of destitution, all the southeastern frontier—which, in turn, intensified the disquiet alongside the St. Johns, now that England had formed an undeclared alliance with Spain, and began to operate northward from the seaports of Florida. An effective English strategy was to incite, with large promises and unlimited alcohol, the bloodthirst of the Creek Indians, who had been England's most formidable allies during the Revolution. Many of these Creeks, upon whose lands American backwoodsmen, without any mentioned authority, had been clearing off and fortifying plantations, joined in with the extraordinarily able sachem, Tecumseh, when, strengthened by the prayers of the Anglican Church, this pre-eminent pagan began to form a federation of all his fellows in totem worship between Canada and Florida.

The forward march of England's copper-colored cohorts was halted by Andrew Jackson, in a battle which developed into a massacre. Yet Jackson was not to be satisfied with a mere defeat of the redskins; he meant to crush their power

forever; to drive these always meddling English out of
Florida; and to compel the Spaniards to control their Indian
population in the same colony. His principles, in fine, were
more American than modern. Proceeding, with the high hand
of James Oglethorpe, into the neutral territory of Florida,
Andrew Jackson carried out all his plans; and as a by-
product, he chased the Seminole Indians into the dense
swamps along and below the St. Johns. In bare time to prevent a Congressional investigation of his disregard for every
known rule of international law, he allied himself with
pirates and routed the English at New Orleans, fifteen days
after the conclusion of peace; and through this double out-
rage became his country's idol, exalted very far beyond any
criticism by common sense.

It was an exploit at once solemnized, with unconcealed
emotion, by Philip Freneau, the "Poet of the American Revolution"—who, in his decrepitude, was still representing the
topmost flights of American literature with an accuracy that
cold understatement can but describe as deadly. The bard
attributes General Jackson's military success, in chief, to the
fact that whenever "He called his thunders from afar, The
thunders answered, 'Here we are!' "—After which phenomena, Freneau inquires (and upon the whole, quite reasonably), "Who dared remain, who dared resist?"

The English, at all events, did not stay to argue with any
such celestial, gross favoritism. They, instead, withdrew,
with an Episcopalian's usual feeling about Jehovah, from the
intrusiveness of these obsequious and vocal thunderbolts.
Quite in vain had Admiral Cockburn made ready an English
fleet to lay waste the American coast from the St. Johns
northward, now that war ceased of a sudden between the
United States of America and England; for the latter country

had desisted from destructiveness in the St. Johns area, as begun by Sir Francis Drake and left uncompleted by Sir George Cockburn.

Conditions along the river, as years passed, changed simply from the unpleasant to the unbearable. Escaped thieves or murderers, after leaving the United States of America, informally and with disquiet, found hereabouts a pleasing broad-minded tolerance; the Patriots of the Republic of East Florida turned outlaws; and the Indians also began, not merely with the connivance of tomahawks, but with muskets nowadays, to share in the general absence of puritanic self-restraint. Affairs had become so disordered by 1817 that President Monroe then openly sent a military force into the area just north of the St. Johns to expel smugglers and slave traders. Declaring that from Florida to Georgia there was a chain of stations through which Negroes were sold and delivered, with businesslike regularity, the Savannah *Republican* dwelt upon the hopelessness of checking this contraband commerce—inasmuch as slave dealers "pushed through uninhabited parts known only to themselves. . . . If ready for forming a caravan, an Indian alarm is created, so that the woods may be less frequented; if pursued to Georgia, they escape into Florida."

In brief, the sole law known to the St. Johns valley was Rabelaisian, now that in those parts each man did what he wished; nor anywhere southward had anarchy become much less an affair of course.

Here is no place to explain the many complicated motives because of which the Spaniards clung to a nominal possession of Florida so long after Spain had lost the power to govern this province. By 1818, though, the decision was made to dispose of, at the best obtainable market price, the empty title of Spanish ownership; negotiations were begun; and Spain delivered to the United States of America, in 1821, the entire peninsula, in exchange for what in those days was the impressive sounding sum of $5,000,000. It is true that, since all this amount was devoted to paying off the claims filed against the Spanish government by American citizens who declared their property to have been damaged or stolen by Spaniards, during the recent period of outlawry on and about the St. Johns River, Spain did not get out of the transaction one penny.

At Monticello, Mr. Jefferson (who would be seventy-eight next month) remarked smilingly, to Mrs. Randolph, athwart a circle of devoted grandchildren and of great-grandchildren that this seemed an even better bargain than was the Louisiana Purchase.

A vast deal had happened (so he reflected benignly) since 1791; yet nothing unforeseen had ever upset his plan to get Florida; instead, his plan had worked out, very perfectly and smoothly, through the long space of thirty years; and it had proved, beyond argument, today, to be the right instrument of "delivering to us peaceably what may otherwise cost us a war."

Mr. Jefferson, sitting alone in his library—before selecting, as was his nightly habit, "an hour or half-hour's reading, of something moral, whereupon to ruminate in the intervals of sleep"—allowed himself a full glass of Amontillado. He did not often ascend to this noble wine; but he drank now to a noble nation, all united.

Part Two

THE REPUBLICAN RIVER

At length we see by prudence gained
What jealous Spaniards long retained;
And Florida's secluded waste
Is in one lengthening chain embraced . . .
Honor to those who first designed
This chain of *States* to bless mankind . . .
A region won from selfish Spain,
A golden link in freedom's chain!

—"On the Cession of East and West Florida, from
Spain to the United States," by Philip Freneau

18

Of Fitness and Discretion

THE St. Johns valley was "a grotesque region"—
aloofly remarked Ralph Waldo Emerson, whom bronchitis
had brought to St. Augustine but a brief while after Florida's
enforced acceptance of still other democratic discomforts—
"rapidly settled by public officers, land speculators & desperadoes." Emerson, yet furthermore, was displeased by the
open-air sales of Negroes along with fruits and vegetables; by
the conversational violence of a Catholic priest, who stayed
imprisoned for debt upon weekdays, but was released every

Sunday morning so that he might conduct the offices of his church; and by the profuse public profanity of Judge Joseph L. Smith (president of the East Florida Bible Society), who both brawled and imbibed in many barrooms, declared idle gossip as to this bulwark of religion, who was likewise said to cheat at billiards unskillfully. All these were unpuritanic practices which "not a little scandalized" the then young and provincial Emerson, and which caused him frankly to prefer the more rigorous standards of New England, such as (in Mark Twain's phrase) forbid you to do anything wrong when people are looking.

Emerson must have been revolted in particular, though, by the fact that Zephaniah Kingsley had been appointed one of the thirteen members of the Council to govern Florida; whereas even more astounding seemed President Monroe's reference to Kingsley as one of the "most fit and discreet persons in the Territory."

This Kingsley, it so happened, was an uncle of the mother of James Abbott McNeill Whistler—whom her son's art immortalized noncommittally as an "Arrangement in Black and Gray," before the more effusive æsthetic standards of the United States Post Office Department had found it desirable to improve a masterpiece (after throwing in a flowerpot) by rearranging Anna Matilda McNeill Whistler in three shades of purple, on a postage stamp. Born in Scotland, Zephaniah Kingsley emigrated to North America with his merchant father, who, when in 1780 Charleston was captured by the English, was among the 207 loyalists to honor the invader with their warmest congratulations upon the return of South Carolina to its "proper Political connexion." So lucky was young Kingsley that almost nothing remains recorded as to the more youthful years of his lack of innocence, or as to his affairs in general between the close of the American Revolution and the early part of the nineteenth century, when he acquired in Spanish Florida a grant of more than three thousand acres. It is known only that he had prospered, and was still prospering flagrantly, in the slave trade, not merely in the illegal fields of Florida and Georgia, but in a more liberal Brazil and the West Indies also. By 1817, when President Monroe sent a military force into Florida to suppress the slave trade, Zephaniah Kingsley—who as yet was not, in the president's opinion, one of the most fit and discreet persons thereabouts, but merely a notorious leader in the forbidden traffic—had established plantations on both banks of the St. Johns as far south as Drayton Island, in Lake George.

His own home then stood at Laurel Grove, the present site of Orange Park. There, in a house filled with grotesque mementoes from Scotland, England, Africa, Brazil, the West Indies, and with a generous exhibit of human scalps acquired from his deceased unfriends, through incidents upon which, as befitted an ungarrulous Scot, Kingsley did not often expatiate, he swayed his parochial empire, convinced that in resourcefulness small Zephaniah Kingsley was forever equal to the corrupt practices of Spanish officials, the depredations of white or red outlaws, the assaults of pirates, and the meddlesomeness of the United States army.

His brief stature alone troubled this magnate of the St. Johns River area, as being inadequate to his position in life. So he made the best of his bodily defects, they record, by appearing always in public upon a specially tall white horse. Then, with the further aid of a huge Mexican poncho hat and the large square silver shoe buckles which at all times he

affected, and wearing a bright green riding coat, small
Zephaniah Kingsley became a figure quite sufficiently impressive as he went regally about his ever-increasing domains.

Kingsley had so far yielded to the demands of the
Patriots of the Republic of East Florida as to place at their
disposal his slaves, his boats, and his crops—an abnegation
for which his executors were to recover from the United
States government $73,000 in damages. Foreseeing that the
loose organization of the so-called republic would allow him
free rein in the advancement of his own fortune, this cautious
and dapper rapscallion, whose dwarfed body was remarkably
incommensurate to his intelligence, had co-operated with
President John Houstoun McIntosh docilely; and so well
managed was the alliance, by Kingsley, that in 1817 McIntosh
was near bankruptcy, and the ownership of Fort George
Island, still the most important point on the river, came into
Kingsley's possession. His household goods and his collection
of scalps, as well as some hundreds of his slaves, were then
transferred from Laurel Grove, in a fleet of barges and
schooners, to the mouth of the river; and next to the small
lime-brick house which his ousted predecessor, McIntosh, had
occupied, Zephaniah Kingsley constructed a home befitting
his own special needs.

One of the few surviving landmarks of the Kingsley
empire, this two-story frame building, with its four faintly
Chinese-looking pavilions, one at each corner, still stands at
the entrance of the St. Johns. From its small central tower,
Kingsley was accustomed to watch the furtive progress of his
ships from Africa, as they passed through the salt marshes
and threaded the unmarked channels toward Fort George
Island; and he watched also from this mirador—overlooking

the same beach upon which Father Martínez had become a martyr—for the lurking hijacker waiting to rob the profit-laden barkentines of a genial but enterprising merchant of human flesh.

Immediately beneath this lookout, Kingsley caused to be builded a couple of sturdy prisons, with heavy oak posts in the center of each, to which his not as yet wholly tamed Negroes could be chained. Comfortable and commodious living quarters, furnished, it may have been, a bit too luxuriantly and vividly to meet the demands of Emersonian taste, were provided for Kingsley and his children between the attic prison cells of the frightened, raging, and as yet uncowed savages and the quiet cool basement in which Kingsley kept his choice wines next to a vaulted chamber in which he stored his money and unset gems and raw gold. That his wife resided next door to him, in the former White House of the Republic of East Florida, was not due to any domestic squabble, but rather to the circumstance that she (like Stevenson's Fair Cuban) descended from a long line of kings who, alas! were African. So the law forbade Anna Madegigine Jai, as a Negress, to live under the same roof with her husband; but a cloister which connected the two dwellings prevented inclement weather from checking the demands of affection.

Through this baroque gateway to Kingsley's river empire, which extended for some ninety miles alongside the St. Johns, were received nobody knows how many hundreds of his wife's race. One of his ships brought in ordinarily as many as three hundred captives, but the average slaver was a 50-ton barkentine manned by a captain, two mates, and a crew of from three to six seamen. Inasmuch as the trapped Negroes, while being fetched oversea, were packed (through economical motives) into a relatively small space not more than three feet high, between the deck and a flooring laid over the water casks, those who survived the long voyage were apt, after reaching Fort George Island, to need a great deal of patience and tenderness, in addition to medical treatment, before they could be made fit for sale at a price fairly profitable. Zephaniah Kingsley attended to such requirements with a shrewd ardor; furthermore, he maintained training schools in which skilled overseers instructed very conscientiously each new batch of abducted Negroes as to the minutiæ of plantation labor; and the reward of his charity, here upon earth, was a fifty per cent increase in the market value of his captives. He profited likewise by their work while they were acquiring in this manner, gratis, an education so remunerative to their future owners; and he thus produced, upon his St. Johns River plantations, large quantities of rice, sugar, cotton, corn, peas, potatoes, and oranges, as the by-products of sound pedagogic standards.

Nor did Zephaniah Kingsley ever so far neglect his Negresses as to select a bedfellow outside their ranks. The exact number of female slaves whom he honored with the practical status of a wife remains uncertain, but he distributed them, with the tact of a considerate husband, alongside the St. Johns, each in her own home, at a discreet distance from her rivals in his regard. He visited them all as often as circumstances and his vitality allowed; he continued affably to indulge even those few of his harem who did not repay his affection with offspring; but always over Kingsley's own mansion, at the mouth of the St. Johns, undisturbed by time's passing, presided his first wife, Anna Madegigine Jai, to whom, as has been said, repute assigned royal birth, as a former princess of Madagascar. Kingsley (not ever a com-

municative person) declared only that his "connubial relations" with her "took place in a foreign land, where our
marriage was solemnized by her native African custom";
and he maintained that her "integrity, moral conduct, or
good sense" lost nothing by comparison with any white person known to him.

Even so, his was not a ménage of which Ralph Waldo
Emerson could be expected to approve wholly without reservation.

19

The Melting Pot Simmers

THAT the former Spanish domain between the St. Marys River and the St. Johns River was not any longer to be "the rendezvous, or asylum, for the smuggling and piratical adventurers of every nation, or the secure retreat for the lawless and ungovernable of our state," had been, in 1821, the complacent announcement of Governor John Clark of Georgia, now that two centuries of untiring aggression, upon the part of Englishmen and Anglo-Americans, had culminated in fixing the 1,200-mile coast line of the Floridian peninsula as the southeastern boundary of earth's largest if not yet great republic.

In opposition to the sound oratorical faith of Governor Clark, many of "the lawless and ungovernable" of Georgia did, however, penetrate, almost at once, into the St. Johns

River lands, and aid in adjusting Florida to the least lovely
principles of democracy. It was a migration enlarged in particular, if not overornamentally, by violators of that Georgian law which concerned all who happened "wilfully or
maliciously to cut or disable the tongue, put out an eye, slit
the nose, bite or cut the ear, nose or lip, or cut off or disable
any limb or member" of persons whom they regarded without friendliness.

By this colonial law, first offenders were fined £100 and
made to stand in the pillory for a period not exceeding two
hours. If unable to pay the fine, they received on their bare
backs a hundred lashes; and by nobody was any outcry
raised against either punishment. It was but the customary
aftermath of a Saturday night's simple mirth among the
uncultured, during which at least one talented and partly
drunk "gouger" was apt to twist the hair of a comrade in
revelry around the forefinger of each hand, thrust his
thumbs with great violence against the eyes of his stunned
victim, and expel both eyes from their sockets. Rather than
incur the penalty for a second conviction—which was death
without benefit of clergy—a vast number of, so to speak,
sophomore gougers now elected to become pioneers upon the
banks of the serene St. Johns, where a lack of police protection would ensure their well-being.

Anglo-Americans, whether desirable or detrimental, who
removed into this new part of the United States found it
more or less abandoned by the Spanish Floridians. There was
a fair quota of such notable exceptions as Joseph M. Hernandez, who, renouncing his Spanish citizenship, took the
oath of allegiance to the United States, and was rewarded by
being chosen as the first congressman to represent in Washington the St. Johns River territory; whereas an appreciable

Spanish element remained in the form of a colony of Minorcans who lived alongside or near the river. Yet quite another group comprised people of property whose progenitors had been in Florida for several generations, such as the Fatio family, with large plantations on the St. Johns. But the general level of character, of intelligence, and of refinements among the population, from out of which was to be evolved a civilization very far superior to that of the Spanish empire, left room for regret.

Now that Florida had entered the Union, settlers on and near the St. Johns were arriving from other parts of the South by horseback, carriage, wagon or oxcart, and from the North by sailing vessels. First among them, along with the Georgian gougers, were the vagabonds called "Crackers," who had been defined unfulsomely (at about the middle of the eighteenth century) as "an improvident and lawless set of paupers from the frontiers of Virginia, Maryland, the Carolinas, and Georgia . . . often as bad or worse than the Indians." Generally gaunt, pale, and leather-skinned, they appeared "to know neither necessity nor desire," according to a later account, by Margaret Deland, but "only silent, joyless, painless existence, which is as perfect in its way as a tree or a stone." Their improvidence, however, was cheered frequently by drunkenness and fornication; the perpetual presence of their destitution was alleviated by an absence of moral standards; and inasmuch as no form of law coerced Crackers, any divergence of opinion could be terminated, quickly and healthfully, with the fist.

Clearings of from fifty to a hundred acres replaced the unfenced small fields of these squatters when from out of the north came reputable and industrious planters to evict the

Crackers and the gougers from beside the St. Johns. Huts for more and yet more slaves were now builded upon these clearings, in addition to a larger log house containing four rooms for the master and his kindred. "Within this almost savage habitation," declared Prince Achille Murat, to whom, as the son of a former monarch, the ways of urbane persons were not unfamiliar, "you will find a family as well brought up, and as intelligent, as you do in Boston or New York. Its manners are not rustic; it has left the world for a time, and is engaged in creating a new one around it."

Likewise to the St. Johns came cattlemen. Packing their ponies with provisions (to which, in the form of an after-thought, a great many of these cattlemen added wives), they drove before them their herds to find in Florida a home which was walled by the sky only; and they thus entered into a life eternally discursive in search of superior grazing lands. Convinced that cow stealing was the one really serious crime, these cattlemen stood always ready, in the event of any such occurrence, to lynch the suspected offender as a matter of moral duty, nor did they often fail to weigh the evidence against him, without bias or rancor, afterward.

The Anglo-Americanization of the Floridian frontier brought sharp changes in the regulations governing Negroes. The deplored if imperceptible despotism of an absolute monarchy over free Negroes had encouraged them to acquire property as well as their own slaves, and to enjoy most other privileges of the white man; but the laws of an enlightened democracy were so restrictive as to forbid free Negroes to leave their homes after sundown without having a written permission to indulge in any such outings. Yet other and reputedly supernal influences which the United States patronized, and which disordered the former routine of Negro life, were very much resented by Zephaniah Kingsley; and so enkindled the brisk dwarf as to cause him to increase an already extraordinary list of misdoings by writing a book. He produced, in fine, in 1828, *A Treatise on the Patriarchial System of Society as It Exists . . . under the Name of Slavery,* and he had the satisfaction of seeing this pamphlet run through four editions.

With his thesis "that the Slave, or Patriarchal, System of Society" furthers the strength, the well-being, the morals, and the productiveness of the country concerned, one's interest has of necessity become academic, though it is still impossible, for the unmuggy-minded, not to admire the force and the clearness with which Kingsley states a great many truths which a democracy has to deny. Our concern here is, rather, with Kingsley's own experience.

"I settled a plantation upon the St. Johns River with about fifty new African Negroes, many of whom"—he records, as a certificate to their primal excellence—"I brought from the Coast myself. They were mostly fine young men and women and nearly equal in numbers. I never interfered with their connubial concerns, but let them regulate these after their own manner . . . I encouraged dancing, merriment, and dress . . . Both men and women were very industrious . . . They were perfectly honest and obedient, and appeared perfectly happy . . . In their weekly festivity . . . they always provided ample entertainment themselves, as they had an abundance of hogs, fowls, corn, and all kinds of vegetables and fruits . . . Then a man calling himself a minister got among them."

And the results of this clerical advent, it seems, were deplorable. It was now thought sinful to dance, or to work

corn, or to catch fish, on Sunday, or at any time to eat cat-
fish, because such fish had no scales; if a church member did
any one of these things, then he would be tormented, with
pitchforks and balefire, and his future food would be limited
to brimstone and sulphur. The Negroes became poor, ragged,
irritable, morbid, and dishonest. They would not work unless
beaten, because it was not their duty to work for a person
who held them in unjust bondage; and at their prayer meet-
ings, once or twice a week, they devoured the stolen hogs of
Zephaniah Kingsley with a religious gusto, because it was not
sinful to steal for the church. In brief, the joys of Eden vanished when once a man calling himself a minister had got
among them.

"My object in this long digression," Kingsley explains,
"is to show the danger . . . of superstition (by some called
religion) among Negroes . . . I cannot help regretting," he
concludes, with a quiet resignation toward the misconduct of
clergymen, "that honest, well meaning men should so mis-
apply their talents as to subvert all natural and rational happiness, and endeavor to render our species miserable."

—Whereafter, one makes no doubt, the brisk midget
with an approving conscience put on his green riding coat.
Then after parting with affection from Anna Madegigine Jai,
and kissing his brown children goodnight, he rode down the
east bank of the St. Johns very jauntily, upon the back of his
tall white horse, to look for that special sort of rational happiness to be found in the companionship of his eighth, or it
may have been of his ninth, black wife.

Preachers from out of Georgia and other near-by states
saw to it that white Floridians also should be exposed to correct doctrines. Soon after 1821, Methodist circuit riders began

to make their devout long journeys about the sparsely settled St. Johns area. These evangelists traveled alone, upon horseback, each fetching with him his clothes, and books, and food, and a sack of corn to feed the horse; nor did success always reward their self-sacrifice. One of them records, in fact, with a tinge of despair, how very difficult he had found his task to maintain, among the communicants of his denomination at a small settlement on the St. Johns, enough common decency to restrain many of them from succumbing to the obscene perils of dancing; whereas not infrequently his sermon would be interrupted by the rowdiness of one or more drunken members of his flock, who then had to be ejected bodily by the pastor, with brute force, before a quiet and profitable resumption of divine worship. Another and more optimistic Methodist minister, however, made bold to believe that at least a few Floridians were "endeavoring to escape the pollutions of the world . . . in this place of moral darkness and desolation."

When to yet a third Methodist circuit rider, the Reverend John L. Jerry, the right of preaching was forbidden—by, as it happened, that same Catholic priest whose manumission remained Sabbatical—then Heaven's Protestant servant pointed to the Stars and Stripes; and he remarked decisively, "There can be no Inquisition where that flag floats." One has no doubt that Rome's pampered hireling went back to his cell in the near-by jail rightfully impressed by this information.

Upon yet another occasion, when his funds had been reduced to one silver dollar, the Reverend John L. Jerry—so declares the record—stepped into a cluster of bushes in order that, after the discharge of an inferior need, he might indulge in prayer. Then "seeing something glitter in the sun-

shine, and supposing it was a button dropped by some Cava-
lier of the olden time, he thought he would go and pick it up
as a relic. But what was his surprise when, on taking it in his
hand, he found it a Spanish doubloon ($16)!!!! This met all
his wants until Quarterly Conference, when he received his
installment of missionary money. Beyond this"—the account
continues crescendo, toward a proper moral—"it established
in his mind that faith in God's special promises which he
never lost."

Considerably south of the Kingsley plantations on the
St. Johns stood "Hope Hill," opposite the old Indian trading
post at Volusia. This was part of yet another private empire,
founded upon principles not wholly akin to the ideals of
Zephaniah Kingsley, inasmuch as the head of this second enterprise was Moses Levy; and he, according to Achille Murat,
was "a Hebrew visionary" desirous to establish in Florida a
colony for Israelites, "provided that he is permitted to substitute Deuteronomy for common law and the Prophets for
statute law." When the St. Johns River lands were nearing
freedom from a period of no law at all (during which the
Kingsley fortune had been accumulated without any awk-
ward need to explain its sources), then Moses Levy began to
become a more and more conspicuous figure.

Born at Mogador, in Morocco, the son of a grand vizier
of the ruler of that country, Levy was descended from a
distinguished Portuguese Jewish family. His youth, like that
of Mrs. Marion Bloom, was spent at Gibraltar, but without
causing, so far as we know, the same tendency toward the
duo intérieur. He emigrated, indeed, to the Virgin Islands.
There, and in Cuba, Levy prospered in the lumber business;
and as his bank account increased, he became a contractor

for the Spanish government. Through his Spanish colleagues he grew interested in Florida, and he dreamed of creating in this peninsula, as a by-product to such wealth as would appear noticeable even in a planet teeming with Semitic multimillionaires, a refuge for his oppressed race.

Levy visited the United States, and he there made two observations destined to change his life and to exert much influence upon the future of the St. Johns. The first of these observations was that in the United States of America one enjoys that peculiar freedom of speech which permits every license except only a collective criticism of Catholics or of Jews. The second was that the lands about the St. Johns, which well suited both his commercial and his religious projects, were fated very soon to become a part of the Republic to the north. So Moses Levy purchased more than fifty thousand acres on or near the St. Johns, for slightly less than a dollar an acre, and he thus became automatically, in due course, a citizen of the United States.

Plans for his Jewish refuge took him to Europe often; and in time he drew to Pilgrimage, as he named his Floridian settlement near the present city of Gainesville, Hebraic settlers from German and French ghettos, as well as yet other groups from New Jersey and New York. Houses were built; much land was cleared; and a cargo of sugar cane was brought in from Cuba, as well as quantities of tropical fruits, roots, and seeds. A tentative cultivation of products similar to those grown in the south of France began at Pilgrimage; and a road was cut through the forest to connect the settlement with the St. Johns and with St. Augustine—all which involved an expenditure of some $18,000. Meanwhile, near the present village of Astor, upon the west bank of the St. Johns, Levy had established also the afore-mentioned plantation called "Hope Hill"; and there he raised sugar cane when he was not abroad raising much public disturbance by his pro-Jewish and antislavery lectures.

Prospects for the building of a great state out of the former Spanish colonial province of Florida, in short, appeared to be wholly bright in the early 1820's, with so many diverse elements prepared each to make its own special strange contribution. Yet such were circumstances that much progress was to be halted by racial difficulties which had existed for more than two centuries between the red men and the white men, and which now had been complicated yet further through the introduction, along with the plantation system, of many peoples at least half of whom were black.

20

A River Rediscovered

N̲o MAN would immigrate into Florida—no, not from hell itself," declared John Randolph of Roanoke, in opposing the movement in Congress to build roads and to provide yet other internal improvements for those newly annexed areas about the St. Johns.

Even in addition to being "a land of swamps, of quagmires, of frogs and alligators and mosquitoes," as Randolph derisively described it, the Floridian peninsula shared very few characteristics with Randolph's Virginia, or with any

other states of Anglo-Saxon origin. The inhabitants of
Florida, indeed, could boast hardly a trace of that mixed
Teutonic blood then regarded with adulation by its in-
heritors; and were forced, at a period when all virtues were
admittedly made in Germany, to confess humbly an origin
from sources less barbarous. A bit of the civilization of
Spain had been transplanted to the banks of the St. Johns
about forty-two years prior to the placing of an English
settlement, partly penal, upon the banks of the James in
Virginia; and St. Augustine had been the home of hidalgos
for some three-quarters of a century before the intimidated
Algonquins abandoned Plymouth to savage Puritans. It resulted that the traditions and mores of Florida, whatsoever
their minor merits in the way of good breeding, were alien to
those of the United States at large.

Anglo-Americans remained unimpressed, therefore, by
the two and a half century background of the St. Johns
valley. It was all too far away, in a "tangled mass of vines
and a labyrinth of undergrowth"; nor was New York or
Boston or Richmond, amicably absorbed in the morning
papers, much interested by the history or the literature of "a
wild jungle," so variously and so outlandishly expressed in
Latin, or Spanish, or Portuguese, or French, or correct English. Such being the frame of mind and the substitutes for
culture among the overlords of the new territory, it remained
for the St. Johns River to be rediscovered by admiration in
the more tangible terms of greatness through sheer bigness
and of wealth gained through speculation.

Andrew Jackson, that idolized heckler for the unshaved
frontier, who was now beginning to dominate the United
States as an epitome of their national failings, was sent by

President Monroe to make Anglo-Saxon the Floridian peninsula—after, it so developed, somewhat the primal methods of Horsa and Hengist. Then in the full enjoyment of the first decade of public adulation following the illegal victory at New Orleans, Jackson accepted the military governorship of Florida without hesitation; and he proceeded without dignity to antagonize its inhabitants. His disposition, to begin with, was embittered by the discovery that he did not even have the power to appoint his own relatives and personal friends to many of the better paying offices—which, as Mrs. Jackson stated with a disarming simplicity, "I thought, was in part the reason for his coming." Moreover, Jackson did not like the Spanish; his nature prevented him at all times from dealing justly, or even rationally, with institutions or persons that he disliked; and so, in a position which demanded the highest reach of diplomacy, he displayed the asperities of an ogre. The quite openly despised and daily browbeaten Spaniards—it must be recorded with regret—began to regard Andrew Jackson without warm affection.

Within a few months, Jackson tired of his Floridian adventure; and characterizing the entire affair as "a wild goose chase," he relinquished the governorship. He returned to Tennessee; and so great (one infers) was the relief of all Florida that during the following year a beginning settlement upon the St. Johns was named Jacksonville in his honor.

The new town was laid out upon the north bank of the river, where, turning abruptly toward the Atlantic, it so narrows as to form a natural fording place. In the 1740's, the Spaniards had erected to guard the passage a fort which they named St. Nicholas. Indians had found this shallow bend so convenient for getting their cows across the river that they called it Wacca Pilatka, which meant "cows crossing"; with the coming of the English in 1763, it thus acquired, naturally enough, the name of Cowford; and a ferry (called the Ferry of St. Nicholas) was established here in connection with the building of the Kings Road, from New Smyrna and St. Augustine to Cowford, leading thence to the north.

Traffic at Cowford multiplied very rapidly after Florida became a territory of the United States, now that so many settlers came southward through eastern Georgia. Farms and plantations sprang up in the neighborhood, so that in 1822, when the name of Jacksonville was substituted for the less elegant Cowford, this sharp bend in the St. Johns had assumed the appearance of a thriving frontier community, with stores and brothels and churches to serve all comers and many inns to accommodate the traveler.

As the number of travelers became ever larger, the resources of these barnlike forerunners of the modern hotel were often taxed to their utmost capacity. Nightly, it stays recorded, an innkeeper would welcome, to a dozen beds, "twice that number of occupants; those who cannot find better room, extend themselves, in their bedclothes, on the floor. No places are reserved for dining or sleeping; we are too much of republicans for that. Everyone pays his dollar, and has a right to eat and sleep where he pleases, provided he does not disturb a former occupant. It is understood that a bed contains two individuals; and nobody is so ridiculous as to trouble himself about who is next to him."

Contrary to John Randolph's prophecy, immigration to Florida increased in proportion to the rapid rise in the census lists of the nation; and was swept forward, to an appropriate distance beyond logic, by the sleek huge current of expansion and speculation which throughout the 1820's and the early 1830's inundated the United States. Cotton-mad planters from the southern states had soon transformed the rank jungles about Florida's new capital, Tallahassee, into the recognizable cartoon of a plantation area; much cotton moved from this newly enriched section, by oxcart, toward the deepwater port of Middleburg; and was carried thence, upon sailing vessels, some twenty miles down the winding course of Black Creek, into the St. Johns, and so to Savannah or Charleston.

In leading periodicals a great many descriptive articles, in a style which zestfully adapted the time-approved Tyrian purples of James Grant and of Jean Ribaut, now called attention to the encyclopedic merits of the St. Johns. "The River Saint John's seems by nature intended as the marked and eternal division of this varying and diversified country," proclaimed, for example, the widely read *Farmer's Register* of Virginia; and even though just what significance the writer of this pronouncement may have meant to convey must now remain forever a riddle, yet the words rang impressively. Still other palladia of paid advertising matter became eloquent; and the polite unwillingness of the American public ever to distinguish between reiteration and veracity produced its usual result; so that but a dozen years after having sent the first steamboat across the ocean, the merchants of Savannah attempted yet another epoch-making experiment by dispatching the steamer *George Washington* upon an excursion to Jacksonville, a trip which consumed all of thirty-four hours.

The shipment of cotton and other products from the plantations west of the lower St. Johns, combining with the traffic of Jacksonville and other river settlements (but more especially of Picolata, as being the river port of St. Augustine), led, in 1835, to the establishing of a weekly schedule by the steamer *Florida*, from Savannah to the St. Johns. Shipbuilders then sent down woodchoppers from out of New England so that they might fell live oaks in the late fall when the sap of the trees was low; and these forerunners of the lumber industry passed the winter beside the St. Johns in rude and hastily reared huts; but in the spring they loaded their schooners, and they sailed back happily toward Massachusetts, singing not wholly drawing-roomlike chanties.

21

Birds of All Feathers

Now at this time not everyone came into Florida by his own choice. John James Audubon, for example, returned from abroad, in 1831, not unwillingly persuaded that he was the foremost naturalist of his century, if not indeed of all centuries. Everywhere among the superior races who inhabited England and Scotland, and throughout two whole months in Paris, he had been feted and patronized with an approach to actual politeness. Yet this personage, who, if perhaps unequaled, remained none the less human, stayed inwardly annoyed because, time after time, he had been questioned, by the savants of Europe, as to a part of the United States which he had never seen.

Entirely too many foreign scientists appeared to be

familiar with those absurd *Travels* in which William Burton, or Bertram, or something of the sort, had described as many as 215 species of birds native to Florida. So, even though the matter was, of course, quite unimportant, still Audubon would now have to go to Florida, because of the continued silly stir over the nonsense of that lately dead Philadelphian imposter ... a Quaker, so near as one could remember ...

Not until just before the American Revolution had the St. Johns been visited by a naturalist at all competent to deal with its ornithology. This was William Bartram; and in the birds of Florida he had delighted with his habitual mild-mannered exuberance, recalling a good twenty years later, how when going about his lone voyages, in a small rowboat, through the solitudes of the huge brown river, he was "lulled asleep by the gentle warble of the painted nonpareil" every evening, and was awakened, promptly at dawn, by "the cheering converse of the turkey cocks saluting each other." During this happy period, he likewise, it is mentioned, had applauded "the seraphic music" of the cranes "in the ethereal sky"; for William Bartram in the earlier quoted phrase of his first British reviewer, was not afraid of "luxuriant and poetical language."

In 1818, three years before Florida became a part of the United States, William Maclure, who was then president of the Academy of Natural Science of Philadelphia, had entered the St. Johns at the head of an expedition, which included Thomas Say, by many called the Father of American zoology, and Titian Peale, who at utmost was but the son of a distinguished portrait painter.

"This noble river we ascended as far as Picolata," reported Thomas Say, as the chronicler of the jaunt, "stopping occasionally at such places as presented an inviting aspect & making short excursions into the country on each side of the river."

From Picolata, the Philadelphian scientists then traveled east toward St. Augustine, so as to present their passports to the Spanish governor, Don José Coppinger; and he warned them "it would be the extreme of imprudence to venture any further up the river" (says Say) because of the hostility of the Indians. Inasmuch as this warning came countersigned by the extinction of a river plantation but a few days previously, the Pennsylvanians, in fluttered haste, collected a few specimens for their museum, and no less hastily went homeward.

Peale returned to the St. Johns in 1824, so as to observe and draw its birds in their native habitat for the Prince of Canino (Charles Lucien Bonaparte) in preparation for the colored plates with which the Frenchman was about to adorn the third volume of his *American Ornithology*. One of Peale's more lasting if not solid rewards for this work was the naming in his honor of an egret adorned with a long train of plumes uniformly snow white; but the knowledge he acquired about Florida stayed scant.

It followed that seven years after the Peale-Bonaparte expedition the most famous of all American ornithologists was moved to assure his wife that "no one in the Eastern States has any true Idea of this Peninsula [of Florida]"; for Audubon harbored a marked skepticism as to the benign notions spread abroad by William Bartram that the St. Johns flowed through a land which was but slightly less soul-contenting than Paradise.

When Audubon left Charleston for St. Augustine, in the fall of 1831, the winds were contrary; so, for that mat-

ter, was the blunt captain of the *Argus;* and John James
Audubon soon passed beyond sulkiness into acrimony.—For
Captain Sweazey declined to be properly impressed by his
world-famous passenger; and he so compelled Audubon, in
a letter to his wife, to declare Sweazey "about as poor a
shoat as ever I have seen." Moreover, the costs of living at
St. Augustine were expensive; oranges sold as high as two
cents apiece; for board and lodgings Audubon had to pay
the steep sum of $4.50 a week; and even then, he was forced
to make out on "a miserable fare" of fresh fish and venison.
Most serious of all, however, was the puncture inflicted upon
the proper pride of a personage—a personage who had been
feted by the *ton* of Great Britain, both as a Fellow of the
Royal Society and as the author of a book issued "under the
Particular Patronage and Approbation of his Most Gracious
Majesty", King George the Fourth—by the extreme boorish-
ness of General Joseph M. Hernandez, who had received John
James Audubon without adulation.

Hernandez, like Sweazey, was not suitably impressed.
Hernandez regarded with disapproval the spectacle of a hale-
bodied if sallow person, forty-six years old, who in a city
well furnished with barbers went strutting about in long
black ringlets like a backwoodsman; and who had not any
better occupation than to travel thousands upon thousands
of miles so as to make pictures of such common nuisances as
birds. Joseph M. Hernandez, praise be to fortune, prospered
upon higher levels of life than were infested by these half-
men who might, or who might not, be geniuses, if that mattered. Señor José Mariano Hernandez had been a man of
affairs under the government of Spain; and when Florida was
acquired by the United States, then Joseph M. Hernandez,
Esquire, had been selected to sit in the great halls of Congress,

for two whole years, so as to represent Florida tacitly. While he was in Washington, his portrait had been painted by a real artist, Charles Frederick. Envious persons said that this masterwork flattered Joseph M. Hernandez, Esquire. You, standing regally beside it, were wholly willing to let this Audubon fellow judge for himself, if he really did know anything about high-class painting, in a large and expensive and genuine gold-leaf frame. At all events, you were very busy with the production of sugar. You could not afford to waste good money upon a set of this Audubon's books, so long as rational persons could look at real birds for nothing.

Thus ran the unspoken meditations of General Joseph M. Hernandez, in the while that, as befitted a properly reared Spaniard, he talked rather more courteously, but without any at all becoming ecstasy of enthusiasm, as to the honor, which he felt scarcely able to sustain, of being visited by John James Audubon; and regretted his inability to subscribe for a set of *The Birds of America.*

Infuriated, Audubon wrote, to his much-enduring wife, that this stingy rude scoundrel would not ever see any more of John James Audubon. St. Augustine was, he wrote also, "the poorest hole in Creation." He shook its sands from his shoes, very carefully, lest at any time their reputed magic should be dragging him back to the accursed place; and he sped down the Atlantic coast still snarling. From near the present city of Daytona Beach he traveled inland, with discomfort, "across the wildest, most desolate tract of Pine Barrens, Swamps, and Lakes that I ever saw."

Thereafter, early in the January of 1832, he became, for two days, the guest of Colonel Orlando Rees, at Spring Garden Plantation, near the St. Johns; and when Colonel Rees named an entire island in honor of the naturalist, then the assuaged genius began with delight to appraise the but slightly more wild creatures about him. Setting out in a small boat, he and Colonel Rees were rowed, from Rees's Lake, through a creek, into Lake Woodruff. With an appropriate pleasure, they observed many alligators, and ibises, and gallinules, and anhingas, and coots, and fish hawks, and cormorants. Proceeding to Lake Dexter, Audubon, and his escort, landed upon a small island covered with orange trees—"the luxuriance and fragrance of which," he wrote, as a gracious tribute to the by-products of John James Audubon's Creator, "were not less pleasing to the sight than the perfume of their flowers was to smell. . . . Under the shade of these beautiful evergreens, and amidst the golden fruits that covered the ground, while the humming-birds fluttered over our heads, we spread our cloth on the grass; and with a happy and thankful heart, I refreshed myself with the bountiful gifts of an ever-careful Providence," declared John James Audubon—who, under the infrequent influence of good temper, could become quite as luxuriant and poetical as William Bartram.

Divers officials in Washington were somewhat more interested in the work of John James Audubon than was General Hernandez. They placed at Audubon's disposal the schooner *Spark*; and boarding it, he started upon a tour of the St. Johns River. He found the circumstance not unpleasant that he traveled with official pomp, at the expense of the government, where that humbugging Quaker, William Somebody-or-other, had been compelled—as befits one who, through prenatal offenses, annoys his betters—to sail or to paddle, unaided, a shabby, and quite probably stolen, rowboat.

Audubon then contracted a most violent dislike toward the captain of the *Spark,* after having heard that the latter deplored being taken off his patrol duty along the coast so as to waste a full two weeks upon such absurdities as birds. Apart, however, from the decision of John James Audubon that the St. Johns was "a dingy looking river," everything went smoothly enough for the first hundred miles of the genius's journey. After that, he began yet again to grumble. "I have been deceived most shamefully about the Floridas," he wrote, still to that luckless woman who had married John James Audubon. "Scarcely a Bird is to be seen, and these of the most common sort—I look to the leaving of it as a Happy event—I am now, truly speaking, in a wild and dreary and desolate part of the World." Recalling those embarrassing questions put to him in Edinburgh and in London about the Philadelphian scientist, he then added, with a pen which dug past syntax into the undefended, supine note paper, "My account of what I have or shall see of Florida will be far, very far, from corroborating the flowery sayings of Mr. Barton."

Apart from this so frankly premature verdict as to anything which "I shall see of Florida"—all which is condemned, wholesale, in advance—nobody who knows genius will doubt that John James Audubon misspelled the name of his great predecessor for precisely the same reasons which induce a spoiled child to sit down upon the floor and to scream when the dessert is not quite what had been expected.

After that, in a tantrum, he quitted the government boat. He yet later fulfilled his own prophecy by describing the St. Johns area as a district where "all that is not mud, mud, mud, is sand, sand, sand; where the fruit is so sour that it is not eatable; and where in place of singing birds and golden fishes, you have . . . alligators, snakes, and scorpions."

Leaving "the *Spark* blackguards," Audubon returned toward lands which he found more affable, including Labrador. His belief, that he had ascended the St. Johns to its headwaters, stays so far unendorsed by geography that it is now certain Audubon did not come within a fair hundred miles of the upper St. Johns; and his disappointment with the river's bird life is thus made understandable. The birds of the lower St. Johns did not then, and they do not now, differ from those in other Southern areas. But the upper reaches of the St. Johns, between Lake Harney and the river's sources, display, even for the most captious bird lover, an opulence of attractions, inasmuch as these huge marshes, of sawgrass and myrtle and pickerel weed, afford homes to many of the most lovely and the least often seen birds of America.

Among them one finds the everglade kite, or snail hawk, which is now existent in considerable numbers nowhere else in the world. Another native bird that appears more commonly in these swamps than elsewhere is the limpkin. Related to cranes and rails, it is brown with white spots, and has a long, slightly curved bill. Limpkins are called "crying birds," because of the wide variety of their weird wails, heard not infrequently in the night. The stillness of the St. Johns headwaters is broken also, very often, by the wild call of the Florida crane, which under favorable conditions is audible at a distance of three miles. This bird belongs to the race of sand-hill cranes, and its distinguishing mark is a brilliant crimson crest.

Still another disturbing sound in these solitudes is that

of the hoot owl. It has gray-brown, barred plumage and a voice that booms out early in the night and again before sunrise. In the palmetto prairies is to be found the burrowing owl, which greets the rare passer-by with a series of profound and deferential bows while standing on guard before its nest, which is builded inside a hole in the ground.

One of the most striking of all the St. Johns avian colony is the white ibis. As many as fifty thousand are believed to foregather during the nesting season at Lake Washington, where their intake of daily food, in addition to countless grasshoppers, is estimated at forty thousand water moccasins eaten as hors d'œuvres to a main course of crawfish. Not unlike the stork, the body of this ibis is white, with black wing tips; its bill as well as its feet being stained a bright orange-red. The wingspread of these birds is not less than a yard; and by ordinary they fly in flocks with their necks straight out, in marked contrast to the heron, which flies with its neck folded back.

Upon the St. Johns, from November onward, there are probably more ducks than any other species of birds; and of these, the wood duck and the Florida duck are unique. The first-named is conceded to be the most beautiful duck in America, whereas the latter offers perhaps the most delectable food known to humankind. Winter after winter, their flocks concentrate in the St. Johns valley, where about fifty per cent of these tourists in feathers remain from the last of February to the middle of April.

Yet possibly the best-known bird of all this area is the Audubon caracara, or Mexican eagle, the national emblem of Mexico, so extensively represented in that country, upon postage stamps, and flags, and serapes. It is usually pictured as standing upon a cactus and holding in its beak a serpent, because it is reported first to have been seen in this posture by the Aztecs upon the site where, later, they erected the City of Mexico. Alongside the St. Johns very many of these large black-and-white eagles habitually build their nests in the tops of cabbage palmettos; and equally often seen beside this river is the official bird of Florida—the "gay mocking bird who, vocal and joyous," according to William Bartram, "mounts on silvered wings, and fulfills the moonlit night with rich melodies."

It really does seem a distinct pity that all these strange rare birds should have been denied the pleasure of meeting John James Audubon merely because the captain of the *Spark* was not so tactful as to grovel before a Fellow of the Royal Society of London, England.

22

Alarums and Excursions

THE coming of such varied cohorts of white persons into the St. Johns valley, in areas at least partly occupied by Indians, soon begot trouble. Relations between planters of the adjoining states and the Seminoles of Florida had often become tumultuous, it may be remembered, because runaway slaves found among these tribes an hospitable refuge, in addition, sometimes, to a working substitute for the comforts of married life. Now that planters also had begun to move into the Seminole territory, with a cold air of permanence, mutual distrust led to still further misunderstandings, as well as to frequent quarrels and bloodshed. Outlaws, both white and red, began flamboyantly to commit outrages; yet although marauding Indians became guilty of cattle thefts now and then, or killed rather casually, so as to rob travelers with an unhurried thoroughness, such depredations were far more often begotten by immunity upon the loose principles of white desperadoes, who, in the uncertain borderlands of civilization, found freedom to indulge in pretty much any crime which might take one's fancy.

Two years after the acquisition of Florida, the federal government removed the Seminoles (or, as it was charged, bribed and intimidated them into self-removal) from out of the northern portions of Florida, into lands south of St. Augustine; and the majesty of the law empowered the vigilance of the police to lay thirty-nine lashes upon the bared backs of any Indians discovered outside this reservation. For the maintenance of the dispossessed Seminoles until they could adjust themselves to their new quarters, Congress appropriated a fair sum of money, which in turn was appropriated by the dishonesty of very many minor federal agents, so that the Indians received hardly anything.

An accumulation of wrongs, both fancied and substantial, thus resulted in that special sort of excuse for breaking all promises such as governments term a crisis; and since the robbed and, in part, imprisoned Seminoles appeared unwilling to accept destitution as an additional favor, it was decided to remove both them and their ungrateful complainings into the western prairies of America. Determined to remain in those Floridian lands which custom and rationality alike decreed to be their legitimate homes, the Seminoles did not any longer— in William Bartram's fine phrase—repose under the odoriferous shades of Zanthoxilon. They, instead, acted with an impetuous swiftness unadulterated by compassion; for in 1835, near the upper valley of the St. Johns, they surprised and murdered more than a hundred American soldiers under the command of Major Francis L. Dade. In this manner began the unfortunate farce comedy which was called, afterward, the Seminole War.

Should it be possible, for the more highly imaginative, to fancy that at any time the government of the United States has muddled matters, then this unique national error took form, it is likely, in handling the Seminole War. Nobody denies, however, that, to begin with, this experiment, trumpeted as wholly noble in motive, to set free the Indians from the obligations of owning real estate, impressed a great many highhearted if reluctantly drafted crusaders from out of the North as being a not unpleasant vacation.

"Everything wears the aspect of mid-summer," wrote lyrically a young West Pointer, as to his first winter experience in Florida. "The soft balmy air, the genial warmth of the sun, and the beautiful green foliage which presents itself to the eye, all serve to strengthen the illusion and add to the beauty of the scene."—For one did not merely write letters, it may be noted, in the 1830's; one conducted a correspondence. Even Lieutenant William T. Sherman (who in a later war was to achieve fame by epitomizing all possible wars tersely) so far unbended toward this particular conflict as to rejoice that because of it he possessed an independent command at Picolata, upon the St. Johns, in "a large good house, and what is better than all, mails twice a week ... with all the advantages of both town and country; for with a good horse I can ride over [to St. Augustine] at any time, in a couple of hours, get books, see ladies, etc." In short, the Seminole War began, upon the American side, with the aspect of an agreeable brief outing endorsed by the very best principles—such, let us say, as grace the bush-screened, coeducational pleasantries of a church picnic.

Inasmuch as the St. Johns afforded the one means of transporting troops and supplies toward the almost impenetrable lairs of the Indians, this river became of instant importance toward the conduct—not here to say the inane conduct—of many American campaigns. The *Essayon,* the *Camden,* the *Santee,* and yet other small steamers were pressed into military service; blockhouses for the protection of river settlements were erected; and log forts, bearing the names of Peyton, Gates, Butler, Florida, Kingsbury, and Mellon, now fortified the St. Johns.

As the conflict progressed, it developed into guerrilla warfare, and became a not ever ending, foiled struggle to overtake the red rebels as they moved nimbly, but always farther southward, along the upper parts of the river. The two large lakes immediately beyond Lake Monroe were thus reached by American forces; and were called Lake Jessup and Lake Harney, in honor of army officers. From Fort Lane, upon the latter body of water, row barges now carried men and supplies, through a serpentine channel winding among marshes, to a small lake nearer the source of the river; and this was named Lake Poinsett, for Van Buren's secretary of war. Here, it seemed, "the river ceased to be subservient to the purposes of transportation"; and in consequence, oxcarts were used to supply the three minor stockades—called Christmas, and McNeil, and Taylor—which paralleled the upper waters of the St. Johns.

Even so, after never so much of American derring-do and of squandered money and young lives, at the conclusion of the first three years of war no special progress had been made in subduing the Indians. Though many of them had been captured and deported westward, yet hundreds of intrepid and vigorous warriors retained their freedom; and through a steady increase in ferocity they offset the uncertain diminishing of their numbers. Scarcely a building upon either bank of the St. Johns remained occupied by white men, for those who had not fled had been massacred; their slaves and cattle were stolen; the orange groves and sugar fields of the valley lay in ruin; and still the Seminoles stayed unconquered.

"The prospect of terminating the war in any reasonable time is anything but flattering," reported the commanding general, Thomas S. Jesup, to the War Department; and he added, with a displeasing flavor of common sense, such as, during wartimes, no branch of government has ever found to fall short perceptibly of high treason: "We have committed the error of attempting to remove . . . [the Seminoles] when their lands were not required. . . . To rid the country of them you must exterminate them. Is the Government prepared for such a measure? Will public opinion sustain it? If so, resort must be had to the bloodhound and the northern Indian."

The frankness of General Jesup was rewarded by depriving him of his command and acting upon his advice. Without pausing to be flustered by the dubious counsel of public opinion, Zachary Taylor was sent into Florida to prosecute the war with a more brutal vigor. He followed his instructions; and at the Battle of Lake Okeechobee, near the source of the St. Johns, he won an inconsequential but well-advertised victory which served as the first step in his journey toward the White House.

Yet neither the future hero of the Mexican War nor thirty-three bloodhounds fetched in from the West Indies at all availed to evoke any least phantom of order out of the chaos which enveloped the upper St. Johns. "That this contest has endured so long is to be attributed to causes beyond the control of the Government . . . [namely] the nature of the country, the climate, and the wily character of the

savage," declared President Van Buren, in the fifth year of
this futile hide-and-go-seek skirmishing. The American army
could not get at the Seminole in his swamps; and although
he did come out of these swamps, with an annoying frequency, so as to conduct cattle raids or massacres, this unscrupulous Indian could not ever be induced to march out
openly, like a self-respecting soldier, and be destroyed in a
fair battle by his superiors. It followed, from the sullen ob-
tuseness of the Seminole as to the correct rules of warfare,
that, in 1842, President Tyler declared any "further pursuit
of these miserable beings . . . to be as injudicious as it is un-
availing"; and that, although driven back into the unexplored recesses of the Everglades, the Seminoles remained
there unconquered.

Throughout this futile seven years' war, the American
public had been edified with a great deal of vivid misinfor-
mation as to the St. Johns valley, in the form of official
reports, and of editorials (all which seemed to have been
modeled religiously after the prophet Jeremiah, in his less
hilarious moments) and of letters from fever-ridden or
wounded or homesick soldiers. A nightly prowling of ser-
pents and alligators and sudden murder by invisible enemies
were declared to be merely the more customary features of
existence in this vermin-infested country, wherein, it was
furthermore pointed out, not even any safe drinking water
could be had. Army officers were thus robbed of their favorite beverage with disastrous results. "Almost every day some
officer recently from Florida may be seen in this city with
enfeebled health and ruined constitution," one public journal
reported sadly; and for once, John Randolph of Roanoke
appeared to have deviated into speaking with moderation.

Moreover, that disastrous year of ungrace, 1835, which marked the beginning of the war against the Seminoles, had brought other and more permanent ills to the St. Johns valley. Early in February, the temperature dropped, overnight, to eight degrees Fahrenheit; and when the sun rose the next morning, its light had revealed everywhere along the river's shore line a thick coating of ice. All vegetation was frozen; hardy forest trees were killed; and the century-old orange groves of the St. Johns were destroyed. An incalculable loss was the grove of Zephaniah Kingsley upon Drayton Island, in Lake George, where alone had flourished the seedless and fine-flavored navel orange. This prodigy in the way of fruit had been introduced with success, by the now aging and almost perceptibly reformed small rascal, from out of Brazil; and its sudden extinction in Florida checked the entire orange industry of the peninsula for a generation.

Inasmuch as the lower section of the St. Johns was cleared of danger from Indian attacks considerably in advance of the formal close of the Seminole War, in 1842, it was thereabouts that life first assumed normal aspects; and that both settlers and excursionists began, in the light of evidence furnished by their own senses, to reappraise America's wholesale condemnation of Florida. When William Cullen Bryant, that most eminent of literati, who had written a virtually unlimited number of volumes which not many Americans had even read, reported, in 1843, to a shivering New York, that from out of its rough April he had stepped overnight "into the middle of summer," a yet more respectful, if still aloof, attitude toward Florida came into being.

"The dark waters of the St. Johns, one of the noblest streams of the country, in depth and width like the St.

Lawrence, drawing upon almost the whole extent of the peninsula," had been conceded, by the author of *Thanatopsis* as well as of some much-admired lines about wildfowl and blue gentians, to be "flowing under my window" even in the same instant that he composed his letter to the New York *Evening Post*. It was a circumstance which elevated the St. Johns appreciably toward the waters of Hippocrene. Besides, Mr. Bryant, since stepping "into the middle of summer," had yielded to a chaste admiration of swaying palms and of gaily colored flowers. The lumber business, he continued, so thrived in Jacksonville that the schooners in its harbor, while being laden with pine logs for both domestic and foreign markets (the bard stated, with a correct touch of poesy) resembled a forest of towering masts; whereas—for all that these attractions were not unbecomingly stressed by Mr. Bryant—the conveniently adjacent bars and gambling parlors and brothels and dance halls, along Bay Street, nowadays evoked praise from virtuosi.

In most quarters of the growing city, during this same year, and after investigating, it remains possible, fields rather less wanton than Bay Street, the Reverend H. B. Whipple, a future Episcopal Bishop of Minnesota, likewise observed many praiseworthy improvements, during his own excursion into Florida, even though he did not accredit the people of Jacksonville, as a corporate whole, with unflawed perfection. "Nowhere this side of Texas can you find so many rascals who live by their wits," he stated, in an ambitious attempt to grant Jedwood justice to two parts of his country in the same sentence. "One half the population . . . are ruined spendthrifts, and too many of the balance are rogues and scoundrels . . . but they are fast disappearing." From this rapid demolishing of the loose-living, Dr. Whipple inferred as to Jacksonville that, through the kindly assistance of God's anger, its "coarse, backwoods crackerism is giving place to refinement and civilization . . . [with] the continual influx of new settlers from other states."

Among yet other excursionists who came to Jacksonville —in this special case, upon the steamer *St. John*, at about the middle of the February of 1855—was Lady Amelia Murray, a maid of honor to Queen Victoria. Lady Amelia was interested in finding the extent, if any, to which Florida was making its own proper and rightful contribution toward progress as defined and directed by Victorian standards; she desired, in particular, to settle, for the good of America, the rights and the wrongs of slavery; and so, ascending the St. Johns as far as Picolata, she drove overland (wearing her lavender barred muslin, for the day was warm) to inspect, with disapproval, a "bare and dilapidated" St. Augustine.

Returning to Picolata, she boarded the *Carolina*— which turned out, vexatiously, to have been builded with an amount of forethought so deficient as to afford for Lady Amelia Murray "no pleasant place upon which to sit upon deck." She endured with patience the omission; she spent the night at Palatka; and from this regrettably un-English village (wearing her second-best Paisley shawl, and accompanied, of course, by her maid) the intrepid explorer of native customs started forth, at nine the next morning, in a bumping bare mail carriage, upon the 70-mile journey toward Silver Springs, near the head of the main tributary to the St. Johns.

"If I had known," the English gentlewoman admits, with a modest underevaluation of the vigor of her sense of duty to set right the slavery question, "that we should not

arrive there till after midnight, with one man driving four
horses through a pine-barren which harbours wolves, bears,
and panthers, my courage would have failed me."

One doubts that, if but because the courage of a virtuous woman, in settling the affairs of other people, dreads
nothing. One knows only that after seeing Silver Springs and
Ocala—where the lodging houses, alas, were far from
weatherproof and the outhouses not such as politeness would
care to describe—Lady Amelia Murray returned, either in a
huff or a dudgeon, to her steamer; for she was now free to
leave Florida, after having deduced from a survey of its
manners and institutions, within less than five days, a decision that "commercial remedies are the only certain and
legitimate slavery preventitives"; and that by making use of
such remedies throughout the peninsula, "we should save
white lives as well as black lives, and white money as well as
black interests."

The considerate reader will bear cautiously in mind the
circumstance that to both statements Lady Amelia Murray
may have attached, at least possibly, some definite meaning.
She, at all events, now prescribed to the state at large, as a
quite simple cure for the evils of slavery, that each citizen of
Florida, according to his means, should purchase slaves and
pay for their deportation back into Africa—inasmuch as one
might as rationally "attempt to improve the morals and add
to the happiness of idiots by turning them out of asylums as
to imagine you can benefit the 'darkies' by abolitionism."
The exact blessings which a former butler or a freed cham-
bermaid would find making roseate their destitution in Sierra
Leone, or among the swamps of the Congo, are not
specified.

With the no longer abstruse difficulties of the slave question thus finally settled, Lady Amelia Murray went back to Jacksonville; and was transferred thence, as well as from the fields of sociology, to the stately gaslit drawing room, hung startlingly with red-and-gray tartans, of her queen's new Highland home at Balmoral.

23

"The Smallest Tadpole"

ON ACCOUNT of (it stays possible) the obtuse failure of Florida and of the United States at large either to comprehend or to follow the cryptic counsels of Lady Amelia Murray, Fort Sumter was fired upon within fewer than six years; and thus began yet another one of those parochial misunderstandings such as the twentieth century's more fanciful and more fortunate predecessors were accustomed to describe as a war. Like most of mankind's national aberrations into valor, the War Between the States was begotten by the mentally crippled, and it left as its heir dishonesty. Even so, as one needs always to remember in extenuation of this conflict's futility, it produced—among divers other but a little less incredible offshoots—the Grand Army of the Republic's pension rolls, the unquenchable Confederate orator, the legend of Abraham Lincoln, the ineptness of Jefferson Davis, and the Floridian exploits of Colonel T. W. Higginson, U.S.A.

To admire the last-mentioned we turn with befitting awe.

Never since his first formal introduction to depravity (above blonde auspices, near Harvard, and among circumstances which here need embarrass nobody) had tall, slender, and ascetically featured Thomas Wentworth Higginson been so excited as when, upon the morning of March 10, 1863, he entered the delta of the St. Johns River.

He indeed had cause; for the former Unitarian pastor had but lately risen from holy orders to the rank of colonel of the First South Carolina Volunteers, then the one regiment in the entire United States Army composed of Negroes; and the "noble enterprise" (as described, and outlined, by his commanding officer, Brigadier General Rufus Saxton), which had been entrusted to the newly made colonel's large genius for preserving a respectable superficies, was: "to carry the proclamation of freedom to the enslaved; to call all loyal men into the service of the United States; to occupy as much of the State of Florida as possible . . . and to neglect no means consistent with the usages of civilized warfare to weaken, harass, and annoy those . . . in rebellion against the Government of the United States."

The fact had likewise been communicated to Colonel Higginson, officially, that "the blessing of our Heavenly Father" was certain to hallow and to assist each one of his endeavors now that Florida had become, from a geographical point of view, the tail of the Southern Confederacy—or, as the New York *Herald* more picturesquely expressed matters, "the smallest tadpole in the dirty pool of secession."

For the blessing of his Heavenly Father, as a source of any specific aid, Colonel Higginson in latter years appeared to be rather less grateful than for the co-operation of Admiral S. F. duPont. The last-named, merely mundane official, who was then commander of the South Atlantic Blockade Squadron, had proved to be both constant and efficient in providing the proper naval protection for those three vessels of divine wrath—namely, the *John Adams,* the *Boston,* and the *Burnside*—which brought the black troops of Thomas Wentworth Higginson from out of South Carolina to the mouth of the St. Johns River, after an uneasy voyage during which the co-operancy of the King of Kings, although of course overhovering, remained less explicit.

Meanwhile, after reaching the St. Johns, "we had several hours of fresh, early sunshine, lighting up the green shores of that lovely river, wooded to the water's edge, with sometimes a verdant meadow opening a vista to some picturesque house—all utterly unlike anything we had yet seen in the South, and suggesting rather the Penobscot or Kennebec."

These facts did Colonel Higginson at once record, in his red imitation-leather diary, without forgetting that, like Cæsar, one might find in a quest for military glory the material for a book.

Colonel Higginson then paused frowningly; and for "a verdant" he substituted "an emerald." Yes; that was much better. He put up his notebook and made ready for carnage.

"The die"—he remarked, like Cæsar—"is cast."

In brief, "it was a delicious day, and a scene of fascination" (Thomas Wentworth Higginson resumed, at a later period, of somewhat less sanguinary promise) when his three ships rounded the point just below Jacksonville, and when, in a devout but truculent jiffy, they prepared to demolish this stronghold of rebellion.

"We . . . saw from afar its long streets, its brick warehouses, its white cottages, and its overshadowing trees—all peaceful and undisturbed by flames . . . and all discipline was merged, for the moment, in a buzz of ecstasy . . . None knew what perils might be concealed behind those quiet buildings . . . We drew momentarily nearer, in silence and with breathless attention . . . and"—there is nobody but must fidget before the abrupt anticlimax—"and the pretty town was ours."

—For (still like Cæsar) Colonel Higginson had come and seen and conquered, through a triumph so far flawless that, without any least faltering, his untrained but intrepid troops, still in a buzz of ecstasy, had captured an undefended city.

Twice before this display of heroic but unopposed virtues upon the part of Colonel Higginson's as yet blameless Ethiopians had Jacksonville been attacked by Federal forces; and twice had the city been evacuated without any at all violent resistance. Inasmuch as a large part of the settlers along the St. Johns had come from the North, many of them remained loyal to the Union, at least tepidly. Moreover, the St. Johns River lands had a not stringently crowded population ranging from some two to, at most, some six persons to the square mile; and of these but few were slaveholders.

It followed that after Lincoln's elevation into a seat so

august as once to have been warmed by the trousers of Franklin Pierce and of Millard Fillmore, the prevailing attitude of both Northerners and Southerners in the St. Johns area had been expressed with tact by a former Floridian governor, Richard K. Call—who in debating secession had asked, with an oratorical pious deference, of the zenith:

"Is the election of a sectional President by a sectional party, consisting of less than one-third of the political strength of the nation, sufficient cause for justifying rebellion and revolution?"

The zenith did not at once reply; but a fair amount of human applause obscured the omission.

Florida, in short, did not regard Mr. Lincoln with approval; yet many Floridians now appraised with a sane abhorrence the magnanimities of a war from which Florida could not hope to obtain any special advantage.

The once reverend Higginson's capture of a dispopulated city was so quiet, and for a military exploit, so plainly unmilitary, that he expected the misled rebels at any moment to uplift their disregard for propriety to the apex of assaulting an aforetime pastor of the First Religious Society (Unitarian) of Newburyport and of the Free Church at Worcester; of which towns it is reported that both grace Massachusetts. Divine Providence, however, so praiseworthily extended Its protection that throughout the ensuing night the half-dozing alertness of Thomas Wentworth Higginson was disturbed by nothing more formidable than a continued singing of mockingbirds—"their notes," so he recorded, sitting half erect in bed, "seeming to drift down through the sweet air from amid the blossoming boughs, like those of the nightingale."

Frowningly, he changed "drift" to "trickle"; he put

aside his notebook; he turned out the kerosene lamp; and the author of *Malbone: an Oldport Romance* yet again lay down in the dark, invincibly protected by the knowledge that even though, in Massachusetts, he had heard few nightingales, he had read all the correct poets.

—Whereafter he rested with contentment upon his laurels, while applausive northern newspapers, with a tincture of the imaginative, described his entry into an unoccupied city as "a great volcano about bursting, whose lava will burn, flow, and destroy." President Lincoln likewise, in strains somewhat less rhapsodic, was "glad to see the accounts of your colored force at Jacksonville"; and added, with Mr. Lincoln's customary licentiousness in matters of syntax, "It is important that such a force should not take shape and grow and thrive in the South, and in precisely the same proportion, it is important to us that it shall." Remiss fortune, however, so arranged matters that Colonel Higginson's perhaps unavoidably fishy pursuit of the smallest tadpole in the dirty pool of secession aroused but a slight effect throughout the South, beyond making more feeble the loyalty of Florida's native-born Unionists—who, for one reason or another, regarded with an unregenerate dislike the North's proposed plan to put Africans in control of them and their fellow Americans.

To the enslaved, Colonel Higginson, as per army orders, carried a proclamation of freedom to unshackle themselves from the dull and tedious drudgery of farm work in favor of a year or two's military service under the more noble excitements of gunfire; yet, somehow, his enlistments, among these unappreciative Negroes, who described him as being "poor white trash," remained negligible; and the dark armaments of the God of Sabaoth managed to occupy but a small part of Duval County. Even so, the now uninhibited clergyman was successful in his mission to weaken, to harass, and to annoy; so that, as he records complacently, when narrating his exploits around Jacksonville, he, both in theft and in destructiveness, approached "the dignity of a fine art."

A gunboat, amply equipped with supplies and reserve troops, accompanied his crusaders up and down the St. Johns. From its plantations, many horses, hogs, and all kinds of cattle were stolen by the First South Carolina Volunteers; smokehouses and corncribs and women were stripped intrepidly; much household furniture, of an unrepublican ancestral nature, was emended with hatchets; barns, mansions, and privies were burned with gay playfulness; but in particular did the black champions of an undivided Union develop their innate talents as chicken thieves.

When the ship returned to Jacksonville, Colonel Higginson merrily reports, it resembled "an animated hencoop." "Live poultry hung from the foremast shrouds, dead ones from the mainmast, geese hissed from the binnacle, a pig paced the quarter-deck, and a duck's wings were seen fluttering from a line which was wont to sustain duck trousers," wrote Colonel Higginson, with that troubling imitation of humor which but too often appears to aid the clergy, even when retired, in debasing religion.

Still more strategic attacks upon unguarded pullets somewhat farther up the river had been mapped out, and the supporting artillery made ready, when of a sudden an official army order recalled northward both Thomas Wentworth Higginson and the inferior blackguards who served under him from this highhearted career of arson and theft. In the garden of his former headquarters, he then, with a poetic touch, culled for his lapel a white tea-rosebud, to be a memento of Jacksonville, which he left on fire.

Colonel Higginson remarked later that the next quarter of an hour, when thus florally decorated he returned alone to the wharf in order to rejoin his already embarked "brave hardy fellows," and observed the rebel city to be "only very partially burnt," appeared to his Heavenly Father's foiled protégé "the only time since I entered the service when I have felt within the reach of tears ... To think that this was the end of our brilliant enterprise . . . was a more depressing occurrence than wounds or death."

He then, reflectively, altered "a more depressing occurrence" into "a sadder thing." Yes: that improved matters; for an heroic patriot, in making ready to peddle his more noble emotions in book form, needed simplicity.

Thomas Wentworth Higginson does not seem ever to have thought about his Floridian pleasantries, as a freebooter, among terrified women and poultry, with blushes. He instead published, in 1870, a candid and complacent recital of his success as a nuisance, called *Army Life in a Black Regiment*. He likewise published, during the next thirty-five years, a great many other volumes, about his Puritan ancestors, and The Afternoon Landscape, and Margaret Fuller Ossoli, and The Procession of the Flowers, and Henry Wadsworth Longfellow, and Cheerful Yesterdays, and John Greenleaf Whittier, and yet other sedatives which Massachusetts found edifying. He contributed, upon several occasions, to the *Atlantic Monthly*. He corresponded with Edmund Clarence Stedman, with Miss Louisa M. Alcott, and with Mrs. Julia Ward Howe. Archæologists report that his writing shows a deep love of nature and art and humanity.

24

The River at War

WHILE Colonel Higginson and his fellow patriots stayed busied among the henroosts of the St. Johns River, the Confederates were making of their slender numbers and scant materials the utmost. Captains Ramon Canova and Adolphus Pacetti, and yet other descendants or connections of old Spanish families, who for generations had sailed in and out of the secretive inlets, bays, and bayous of the Florida coast, now organized a fleet of small schooners; and these began with success to pass the Federal blockade. Under darkness of night, cotton from the large plantations west of the St. Johns was ferried across the river, at Palatka and Volusia, before being carried in oxcarts to New Smyrna, or to some other near-by port, for shipment upon these schooners, to Nassau or to Cuba. Munitions, medical supplies, and other necessaries, as well as a few luxuries, were brought back on the return voyages. At least two small steamers, the *Hattie Brock,* and the *James Burt,* transported cotton from the Oklawaha, up the St. Johns, to Lake Harney, from which it was carted to the Atlantic coast, near the present city of Titusville.

Now that the trade of blockade-running increased, alike in success and boldness, to this fleet were added two ocean-going steamers, the *Cecile* and the *Carolina*—which last-named, it may be remembered, had disappointed Lady Amelia Murray *a tergo.* These touched at various ports in Florida; and some smaller steamers began even to take aboard their cargoes of cotton from the banks of the St. Johns. One of them, the *Governor Milton,* was soon captured. Another, the *St. Marys,* at first eluded Federal pursuit by running up Trout Creek; but when the gunboat *Norwich* had trapped her, beyond hope of escape, in McGirt's Creek, then the Confederates burned the *St. Mary's* cargo; and after sinking the vessel by opening valves, fled through the moss-draped, dim woods toward the more genial comforts of Jacksonville's water-front saloons.

Most famous of all the blockade-runners connected with the St. Johns River was the yacht *America*—the winner, in 1851, of the international races held by the Royal Yacht Squadron around the Isle of Wight in England. Having come into the possession of an English owner before the War Between the States, and being rechristened the *Camilla,* she was sold to the Confederates, who renamed this yacht the *Memphis;* and for about a year they made excellent use of her then unexampled speed so as to bring in medical supplies for southern hospitals.

In order to avoid capture, she was scuttled by her crew in Dunn's Creek, a tributary of the St. Johns; where, for all that she lay three fathoms deep, her tall masts protruded and were easily observed by two Federal boats, the *Darlington* and the *Ellen*, in the March of 1862. The finest yacht of her era was then raised by a week's hard work, towed north, and refitted. After being renamed the *America*, the former blockade-runner, through a neat touch of irony, re-entered service as a part of the South Atlantic Blockade Squadron, for the remainder of the war; and later ended a remarkably varied career by figuring for a long while as a training vessel of the Naval Academy at Annapolis.

An odd adjunct to these blockade-runners was a small cavalry corps under the leadership of Captain J. J. Dickison, who operated along the St. Johns River with results such as may yet thrill that class of after-dinner enthusiasts whom unleashed orators address as Southrons. When, for example, Captain Dickison and his band of guerrillas captured Federal posts at Welaka, about the mouth of the Oklawaha, and near Volusia, the steamer *Columbine* and the gunboat *Ottawa* were sent up the river to reprove these rebels. At Brown's Landing, Dickison and his men opened fire, upon both vessels, in a surprise night attack. The *Ottawa* returned fire, but after having sustained injuries, moved northward, while the *Columbine*, with a rapidity such as in her commander's official report alone can be distinguished from panic, steamed south.

When during the following afternoon, the *Columbine* attempted to withdraw down the river, and so came within sixty yards of the Confederates hidden on the shore at Horse Landing, Dickison's troops yet again fired upon her. Almost immediately disabled, the *Columbine* struck a sand bar, and after a 45-minute interval of mutual human destructiveness, she hoisted her flag of surrender. Only sixty-six of her 148 men were found alive when the victors came aboard, and of these survivors fully one-third were seriously wounded. After the guns, the ammunition, the equipment, and (as an afterthought) the injured Yankees had been removed from the demolished steamer, the Confederates burned the *Columbine*—which was perhaps, in all naval record, the sole ship of war to be taken by cavalry.

Since Dickison's men won many other, if less eccentric, victories, they became so idolized alongside the St. Johns that their glory by-and-by entered the domain of verse, upon exceedingly infirm feet. "They have sworn an oath, and the foe shall feel," remarks one of these pæans, "[that] they have merciless hearts and pitiless steel, those horsemen who sweep by the St. Johns river." It is a diploma in the praiseworthy before which southern-born writers can but blush, and pass onward hastily.

So large, at all events, became the gratitude of the women of Orange Springs for the defense of their homes and chastity and household goods by the valor of Captain Dickison that, against his possible requirements in attacking yet another Federal battleship, they presented to him a pair of spurs—"made in our little village, from old heirlooms and relics of silver long preserved with scrupulous care, melted in a crucible cut from a firebrick, and fashioned entirely with a hammer."

It was a picturesque tribute to which the hero of Horse Landing responded in the well-nigh incredible vein of his epoch. He remarked at outset that the kindly remembrance and the touching expressions of the friendship of the fair

maids and matrons of Orange Springs, when accompanied by
the sweet breathings of sympathy which rose from their pure
souls, in a pious and heart-thrilling refrain, were peculiarly
soothing to man's spirit in an hour when Fate, treacherous to
Nature, seemed to conspire with the powers of Darkness, and
to give to Might the sacred privilege of Right. Yet (Captain
Dickison continued) the prayers and the words of gentle
encouragement of the ladies of Orange Springs—such as Mrs.
F. L. Freyer, Mrs. J. W. Fearson, Mrs. H. L. Hart, and
others—served as an ever-present inspiration in this time of
danger. Even at an instant when the star of peace was
shedding no beauteous light upon the oppressed Southland's
darkened pathway, their gracious smiles and their generous
plaudits were, to the very best of his judgment, a most
precious guerdon.

"The memorials of your virtue," he then stated, to the
ladies of Orange Springs, in conclusion, "will be engraved
forever upon my heart; and that your names may be recorded
in the 'Lamb's Book of Life,' is the earnest prayer of your
loyal friend and obedient servant."

For thirty-seven years after these imposing ceremonials,
even until the end of his noble career, as a professional Confederate veteran, in the August of 1902, J. J. Dickison was
revered throughout all Florida as the Knight of the Silver
Spurs.

While Floridians in such places as Orange Springs supported the Confederacy, yet others were abetting the Federals, and one thousand of the state's people who condoned
the political compromises of Abraham Lincoln as to his more
early convictions could be found enlisted in the Union army.
It followed that when yet other strange subterfuges were

being shaped for his renomination, in 1864, the New York *Herald* suggested a plan for using Florida so as to provide three delegates—then very greatly needed by Lincoln—through maneuvering the partly Federal inclinations of this nominally Confederate state. So too did it happen that Major John Hay of Salem, Indiana, then Lincoln's secretary, prepared to foster the political repentance of Florida through buying a house near St. Augustine. In this way only, it should perhaps be explained, could the exploiter of "Little Breeches" hope to become eligible for the toga of a congressman from the St. Johns area.

Hay made his headquarters in Jacksonville; and he there explained Lincoln's promise that if Floridians to the number of one-tenth of those who had voted in the presidential election of 1860 would take an oath alike "to support, protect and defend" the Constitution of the United States, and to disregard it by accepting the new slavery legislation, then the regenerated state would be welcomed back into the Union by her sisters in unreason. Or else! it was added, warningly, in the more dignified phrasing of a political utterance.

Soon afterward came to Major Hay's office, he reports, "a dirty swarm of gray coats, and filed into the room, escorted by a Negro guard. Fate had done its worst for the poor devils. Even a nigger guard didn't seem to excite a feeling of resentment. . . . They all stood in line and held up their hands while I read the oath. As I concluded, the Negro sergeant came up, saluted, and said, 'Dere's one dat didn't hole up his hand.' They began to sign. . . . Nearly half made their mark."

No tact or diplomacy, nor even common sense, one infers, was able to dissuade John Hay from the victor's lust to insult yet a bit further the unfortunate who were thus planning perforce to submit to the unscrupulous.

Back of this Lincoln-Hay proposal for political reconstruction was the force of between five and six thousand Federal soldiers who came with Major Hay into Florida so as to advance the Republican party, and in spare moments, to protect the Union. While at Jacksonville he spoke handsomely, as to peace and forgiveness and the universal brotherhood of humankind, howsoever tinted, not a few of his troops were conducting savage raids beside the St. Johns; and many aforetime Confederates, who had deserted from the army and concealed themselves in quiet swamps alongside the river, now came out of hiding to join the Federal forces, as being no less trustworthy companions than alligators.

The main body of Union troops stationed at Jacksonville by-and-by marched toward the interior; and at Olustee, February 20, 1864, was fought the most important battle of the war, so far as the war involved Florida. Disastrously defeated, the Federals lost almost one-third of their numbers, and provided unwelcome evidence, to the politicians in or about the White House, that their hopes of Florida's early return to the Union were nonsense. John Hay discovered also that a majority of the St. Johns River inhabitants displayed frank abhorrence toward signing his conciliatory oath, upon the ground that, while secessionists from the vote-getting creed of black races' being in all respects the equals of white races might be rebels against the first principles of sound politics, they were not repentant rebels.

The loss of near two thousand men in this expedition directed much harsh criticism toward Lincoln, who was accused, by an acrid representative of the northern press, of being incited by "the selfish, gross cheap motives of a back-woods thimble-rigger" in making possible the Floridian fiasco. The New York *World* yet furthermore asserted that the "conquest of Florida would do no more to put down the rebellion than would· the occupation of Yucatan or Coney Island. The object is political. Florida has been marked out as one of the rotten boroughs which are to make Mr. Lincoln President."

Displeasing also, in the North's eyes, was the loss of several Federal transports upon the St. Johns River during the late spring of 1864. First in this series was the *Maple Leaf,* which was blown up off Mandarin after having struck a log filled with explosives. Five days later, the *General Hunter* went to the bottom of the river, at virtually the same place, in a similar manner. Shortly afterward, the *Harriet A. Weed* and the *Alice Price* were destroyed, by mines or torpedoes; and bleak doubts arose as to whether or not the marching of the bleak soul of John Brown of Osawatomie was being continued according to its choric program.

Within less than a year, the fall of Richmond was hailed, throughout the North, as promising to replace the hurried bloodshed of war by the more leisurely cruelties of revenge. Inasmuch as Jefferson Davis and his Cabinet, along with yet other pre-eminent fiends in the Confederacy's pandemonium, had fled toward the lower South, it was assumed generally they would seek refuge from Heaven's anger in Mexico or in Cuba, or perhaps even in the still more God-forsaken British West Indies. When Davis was made prisoner in Irwinville, Georgia, by Lieutenant Colonel B. D. Pritchard, and had been furnished by calumny with petticoats, the New York

Herald regretted that "General Breckinridge, the rebel War Secretary," was not captured; but gave assurance that "such disposition of the national cavalry had been made as, it is believed, will completely cut off the escape of Breckinridge ...and other Cabinet officials and fellow criminals." Meanwhile, John Cabell Breckinridge was well upon his way toward Florida.

Protected by loyal Confederates, Breckinridge arrived at the St. Johns River, near the present settlement of Astor, on May 26, 1865. Awaiting him there were three of Captain Dickison's men, with a four-oared cutter, which they had salvaged from the wreck of the *Columbine*. Rowing when wind did not make possible the use of their tiny sail, the party began its laborious progress up the St. Johns, which Breckenridge regarded as a bewildering body of water.

"The boat's head," he records, "pointed to every point of the compass, and we were often puzzled and led astray by false channels that ended in nothing. . . . [The river] abounds in cranes, pelicans and other water fowl, and great numbers of crocodiles. . . . I shot one with my pistol, and after we got him ashore, it required three more balls through the place where his brains should have been, to finish him. . . . We caught some fish in this river, and found some sour oranges in a deserted orchard."

Such was the fugitives' slim diet; and Dickison's once fearless warriors were so far appalled by the mosquitoes of the St. Johns, against which neither a merciless heart nor pitiless steel afforded protection, that at night the Confederates anchored the boat in midstream, sleeping there fitfully. In a fashion so unluxurious did the party contrive, somehow, to reach Lake Harney, four days later.

Near the mouth of Lake Harney, Breckinridge left the

St. Johns, and his boat (for which one of his companions, Private Murphy, who with loyalty combined thrift, now demanded of General Breckinridge the stiff price of $100) was carried overland by oxteam to the Atlantic. Sailing down the inland passage which is called Indian River, he then got safely to Cuba (after a brief career as a pirate) and so, by-and-by, to England.

Among Unionists, the unrepentant and rebellious escape of General Breckinridge, from the varied punishments that had been made ready for him, added a vast deal of fuel to the hysteria which, like a forest fire, was sweeping all the north parts of America now that the pistol of John Wilkes Booth had removed Abraham Lincoln from the stage box of Ford's Theatre into incalculable octavos of imaginative biography. At this special instant, indeed, no former member of the Cabinet of Jefferson Davis was regarded anywhere in the North with complete affection, or might hope to be coddled. As the Boston *Transcript* phrased the North's public opinion, with that self-restraint for which Boston stays famous, "The whole mass of individual murders since Cain has not produced in forty centuries so much misery and ruin as these malignant traitors [that is, Jefferson Davis and his Cabinet] have wrought in four years."

John Cabell Breckinridge, in brief, was remarkably lucky to have got out of the yet again United States of America, at this precise moment, the more thanks to the St. Johns; for the St. Johns alone had preserved him from the divine anger of editorials and office-holders. So does it become edifying to observe how the brown river's redemption, from any yet further indulgence in a kindness which was not public-spirited, would seem to have been started at the Battle of Gettysburg, almost two years earlier.

25

As to Frederick in Patmos

I<small>T WAS</small> at the Battle of Gettysburg that Captain Stowe—then somewhat actively employed, with his saber's help, in the destruction of a Confederate private—lost consciousness. Captain Stowe very often wondered, afterward, whether or not the head did come off? and just how many days it had been since the old rebel shaved? His twitching lank high cheekbones, which glittered in the sunlight like hoarfrost, were the last matters actually noticed by Captain

Stowe before the Battle of Gettysburg was obliterated, by a quiet dark flood, by a most soothing sort of flood, from out of which you emerged painfully, by-and-by, to find yourself in the narrow bed of a hospital; and in which black flood you had lost much, including even some filial feeling.

So did it happen that, in a Connecticut barroom, Captain Stowe decided, over three double-size glasses of whisky, he would like to go south, into Florida, a safe distance beyond the reach of Mamma's amiability.

Mamma, in sweet level tones, chose not at all to understand this desire; for whatever her Frederick wished to learn about the misled South she would be wholly willing to explain. . . .

Never at any instant during the period that she was composing *Uncle Tom's Cabin, A Tale of Life Among the Lowly,* had it been necessary for Mrs. Calvin Ellis Stowe to leave Brunswick, Maine, in order to explain or to describe or to denounce anything concerning the South. Each portion of this book had come to her in a vision from Heaven, so that she had needed merely to put down upon paper, one by one, these forty-three divine communications, which reached her always in good time for the next week's issue of the *National Era.*

"The Lord Himself wrote *Uncle Tom's Cabin,*" Mrs. Stowe confessed frankly, upon a number of occasions, "and I was but an instrument in His holy hand."

The considerate will not fail here to note the direct link with St. John, who at Patmos was the last preceding person upon record thus to be assisted in the composition of romance; nor will the reflective hold it against Mrs. Stowe that she accepted all moneys earned by *Uncle Tom's Cabin,* with-

out ever offering, so far as is known, to divide with her
fellow laborer, in view of the inaccurate fustian which from
above was dictated in regard to southern scenes and customs.

As an alternative to the wild supposition that at any
time in her life Mrs. Calvin Ellis Stowe may have been mis-
taken, one can but infer that the south portions of the
United States of America had not recently been visited by
the Lord God of Hosts, in 1851, when Mrs. Stowe became an
instrument in His holy hand; and when she thus enabled
Him to repudiate His youthful error, in a more early collaboration, of decreeing slavery to be a just punishment for
the descendants of Ham. It appears enough to say that in
Uncle Tom's Cabin, which was His first full-length novel,
Jehovah, in the same instant that He demolished His reputation as a stylist, added immeasurably to His already wide
popularity as an anthologist of short stories and poems; so
that Mrs. Stowe, as His amanuensis, earned a fortune. Almost
instantly (records a biographer of this virtuous and amiable
gentlewoman) her book "was translated into French, German, Italian, Spanish, Russian, Danish, Dutch, Flemish, Polish,
Portuguese, Bohemian, Hungarian, Servian, Armenian, Illy-
rian, Romaic, Welsh, Wallachian, Finnish, and Siamese." It
was not ever put into English, some purists complained; but
in Great Britain a million and a half book-buyers wept copi-
ously, between shrugs, over the quaint American version.
Almost everybody upon earth, in short, who happened to
know even a little bit less about the South than did Mrs.
Stowe was induced to condemn the South's manner of living.
War followed; the South was devastated; and slavery was
abolished.

A yet further result was that when, in 1865, Mr. Lincoln's admired "little lady who caused this great war," was

privileged to note the gratifying end of a conflict which she more than any other person on earth had helped to incite, Mrs. Stowe noted likewise that among its casualties she must rank the sobriety of her son.

Captain Frederick Beecher Stowe, dear reader, had lost consciousness at Gettysburg, whilst gallantly defending his country's cause, because of a fragment of shell which during the thick of the fray, had entered into his right ear. His wound healed, to all seeming; but it left disturbing results.

"It has made of me a philanthropist, Mamma," he stated to the better known of his parents, "in so far that people who do not like Harriet Beecher Stowe—and there are many of them as yet undemolished by divine wrath—derive a great deal of pleasure from the fact that a visitation of this scandalous, almost scarlet nature should have settled down, as it were, upon your doorstep."

"My child," returned the distraught mother, temporarily putting aside the short story which at this instant she was writing, for the *Christian Union,* "it is indeed a circumstance more dreadful than any words can depict, that you, a Beecher, should have succumbed to the curse of strong drink."

"Your news surprises me, Mamma: for until today I had believed that in producing me you had so far stooped as to collaborate with the Professor."

"I fail, Frederick, to understand your remarks; the principle, in any case, is the same; and almost daily I receive anonymous letters telling me when and where you were last seen under the influence of intoxicants."

"Which shows, I submit, Mamma, that a great many people do dislike you. And for the rest, I had meant only that you and Uncle Henry—like Byron and Byron's sister—have not wholly escaped the tongue of slander."

"I do not at all grasp the meaning of your lewd insinuations, Frederick—"

"And in fact, Mamma, it is one source of your strength, that you do not ever understand anything which you prefer not to understand."

"I know, in any case," she replied sadly, "that I can no longer take pride in, or understand, my own son."

He was touched, somewhat, in spite of himself; and he patted the back of her plump small hand.

"But my head hurts me, Mamma. My head is always hurting me until after I have had a drink or two drinks. Then it stops hurting; and I begin to think something highly agreeable is going to happen tomorrow. My debauches ought to be weighed, in consequence, as medicinal and based upon the main principles of religion. Meanwhile, as I was saying, they afford to most people a great deal more of pleasure than they give to me, because so very many persons do enjoy seeing you, of all women, disgraced by a drunken son."

"I am accustomed to persecution, my poor Frederick."

"And in all likelihood, Mamma, you will always have your fill of it, to digest piously, because while we lesser mortals cannot avoid terror before the unbridled good-will of Harriet Beecher Stowe, it really is not possible to like you."

"Frederick, but how can you thus address your own devoted mother?"

He replied moodily: "I have seen your war, Mamma. I have been through your war, while you sat at home, alongside a canary-bird cage, writing your hymns. And your war has changed me. I can see nowadays—in the disengaged cool light which alcohol produces always when taken moderately and continuously—that you are a quite dreadful person. You are virtuous; you are well-meaning; and you are wholly ignorant as to your fellow creatures. You do not care to know what they are like. You know only what you would prefer them to be like. And there are God knows how many of you reforming women made ready to tyrannize over all America, in the drunkenness of your ignorance and of your high-mindedness! For one, I prefer the more genial drunkenness which comes out of a bottle."

The emotions of poor Mrs. Stowe in the presence of her son's callous levity can perhaps be more easily imagined than described. Her sole comfort, as she mentioned before reverting to her literary employment, in behalf of the *Christian Union,* was that by uttermost distress alone had the Captain of her salvation been made perfect as a Saviour.

A half hour later, with her short story completed and punctuated properly, Mrs. Stowe decided that there, after all, might be in Frederick's notion some merit. Two of his unhappy comrades in dissipation (we must here explain) after having been mustered out of the Federal army in Florida, had leased in that state a 1000-acre plantation called Laurel Grove. This once had been the home of a notorious slave trader, named Zephaniah Kingsley, concerning whom stories of a peculiarly revolting nature had reached the ears of our distressed heroine. Yet Frederick, with the aid of a fond mother's incessant prayers, might still find, even at Laurel Grove, the True Way—what with the open-air life, and the never-failing kindliness of Heaven, and the remoteness of saloons—and he would thus become once more the lighthearted, gallant Christian lad whom she remembered. At all events, he would not grieve daily his own mother.

Mrs. Stowe then summoned both the young veterans into her presence. She explained to them the terms upon which Frederick was about to become the superintendent of their plantation, of which, she told them kindly, she meant to purchase a third interest. They were much surprised to hear of her arrangements concerning their property, but they did not argue. They felt, perhaps, that to argue with Mrs. Stowe would be profitless.

She dismissed the three young men into Florida, after bidding her son an affectionate farewell; and then fell into meditation.

"This investment of my money," Mrs. Stowe reflected, "while in no sense a worldly enterprise, yet involves the not negligible sum of $10,000. The profits promise to be considerable; even so, they would not be lessened should a woman of suitable moral and religious principles be at hand to keep an eye on the business; and indeed it is with no ignoble thought of making money that I shall travel south. For many years I have cherished a longing to do Christ's work upon earth in fields more urgent than are afforded by Connecticut. My heart is with those poor black people whose cause I have tried to plead in words, and whose welfare I shall seek now to further through religious education. Yes: I by all means must see to it that they are united with the Episcopal Church; for, ignorant and docile, they are now in a formative state in which whoever seizes them has them."

Removing her attention, momentarily, from the obligations of a Christian gentlewoman toward Heaven, Mrs. Stowe considered the debt of an authoress to her public. Undoubtedly, the winters of New England tended somewhat to stupefy her genius. In fact, it became clear that she had always suffered quite dreadfully from the bitter cold of the

North. She must have warm weather in which to exercise properly the talents entrusted to her by Providence; and so, from all points of view, was Mrs. Stowe compelled to grant it was her moral duty, alike as a mother, as an authoress, and as an investor in the citrus industry, to spend the ensuing winter in Florida.

In the March of 1867, the indomitable, small, ever-smiling woman (after having committed, without much optimism, the care of all six canaries to her husband's charge) obeyed the dictates of her conscience. With a hint of acerbity, the Tallahassee *Sentinel* informed its readers that "Harriet Beecher Stowe has purchased a plantation on the St. Johns river; and will reside hereafter among the people whom she has represented as worse than barbarous."

She was enchanted, to begin with, by the climate, because it contrasted so sharply with that of Connecticut in winter. Her admiration became ecstasy when once she had been rowed up the river to Mandarin—a village standing some fifteen miles south of Jacksonville—so as to obtain the mail, which arrived every week by way of the steamer from Charleston. Cherokee roses were massed along the boardwalk near the landing; and beyond their delicate pale beauty, Mrs. Calvin Ellis Stowe observed with approval a thick grove of live oak trees, reputed to be the largest in America. Here, "in a setting more lovely than Italy," she found also, through the benevolence of Heaven, a cottage for sale—"a dream place."

Mrs. Stowe purchased it; and became exuberant, in a letter to George Eliot, as to this new home, "built close to a great live-oak twenty-five feet in girth, and with over-arching boughs eighty feet up in the air, spreading like a firmament, and all swaying with mossy festoons. . . . In front, the beautiful, grand St. Johns stretches five miles from shore to shore . . . [with] steamers plying back and forth to the great world. . . . On all sides are large orange-trees with their dense shade and ever vivid green."

Toward the local birds and flowers she extended a similar quality of enthusiasm.

She then investigated the Laurel Grove plantation and found that her son's partners, who had but little experience of farming methods in the South and even less control over the former slaves whom they had hired, were said, by local scoffers, merely to be running "a free boarding house for a gang of lazy Negroes." Mrs. Stowe retrieved from the unpromising enterprise, with a serene smilingness, her misled son. Henceforward, Captain Stowe remained in his mother's fond keeping at Mandarin, where Mamma, for the instant, was busied in repairing and altering and enlarging her dream place "around the trunk of the tree, so that our cottage has a peculiar and original air and seems as if it were half tree or a something that had grown out of the tree. We have thrown out gables and chambers as a tree throws out new branches, till our cottage is like nobody else's."

Meanwhile, at odd moments, she fostered American literature by adding to its classics yet another wholesome volume, entitled *Old Town Folks*.

No one of these avocations was allowed, however, to divert the attention of Mrs. Stowe from her more lofty task to establish a line of churches along the St. Johns River for the benefit of the Negro race. This laid upon her the duty of instructing the Right Reverend J. F. Young, then the Episcopal bishop of Florida, as to those especial merits of his church which made it for her purpose a fit instrument.

"Even if my tastes and feelings did not incline me toward your Church," she wrote affably to the bishop, "I should still choose it as the best system of training immature minds—"

"Now, but really, Mamma," said Captain Stowe, to whom she was dictating this letter, "do you think that is a quite tactful reason for your decision to permit the Episcopal faith to continue its existence?"

She inspected what he had written.

"Why, but indeed, my dear Frederick," she admitted, "you are right. One must not be inconsiderate. So let us say, 'of training immature minds such as those of our Negroes.'"

Afterward Mrs. Stowe went on to explain to Bishop Young that inasmuch as his church "was composed with reference to the laboring class of England, at a time when they were as ignorant as our Negroes now are," this, as it were, crude kindergarten sort of religion would serve quite well enough as an instrument in the hands of Mrs. Stowe.

"Now, my son," she continued, "do you write to our cousin in South Carolina, Spencer Foote. Instruct him that he is to come at once to Mandarin, to my own Patmos, so as to superintend our dream home. You will assist him. Each box of fruit shipped from the grove will be stenciled, in rather large white letters—since white, after all, is the emblem of purity—'Oranges from Harriet Beecher Stowe, Mandarin, Florida.' In business matters one ought not to be unbusinesslike; and my not unknown name will help to sell the fruit."

"It would have helped a great deal more," replied Captain Stowe, "if you had not published in the *Atlantic Monthly* that absurd article about Byron and his sister. The power of your name, Mamma, is at this instant open to question, now you have come so near to wrecking a respectable magazine through your need to be reproving iniquity twenty-four hours to the day, even when you have to invent your facts."

"Lord Byron, my son, was guilty of unmentionable conduct with his own wretched sister."

"And so, Mamma, because his conduct was unmentionable, you felt it your duty to mention it. That is wholly like you."

"I do not understand you, Frederick—"

"And I, Mamma, I am enough like other people to yield, as always, to your preference as to what Harriet Beecher Stowe may prefer, or prefer not, to understand or to believe."

"Very well, then," she resumed pleasantly. "Instead of retracting the article, I shall expand it into a book. But come now, my dearest, write next to your Uncle Charles Beecher. Tell him I think it would be far wiser for him to give up those strange notions of his as to the pre-existence of the human soul, and become an orthodox Episcopalian, slightly High Church. He can then be our clergyman here at Mandarin. He is just the man we need. I can manage also, you may mention, to have him made State Superintendent of Education. It is an office for which he is well fitted; the salary is sufficient; and I myself will speak to Governor Reed about the appointment."

"You are wholly wonderful," said Captain Stowe; "and the Governor of Florida, as well as Uncle Charles, like everybody else, will beyond doubt obey you."

Thus speaking, the captain arose and embraced his mother.

"Yet I, Mamma, I am not worthy to be the son of Harriet Beecher Stowe. I admire you; I quail before you; but

I simply cannot put up with your smug, sweet-voiced efficiency for an instant longer."

The next morning, he had disappeared. Some said that he went to Chile; there were rumors as to his having been seen in San Francisco; but in mere point of fact, nobody was ever able to say just what did happen to Captain Stowe, now that his hurt ear, like Captain Jenkins' ear, had served handsomely to foster the St. Johns' welfare.

Even though his bereaved mother found the evasion to be regrettable, yet Mrs. Stowe was accustomed to disaster; nor did she ever question, impiously, the wisdom of her Heavenly Father in His well-known habit of chastening those whom He most loved. Her desolation, when thus rightly regarded, became an oblique compliment to one's humble ventures in correct behavior. It followed that, stifling her anguish, she purchased a box of rather broad pen-points; and settled down to the production of a book, in this "my calm Isle of Patmos, where the world is not, and I have such quiet, long hours for writing."

The great Emerson, she meditated, would have done well to insulate himself here and so keep all his electricity; all-gifted Louisa M. Alcott might have developed, at Mandarin, beside the placid St. Johns, a yet wider range of sprightliness; and sublime Hawthorne also would have been improved, it stayed possible, by living in an orange grove. Only in complete quietude could genius display its utmost glory, Mrs. Stowe reflected, as she began to write, for the *Christian Union,* a series of papers about the St. Johns.

These papers were published in book form, a brief while later, under the title *Palmetto Leaves;* and howsoever incoherently Mrs. Stowe may have injured the South some twenty years earlier, now her surprising pæans as to the "lapis lazuli blue colored" St. Johns, and as to the semitropical paradise called Florida—even though quite as loosely based upon facts as had been *Uncle Tom's Cabin, A Tale of Life Among the Lowly*—did result in an immediate and a most profitable increase of tourist travel from out of the North.

Thenceforward, until 1883, all that part of the St. Johns River valley about Mandarin was both hallowed and animated, throughout every winter, by the presence of Mrs. Calvin Ellis Stowe, who not infrequently brought with her, in a white forestry of whiskers, her husband—"my own Professor." Few noticed whether she did or did not; for, like most other persons, he was submerged by the flood of her indulgent kindness.

So amiable remained always the disposition of our heroine that even after Florida had so far passed beyond making the best of her deplored presence as to make of it likewise a font of revenue, she did not ever resent with an undue bitterness the advertising which human nature conferred gratis upon her books. A small steamer, the *Mary Draper*, now began to conduct round-trip excursion parties upon the St. Johns, between Jacksonville and Mandarin, so that virtuosi of literature might observe with their own eyes its manufacture. The "quiet, long hours" of Mrs. Stowe's communion with the supernal were thus timed by the schedule of the steamer.

No sooner had the warning whistle of the *Mary Draper* proclaimed the need of quick inspiration than plump little Mrs. Stowe would trot amicably toward the writing table upon the open porch of her dream home. She would then write, with rapt industry, while the steamer paused before Mandarin; and each passenger, for the trivial sum of seventy-five cents, was allowed thus to admire at close quarters the output of an inspired artist in full blast. Very often, remarks an historian, did chance so favor these excursionists that Mrs. Stowe would grant to them a yet more impressive, full-face view of America's supreme novelist's chubby and serene and vacuous features, when she glanced upward from labor, in search of the *mot juste*, without at all noting the awed tourists. You saw then that her benign attention was riveted, far beyond transient matters, upon the tidings which at this instant were being transmitted from on high; and niggardly indeed must be the observer who did not purchase the next book by Mrs. Stowe after he had thus witnessed its parturition.

Never, as she announced in the New York *Tribune*, did she "receive even one incivility from any native Floridian," although she admitted that her neighbors showed, "at first, no very warm love." That ever, indeed, the sentiments with which they regarded Mrs. Stowe grew to be adoration, is not attested by affidavit. Nevertheless, they were civil; her fame had become for them an asset; and they, like the rest of the world, did that which Mrs. Stowe told them to do.

She continued, in brief, to display every Christian virtue winsomely; and nobody ever presumed to withstand her wishes. None knew why everybody obeyed her, not even Captain Frederick Beecher Stowe—who alone of mere human beings did manage to rebuff the cast-iron will of his brisk and gentle-voiced mother, by running away helter-skelter.

At Mandarin, a wee sweet chapel, with an ornate triptych of stained-glass windows—all parti-colored in the melting Neapolitan ice-cream style of Tiffany's more luscious but for once appropriate manner—perpetuates the memory, along with the ideals, of Mrs. Stowe.

26

The Steamboat Era

THE debt of Florida, alone among the southern states, to Mrs. Calvin Ellis Stowe has been noted. In her *Palmetto Leaves*, and in yet other products of an untiring if inaccurate pen, throughout the course of some twelve years, she elected to become for her adopted state a press agent of the first order, in the superlative, stanch, ancient line of Jean Ribaut and James Grant and William Bartram. Inasmuch as her readers were much more numerous and more naïve than had been the public addressed by her predecessors in the implausible, so now the rhapsodies of Mrs. Stowe—concerning her Isle of Patmos, and its plant- and animal-life, and the beautiful, grand, lapis-lazuli blue colored St. Johns in general—procured for the broad brown river an influx of tourist travel immeasurably beyond the resources of her not typo-graphically color-blind forerunners.

A new and sensible habit was arising among Americans. Many of them began now to imitate Mrs. Stowe (so far as their but human gifts permitted) by spending the cold win-ter months in the peninsula of Florida—where the climate, as this intrepid huntress of the hackneyed did not omit to point out, was no less "balmy" than "salubrious." And as this habit became more firmly fixed upon an ever-increasing number of winter visitors, so did prosperity likewise visit the St. Johns valley, now that many physicians also had begun to suggest, to their patients, an outing in Florida.

—For, as Dr. Daniel G. Brinton, who was then prac-ticing medicine in Philadelphia, remarked (after recording his apologies for approaching "a delicate topic") in his *Guide-Book to Florida and the South*: "A warm climate promises aid . . . in marriages not blessed with offspring. . . . Heat stimulates powerfully the faculty of reproduction. . . . So we can with every reason recommend to childless couples, without definite cause of sterility, a winter in the south. I have known most happy effects from it," he adds com-placently, with a strange flavor of some personal adventure.

Yet furthermore, Dr. Brinton pointed out that, while the climate of Florida very much resembled the climate of Italy, "I am . . . pleased, for the invalid's sake, to say that as for treasures of art, Florida has none. There are no inter-minable picture galleries, or cold, damp churches, or belvi-deres, or other such æsthetic afflictions to visit, the frequency of which in Italy is a serious drawback to the seeker after health."

Such inducements proved irresistible. More and yet more wholesome-minded American citizens, who fidgeted in art's presence, began nowadays to visit the St. Johns River, either with or without their own wives.

As a further by-product of the tourist trade, many permanent settlers, chiefly from the North, were drawn to sites and towns along the river, and to its back country; so that, in the years between 1870 and 1900, the population of Florida, under the annual influence of Dr. Brinton's prescribed tonic, "a winter in the south," became more than doubled. Inasmuch as, until the 1880's, steamboats afforded the only transportation to the one part of Florida known to the general public, or sought by the majority of persons needing new homes, now occurred, upon the St. Johns also, that tumultuous and gaudy growth of steamboat traffic which, at this period, was a feature of American life at large. Always, however, the chief factor during the steamboat era was, in Florida, "the winter tourist trade."

Just as the rowboat and the schooner replaced the aboriginal dugout on the St. Johns after 1562, so had the invention of the steamboat brought about a new mode of travel upon its waters in the early 1830's. As freight and passenger demands increased, a tentative imitation of the more luxurious vessels employed in more metropolitan areas was substituted by degrees for the earlier crude carriers, whose bills of fare had suggested, to at least one victim, the "grub of a mining camp," and whose cabins, so far as went their dimensions and comfort, he had compared (but upon the whole unfavorably) with "a poor house coffin." Then, after the close of the Seminole War, in the early 1840's, trade with the outside world began daily to increase in regularity and in volume. Lumber, cotton, oranges, barreled fish, and yet other Floridian offshoots were shipped to Savannah, and occasionally to more distant ports, upon such pioneer steamers as the *St. Matthews*, the *William Gaston*, the *Ocmulgee*, the *Welaka*, the *Magnolia*, the *Seminole*, the *Sarah Spaulding*, the *General Clinch*, the *Pampero*, the *William Barnett*, the *Thorn*, and the *Zephyr*. And the life of the St. Johns became enriched by the presence of many steamboat captains who have since entered into legend.

Few captains employed upon the St. Johns were more devoutly esteemed than was Louis M. Coxetter. Short and stout, he wore both a moustache and a goatee; and the unfailing profanity of his orders is said to have been remarkably emphasized by the indolent mild tone—flavored with a Dutch accent—in which they were issued. His success as captain of the steamer *Carolina*, operating between Savannah and Picolata, led, in the 1850's, to Coxetter's introduction of a direct service between Palatka and Charleston with a larger steamer, the *Florida;* and this service was increased, later, by the addition of the *Everglade*, the building of which Captain Coxetter supervised, and which he himself ran.

With the beginning of war, in 1861, Coxetter entered the Confederate forces, and his naval career became so acquisitive that he was described by Admiral duPont, of the Federal navy, as being the most skilled and the most formidable seaman upon the Atlantic coast. One of the more valuable prizes taken by Louis Coxetter was the *Alvarado*, with a $70,000 cargo; yet he captured too, not only the *John Welch*, the *Enchantress*, the *S. J. Waring*, and the *Santa Clara*, but also the *John Carver*, the *Mary E. Thompson*, and the *Mary Goodell*. As the skipper of various blockaderunners, such as the *Fanny and Jenny*, the *Herald*, and the *Jeff Davis*, Coxetter was responsible for transporting large cargoes of cotton to the Bahamas and for the bringing back of a considerable amount of general supplies and ammunition.

After the fall of Richmond, he was commissioned, by friends of Jefferson Davis, to convey the president of the Confederacy from the coast of Florida to some foreign port. Coxetter made ready his best vessel; and, waiting the arrival of his fugitive passenger, he kept it hidden in a secret channel near the Indian River until the capture of Davis, in Georgia, had made impossible a most promising chance for Louis M. Coxetter to enact what might have been his most exciting role in a varied repertoire.

Captain Coxetter resumed, after the war, his former activities upon the St. Johns; and ran the *City Point* between Charleston and Palatka. He endeavored also to aid in the reconstruction of the St. Johns valley by founding the town of Coxetterville, near-by Deep Creek, a bit east of where that tributary enters the river. Colonists came from South Carolina, but success did not attend them; and so today the grave of Louis Coxetter's civic aspirations is marked only by the presence of a few small farms, the owners of which, with a republic's famous ingratitude, now call their post office Bakersville.

River traffic had so prospered, by the late 1860's, that several steamers were now making weekly round trips from Charleston and Savannah to Jacksonville and Palatka and yet other St. Johns settlements. Among them was a vessel built in 1857, and christened the *St. Marys*—which, it may be recalled, had ended her harried career as a Confederate blockade-runner through being sunk, by her own crew, in McGirt's Creek. This steamer was raised and rebuilt after the war; and under a new name, as the *Nick King,* she was placed on the run between Savannah and the St. Johns.

When on April 12, 1870, nine years to a day after the firing on Fort Sumter, the *Nick King* left Savannah, on board was the most famous of living Southerners, in the no longer robust person of General Robert E. Lee. He had been persuaded to seek, in climes of which the balminess and salubrity had been vouched for by Heaven's own amanuensis, aid for his failing health, by means of a leisurely journey, during which he was accompanied by his daughter, Agnes. They visited Raleigh, Charlotte, and Columbia, in all which towns General Lee was greeted with an enthusiasm untempered by privacy; so that the Savannah *Republican,* when he reached that city, spoke with concern as to the "inexpressible sadness visible in his features . . . caused by the demonstrations of filial love and devotion shown him by a people whom he has striven in vain to liberate from political bondage."

To the more prosaic, it may appear not unlikely that the invalid, who wanted only quiet, was being pestered with a slight surplus of filial love and devotion; for his private verdict as to this southern journey, in a letter to his wife, displays eloquence.

"Agnes seemed to enjoy the trip very much," he reported—with a striking reticence as to his own opinion of it.

Then, at Jacksonville, the president of Washington College was greeted, yet again, by an official committee, in addition to as many citizens as could possibly crowd aboard the *Nick King.* The old tired hero was forced also, by the disappointed requirements of filial love and devotion, to appear on deck, so that he might at least be seen by his people. The wharves were packed with his people, and not one of them cheered now; for indeed a Southerner of this period would as soon have thought of applauding God. There was, instead, a complete silence; and it was not only the women who wept.

After that, the *Nick King* continued up the river, and General Lee disembarked at Orange Mills. Here he spent the night of April 13, 1870, at the home of Colonel Robert G. Cole, who had been chief commissary of the Army of Northern Virginia, and whom Lee had not seen since their parting at Appomattox. The next day—which was the fifth anniversary of Abraham Lincoln's assassination—the Lees returned to Jacksonville.

"We rode over the town, etc.," General Lee reported, still to his wife, "and were hospitably entertained by Colonel Sanderson. The climate was delightful, the fish inviting and abundant."

Concerning Jacksonville, that is all he records. General Lee, in brief, was an aging, ill, tired man, with but six more months to live; and the filial love and devotion of a people who adored him were, through the highest of motives, taking shape as an interminable nuisance to plague his last moments upon earth. One finds it a bit ironic and wholly pitiful. He returned then to his home at Lexington, in Virginia, where his worshipers permitted him to die unmolested.

At Orange Mills, General Lee is reputed to have bitten into, for the first and only time, an odd sort of citrus fruit which was cultivated there, upon a half dozen or so trees, as a curiosity, because there was not any market for it. Its flavor was a surprising blend of bitter and sweet and acid which at once puckered up the faces of those who tried to eat it. This fruit was several times the size of an orange; and since it grew in clusters, Colonel Cole called it grapefruit.

Even though it did not have any possible commercial future, Colonel Cole liked to raise grapefruit, so that he might surprise his guests by inducing them, just once, to taste this strange freak of nature.

Colonel Cole's was a typical St. Johns River grove of the 1870's, when oranges were beginning to rank among Florida's most important products. The banks of the St. Johns were especially favored as a location for groves, because the soil there was thought to give a particularly fine flavor to the fruit, and because the river tempered the now and then freezing winds. Moreover, the river provided the most handy and virtually the only means of transportation for fruit in any considerable volume.

Each of the larger groves had its own packing house adjoining its own landing—with a gaunt wharf reaching out into the river's channel, where the oranges were put aboard steamboats. The smaller groves were served by a floating packing house, renovated from an old steamer, the *Orange Maid,* which stopped at various landings along the St. Johns and received fruit in bulk. The oranges were then crated on board the steamer, so as to be made ready, before they reached Jacksonville, for shipment north. So universal had become orange raising that during the early 1880's it was estimated $10,000,000 had been invested in the citrus industry, of which the annual yield was about 75,000,000 oranges, selling at an average of $15 per thousand.

For fuel the steamers on the St. Johns used fat pine wood; and so much of this was required that contractors throughout the length of the river were busied in supplying it. Criblike log wharves were built at the edge of the channel; and as more and yet more logs were piled up one upon another, in the style of a log cabin, the foundations became firm. Pilings were then driven into the bottom of the river, at each corner of the crib, and chained to it; split logs were laid across the top of the crib for a flooring; and upon this massive structure was heaped pine wood for the use of steamers.

Attendants remained on duty during the day to conduct the sales of this wood; and at night, the lock box, which was kept upon each wharf, received a memorandum of the names of steamers that had purchased fuel and of the amounts taken aboard. These "wood-tickets," signed by either the captain or the purser, were very often circulated instead of currency, among merchants alongside the river, before being redeemed. In the mean time, while freight claimed so much attention from the river steamers, their facilities for passenger travel were not neglected; and in Florida the tourist began to outrank the citrus industry as the more dependable source of income.

27

"To Amuse and Instruct"

"T IS but a few years," proclaimed one river steamboat line, in the middle seventies, "since the question of a tour of this spendid natural domain . . . via the great highway of the peninsula, the broad and forest-environed St. Johns, presented so many obstacles that but comparatively few travellers had the courage to invade the vast reaches of territory tributary to and accessible by the river. Now things are as they should be. Not only easy and swift transportation, but even the luxuries supposed to exist only upon the northern rivers [are provided]. . . . There is much to amuse and instruct in observation of the various types of the genus homo, not only the homespun 'Cracker' upon the steps of the store at the landing, but the ebony genius who picks his banjo, all day long, for the edification of the deck hands forward."

It appears, to posterity, a choice among delights somewhat unexhilarating. And in point of fact, the recreations of a steamboat passenger were a trifle more varied.

As a rule, these winter visitors to the St. Johns landed first at Jacksonville. Prior to the building of railroads to that city, they came south by rail to Charleston or Savannah, and at these ports boarded steamers for Florida. In 1878 the mouth of the St. Johns was dredged in order to permit the entrance of large oceangoing vessels, such as the *Western Texas;* and after 1886, when the Clyde Steamship Line opened its regular through-service from Jacksonville to New York, by means of the steamers *Cherokee* and *Seminole,* tourists very often made the entire trip south by water.

Jacksonville in the 1880's did not possess a population of more than fifteen thousand inhabitants, but its forty hotels, in addition to yet many more boarding houses, entertained annually some seventy-five thousand patrons from the North. The St. James Hotel, opened in 1869, acquired the reputation of being "The Fifth Avenue Hotel of Florida," and it combined with the Magnolia Hotel at Magnolia Springs and the Clarendon Hotel at Green Cove Springs to establish all correct fashions for the current winter along the St. Johns. Then the Putnam House, at Palatka, inaugurated its season of 1879 with a Grand Ball in honor of General Grant; and yet other resorts along the river entered with prominence into the columns of every newspaper published in the United States when, in 1886, President Cleveland brought his young bride to Florida. Presently Joseph Jefferson, the actor, and still other celebrities, such as the Duke of Newcastle, had chosen the St. Johns for their winter vacations; and the yachts of the wealthy became upon its brown waters bright commonplaces.

These resort hotels were sprawling wooden structures, two or three stories in height, with wide verandas for those patrons who elected to take out-of-door exercise in a rocking chair. Decorations were limited to a half dozen or so mounted birds, one stuffed alligator, a meager collection of seashells, and a few lithographs. The more pretentious hotels possessed a ballroom; but others simply cleared their dining rooms for the lancers, the polka, and the schottische, or for the more formal Washington Birthday Ball, which was the climax of all Florida's social season.

Serious elderly patrons interested themselves in a shared study of the neighboring birds and of the Negro problem, or else dozed in semitropical sunlight. The more energetic preferred croquet. The truly strenuous turned to fishing for bass, or to sailing upon the quiet waters of the St. Johns, or to hunting wild turkey, deer, and quail; but the heroic hunted alligators. So general, indeed, was the practice that small steamers were leased regularly for this purpose. One notes, for example, the *Florida Review,* in the autumn of 1878, as reporting that "the last alligator excursion of the steamer *Mary Draper* was a very successful one. . . . On her arrival . . . her deck [was] decorated with the carcasses of a number of festive gators from Black Creek."

A student of Charles Dickens, howsoever inured to journalese, may here find that the adjective "festive" "by himself surprises."

A pastime of daylong interest to the tourist was to watch the passing of steamboats up or down the St. Johns and to compare the merits of each vessel. Increase in the number of steamboat lines operating upon the river produced keen rivalry; and races were very often conducted between steamers—of which contests perhaps the most notable to take place upon the St. Johns was the final fruitage of a perennial competition between the Post and Baya lines.

The rise of the latter company under H. T. Baya was unusual. The descendant of an old Spanish family, Baya acquired a sound business training in Charleston, to which city he had gone from his native St. Augustine as a boy; and by 1861 he had become a partner in the brokerage firm of Porcher and Company. Upon the outbreak of war, he averted promptly from finance, to become an excellent soldier. He served as a captain in the Confederate army until the South's downfall. Then Captain Baya returned to Florida; he opened a grocery store in Jacksonville; and with a captivating versatility, the aforetime banker and shopkeeper and military officer devoted himself, by-and-by, to running a steamboat.

His first venture was to purchase the *Gazelle*, which although small, was unparalleled, in that she was a propeller steamer, where all her rivals were either side-wheelers or stern-wheel paddlers. The unique *Gazelle* at once became popular for excursions to Mayport, to Fort George Island, to Green Cove Springs, or to yet other points near Jacksonville. So Captain Baya then bought the *Pastime* and the *Water Lily*, both of which, under his direction, carried mail, passengers, and freight, to settlements on the lower St. Johns. Inasmuch as this steamboat business had now become his chief occupation, he was not pleased when, in 1878, John A. Post, who was a Northerner, brought to the St. Johns two large side-wheelers, the *Eliza Hancock* and the *John Sylvester*, and employed them between Jacksonville and Palatka.

This competition, from semipalatial steamers owned by

a Yankee intruder, alike provoked and aroused Captain Baya. He purchased, from the Harlem and New York Navigation Company, the *Sylvan Glen*, which was then thought to be the handsomest of the East River flyers. This impressive side-wheeler was 160 feet over all, and her speed was seventeen and one-half miles per hour. So when brought to the St. Johns, she outstripped the *Eliza Hancock*, but in a race with the *John Sylvester* the *Sylvan Glen* failed utterly.

Captain Baya was now faced with a serious problem; and being but partly successful in the speed of his steamers, he resorted, with an afore-mentioned versatility, to quite other attractions, by entertaining his passengers with an Italian band. It was a coup which Post parried by producing a German band. Thereupon Baya cut his fares; but so too did Post. Furthermore, when competing vessels were sailing at the same hour from the same port, both now began to offer free passage; and if a potential guest appeared undecided as to which steamer he would honor gratis, then porters or even the higher officials of one or the other line would seize on the waverer's suitcases and rush them aboard. The passenger followed his luggage perforce.

From out of this deadlock, through which both lines were approaching bankruptcy, Captain Baya hurried to Philadelphia, where he ordered the construction of a vessel such as, he was confident, could outrace that infernal *John Sylvester*. So large became his faith in the new liner that Captain H. T. Baya gave to it his own name; and early in the spring of 1883, the entire area of the lower St. Johns awaited the supreme test between Baya and Post.

At nine o'clock upon the appointed morning, the *H. T. Baya* and the *John Sylvester* pulled out from adjoining piers at Jacksonville, and started south against the river's slow current. They ran neck and neck until they approached the first stop, which was Green Cove Springs. Here the pilot of the *H. T. Baya* swerved cunningly to the inside just as both steamers rounded the beacon, and the heavy ropes of the *H. T. Baya* were slung to the wharf. When thus slightly bested, the *John Sylvester,* with her ballast barrels rolled hard over to port, at once charged full-tilt upon her rival; her guards mounted above those of the Baya liner; and from this abrupt, smashing onslaught resulted much damage to the upper side-house of the *H. T. Baya.* No one was injured, however; and since the hurt done was well above the water line, the race continued, with the treacherously attacked steamer still in the lead, as far as Palatka.

Both crews there worked like maniacs in loading and unloading the freight and passengers, while half-naked Negroes fed four-foot pitch pine to the boilers of both engines with a prodigality so large that clouds of jet-black smoke now obscured the sky line—"like floating continents." Soot drifted in on the fine new carpets, adorned with crimson roses as big as soup plates, of the *H. T. Baya's* Grand Staircase and Parisian Salon; the oil paintings, all done by hand, were ruined; and so powerful became the vibrations of the ship's engine that the genuine bronze stag upon the pilothouse quivered as if terrified, now that the return trip to Jacksonville had begun. When twilight settled over the St. Johns, the relative position of the two steamers could hardly be determined.

Meanwhile, all male Jacksonville who were not bedridden had lined the long water front of Jacksonville to await the evening's transcendent outcome. Upon one wharf, Captain H. T. Baya, dressed to the nines (as he remembered the great planters of Charleston to have dressed before the war) was the impressive center of an admiring and confident group. Solomon at his glory's height did not go thus appareled, for Captain Baya wore, it is recorded, a Prince Albert coat, with a very low-cut white waistcoat which revealed a red bandanna handkerchief tucked inside it across his stomach, in addition to a frilled stock, a large ruby pin, a couple of ponderous watch chains, a pair of light-gray trousers, and a gleaming black top hat most opulent in curves. He swung jauntily a gold-headed cane. Yet equally certain of victory appeared, upon the next wharf, the no less resplendent owner of the Post line, nor was his cortège inferior, either in numbers or in boastfulness. Bets were placed raucously. Gentlemen fidgeted from one foot to the other; they puffed at black, thin cheroots; and they laughed loudly for no reason at all.

When, at long last, a blaze of deck lights foretold that the great race would soon reach its end, none knew which steamer was ahead. Sparks poured from both of the heavy smokestacks like meteors, while a continued firing of rockets reduplicated, in a highly creditable manner, the élan of a naval bombardment. Then the hoarse whistle of the *H. T. Baya* shrieked proudly as she slid into her dock, with the *John Sylvester*, a discomfortably close but undeniable second; and the peak of the steamboat era upon the St. Johns had been attained.

By long odds the most popular side trip for the St. Johns River tourist was a voyage up the Oklawaha, upon one of Colonel Hart's steamers, to Silver Springs, or to Lakes Griffin, Harris, Eustis, and Dora.

Lafcadio Hearn has very glowingly described the

Oklawaha (in a poetic prose style, of which he appears deplorably remote from being the one casualty) as "a narrow river undulating through the forest like some slow serpent unrolling its hundred coils of green. . . . So sudden and so multitudinous are the turns of the stream that the boat seems ever steering straight for land. But always as she seems about to touch the bank, a wooded point detaches itself from the masses of verdure—a sharp curve betrays its secret—a new vista terminating in new mysteries of green opens its gates to our prow. Narrow and labyrinthine the river is, but so smooth that like a flood of quicksilver it repeats inversely all the intricacies of tangle growths, all delicate details of leaf and blossom, all the bright variations of foliage-color. . . . Near the water the swamp-growth is dwarfed, tufted, irregular, but generally bright of hue; further back, it rises to majestic maturity, offering a long succession of domes and cupolas of frondescence, alternated with fantastic minarets of cypress; behind all, the solid and savage forest towers like a battlement, turret upon turret."

It is good cheap rhetoric; and the conveyed impression in general—that the Oklawaha may be well worth seeing—will arouse, among the tenderhearted, a proper feeling of regret that myopic Lafcadio Hearn himself could not see this river, or anything else which was more than eight inches distant from his infirm eyes.

For the rest, it was Hubbard L. Hart who first undertook to render the Oklawaha navigable, by clearing its deep twisted channel. A New Englander of thrifty habits and considerable distinction of appearance, Hart came to Palatka in 1854. His first enterprise was to conduct a stage line between Palatka and Tampa, through a part of Florida so unessentially civilized that the escort of a government guard was required. He then purchased, in 1860, the small steamer, *James Burt,* with which to begin passenger service upon the Oklawaha; but of a sudden the War Between the States checked his plans. He allied himself, prudently, with the Confederate cause; and upon the *James Burt* he transported cotton from plantations west of the St. Johns to Lake Harney, from the banks of which his cargoes were carried overland to the Atlantic coast, and so shipped, by means of blockade-runners, to Nassau.

Hart built the small steamer *Griffin* in 1866, and he resumed his attempts to navigate the seemingly impenetrable Oklawaha. He succeeded by-and-by; and as a reward he at once got, from his fellow citizens, the indigenous and informally bestowed, but enduring, title of colonel. Very shortly afterward, Colonel Hubbard Hart was the head of a line of steamboats offering to the tourist an opportunity to inspect the wild wonders of the Oklawaha, by means of quaint small boxlike steamers which brought fame to the St. Johns valley and a fine livelihood to the most enterprising of all the colonels then visible in Palatka.

—For Colonel Hart established in Boston a sort of recruiting office for tourists; he advertised widely; he conducted every one of his patrons upon a "special" tour of his thriving large orange grove, upon the point opposite Palatka; he overwhelmed them with all manner of stately courtesies and Old World attentions. For the benefit of his fellow New Englanders, he gave, in brief, upon all occasions, an impersonation of the orthodox southern colonel which was a great deal more impressive than the original; and inasmuch as pleased customers carried back with them a lively approval of his superb acting, into the villages of Maine and Vermont and Massachusetts, and to the farms of Indiana and Ohio and

Iowa, as well as toward all other rural corners of the Union, Colonel Hubbard Hart's repute as a polite mentor for the beginning traveler achieved heroic proportions.

Moreover, was it not through this supreme flowering of the South's gentry that the returned tourist had been made familiar with alligators asleep on reed-grown shores, with water moccasins hanging from vines and trees, with white herons standing like sentinels, and with fried bass for breakfast? Such babbling Sindbads, after a surcease from travel, spoke likewise of how upon the pilothouse of the Hart steamers had been placed a large iron basket filled with burning pine knots, from out of which, at night, burst flickering tall yellow flames. These gilded the obscured fastnesses of that jungle through which the steamer moved slowly; and they so gave comfort to such persons as did not wholly delight in the ominous grave calling of Florida's outlandish birds, in the coughing of panthers, or in the malignant bellow of crocodiles, with all of them so very close to you in the darkness.

With a remunerative gusto, Colonel Hart himself would speak, upon the least possible provocation, as to these marvels wheresoever he went. Then, during the December of 1895— while upon a cultural mission to enlighten the public of Georgia as to the many benefits of what was virtually foreign travel, upon the Oklawaha River—the veteran showman was killed, in Atlanta, by a streetcar. His body was brought to Palatka; and it there lay in state for five days, in the front parlor of his family mansion, so that his many admirers might pay, to the dead impresario, the meed of parting tears. The report appears unlikely, that a small admission fee also was charged.

28

About the Advance of Napoleon

Y ou came back home after the war was over. But at
Cedar Creek there was no longer any home. Some black
soldiers, who were put up to it by a man named Higginson,
had burned down the houses, and the fences too. The big
oaks, which you just halfway remembered, around the place
where your home had been, once, were still there. They were
like charcoal on one side, the side where the houses used to be.
On the side next to the brown-colored broad river, the trees
were all cut up and scarred by shells from the Yankee
gunboats.

The higher-up fields were pretty near covered with chinquapin bushes and live oak saplings. Some of the saplings were as much as twenty feet high. A sapling can do a lot of growing in six years; and you all had been away for six years, nearly six years anyhow, over in Hamilton County. Down in the low fields, it was just tall grass and some myrtle bushes and weeds mixed up together.

Pa had a mighty hard time getting enough ground cleared for a new house. He finished that work, though, by-and-by; and he finished a sort of small log house too; and after that, you all lived in it.

Pa did not have any money to buy mules or horses or cattle. So the Browards all had to work together to clear out the weeds and the bushes down to the riverside. Ma and you and your brother did most of this work while Pa was away somewhere trying to get something for everybody to eat. Sis' Josephine had helped too, a little bit. Then all the Browards who were feeling spry enough, on account of this not being their day to have chills, started right in to dig up the ground with their hoes. They planted some Irish potatoes, and sweet potatoes, and sugar cane, and beans, and some English peas. It was sort of fun, working with Ma. Little Emily stuck a stick under her right arm and just stood around playing she was the state guard, with a shotgun, watching you convicts work. Emily was real cute.

After that, the Browards started a garden, for cabbages and turnips and beets and lettuce and asparagus and onions. None of the other children were old enough to remember how good lettuce tasted when it was fixed up with sugar and cream, the way Ma used to fix it before the war started.

The things that you and Ma planted did not do very well. You planted, for instance, four whole sacks of Irish

potatoes, and you raised only one sackful. The English peas
started out all right, but they turned yellow and died. The
sugar cane did fine. It had seven or eight joints to each stalk,
before a herd of wild cattle got in there one night. They just
ruined the whole patch.

"A divinity that shapes our ends," Pa said.

Then he sort of laughed and took a good snort of corn.
Pa had almost the best moonshine in Duval County, so everybody said. Pa was smart. He used to be sort of famous. He
had been in what they called a State Senate, once, before the
war started.

Anyhow, Pa had got some hogs now. And you and your
brother had a drag seine. With a drag seine, you and Montcalm could catch pretty near enough fish in the river to feed
all the Browards. The Browards kept on having chills and
fever most of the time, though. People said to take tartar
emetic; but that only made all the Browards sicker than ever.
Pa borrowed some quinine, somewhere; and everybody took
lots of it; and some of you got to feeling heaps better. Ma
died, though, and Pa died too, a little while after she did.
That was right bad. You cried some about it at nights.
Your aunts came over from Jacksonville then. Even Aunt
Helen and Aunt Florida came. You had not ever seen them
before. They took all five of your sisters away. But you and
your brother just stayed on in the log cabin Pa had built.
The two of you could run the place all right, now that you
were twelve years old, and Montcalm was almost ten.

The Broward boys lived beside Cedar Creek, upon the
east bank of it, just where this creek enters the St. Johns.
They raised corn and potatoes, and they cared for their hogs,
about as successfully as any two children might be expected

to do. Each of them had a gun; and they had also a couple of half-wild mongrel animals—charitably called dogs—which answered, when they felt like answering, to the names of Lady and Ring. So the boys were able to hunt deers and turkeys and squirrels. The woods were full of deers and turkeys and squirrels. It was pretty hard to find the squirrels up in so much Spanish moss. Still, both of the boys had regular, well-paying work nowadays, because they were making water oak pins to be used for rafting timber. These pins had to be cut carefully, so that they would be just twelve inches long and just one and a half inches thick. A little bit more, or a little bit less, would make the pins not worth anything. So it took you a long time to cut these pins right; but for every one of these pins, after it had been finished, the boys got a cent apiece. That gave them the first money they had ever had.

Nobody else lived less than about two miles from their cabin. It made the nighttimes lonesome, sort of lonesome at least. So at sunset the boys used to bolt both the doors before they even began to cook supper. For supper, almost always, they had some peeled sweet potatoes and hominy and a hunk of pork, all boiled together in the middle-sized iron pot. After they had supper, they used to lean up their guns against the wall, near the head of the bed, and they would each put a bowie knife in a crack of the log wall, where you could reach it easy. Then, by-and-by, before the fire went out, the boys used to get into bed and cover up their heads with the crazy quilt that Ma made. It kept you from hearing the screech owl. They were not afraid of bad people, because both children had their guns and their bowie knives, but everybody in Duval County was skeert of the screech owl. If ever you heard the screech owl, it would bring you bad

luck; and bad luck might be following after you forever
and always.

They lived in this manner for some years, until both the
boys were big enough to begin work at rafting logs.

Now, the older of these boys was called Napoleon Bonaparte Broward. We do not know whether or not, during any
one of those just half-frightened nights beside the St. Johns
River, he heard the wavering and malignant cry of the
screech owl; but we do know that if he did hear any such
omen, the involved owl proved to be an incompetent prophet.

—For after leaving the Cedar Creek cabin (it stays recorded, officially) "Napoleon B. Broward struggled from one
odd job to another, until manhood saw him settled at Jacksonville, as the part owner of steamboats conveying passengers between Mayport and Palatka . . . He entered politics
. . . He was elected sheriff of Duval County, and later, a
member of the City Council of Jacksonville . . . He prospered in the phosphate mining business . . . In 1896, he was
captain of the *Three Friends,* that famous filibustering
steamer which repeatedly ran the blockade to Cuba, with
arms and ammunition for the dauntless insurgents . . . He
was now a member of the State Legislature, in which capacity he proved himself to be a friend of the masses and a
leader of no mean ability . . . He was appointed a member
of the State Board of Health, by Governor Jennings, who had
learned to appreciate his splendid qualities."

That all this is most edifying, and that it affords a complete apologia for the literary methods of the late Horatio
Alger, are points which do not need stressing.

Then, in 1904, Captain Broward himself became a candidate for the governorship. He was elected; and it is granted

by most historians that the administration of Napoleon B. Broward (1905-1909) was the most beneficial which Florida has ever enjoyed since the all-prospering mendacious era of James Grant.

Here, though, it is far beside one's purpose to dwell upon the praiseworthy exploits of Napoleon B. Broward in regard to the advancement of education, to control of the railroads, to finance, to forestry, to the improvement of highways, to the protection of fish and game, or to any other proper, if perhaps slightly unexhilarative, gubernatorial task; nor does it much matter, here, that he got two colleges founded and enough of the Everglades drained to create for Florida a million or more new acres of arable land. The point, here, is merely that he proved a more than satisfactory governor; and that after his term expired, he was elected to be senator. Above him and his senatorial peers there now loomed only, behind the well-known mustache, which was nothing like so majestic as that of Napoleon B. Broward, the official splendor of William Howard Taft.

To such heights had ascended the small, quivering, half-fed boy who was skeert of screech owls. And then, just then, it so happened that all-prospering Napoleon B. Broward died, at fifty-eight, before taking his seat in the Senate.

One desires here, in chief, to avoid any pretension that Napoleon B. Broward was an incredibly distinguished personage, or that his career was epoch-making. He worked hard and honestly. He became the governor of Florida, and he was elected to the Senate of the United States of America. Yet Florida has had slightly more than a hundred governors, since Ponce de León's time, whereas it is likely that no living mathematician could figure out, to the digit, just how many persons have been United States senators. The distinction of holding either office is, therefore, not quite unique; nor would a philosopher contend it is desirable for an heroic being, of exceptional genius, to be elected to either office so that therein he might overgrossly misrepresent his constituents. That both statements apply to every state in the Union no less exactly than to Florida, one makes haste to append.

The important and the impressive feature in the career of Napoleon B. Broward is that it was so very far from being unique. He came out of a log cabin beside the St. Johns, alone and unaided and but one-tenth educated, into the most lofty political stations which were afforded by Florida; and in each one of these stations he served Florida's well-being. He served, indeed, to a degree but humanly short of perfection. Yet this is a performance which, to us of America, has become trite. Never so many of our leaders—charitably called statesmen—have climbed, somehow, from out of just such poverty and hopelessness into hard-earned pre-eminence; most of them, when judged from any standpoint of culture, or even of intelligence, were, through the best of luck, untouched by distinction: yet—by and large—when the chance came, they have served their people, with stanchness, acceptably.

That is the true point.

The land's work, in brief, under a democracy, is done by no genius but by the man of normal mental equipment such as was Broward; and by this average man the work is done soundly. He does not often—he, perhaps, does not ever—obtain stupendous results, or the best possible results. Yet, somehow, he gets his job done honestly and satisfyingly, against unconscionable odds. That, precisely, is what Napoleon B. Broward accomplished, just as precisely as once he had trimmed his water oak pins.

Furthermore, that is what thousands of yet other commonplace persons have been doing, without any ostentation, and as a mere matter of course, alongside the St. Johns River, for rather more than three and a half centuries. That is what quite ordinary persons are doing, ordinarily, at every hour, in all parts of the United States of America. And it is this humdrum truism—or to speak with more justice, it is this great miracle—which may yet keep our democracy immortal.

29

The Upper St. Johns

Tourists who, during the steamboat era, made the grand tour of the St. Johns, after ending their sixteen-hours' trip two hundred miles south of Jacksonville, disembarked upon a 600-foot pier; and so landed to explore what the *Atlantic Monthly*—a magazine then purchased with eagerness by a great many persons who felt humbly, but correctly, that their minds needed improvement—had recently described as "a widespread desolation of houses and shops." This pier projected from the southern shore of Lake Monroe—an oval expanse of the river, six miles in length, and in width but a little less extensive. The "widespread desolation" was the beginning city of Sanford.

Sanford was, for the tourist, the head of navigation; yet the more adventurous could penetrate, under conditions known to but a few seasoned surveyors and engineers, a full hundred miles farther on, slightly east and then south, toward the indefinite sources of the St. Johns River. Concerning its uncharted streams, its bogs of sawgrass, its unending palmetto hammocks, and its broad treeless stretches of empty and infirm meadowlands, no assured knowledge existed. One knew only that this wilderness was the home of alligators, of bears, of raccoons, of deer, of wild turkeys, of snakes, of frogs, of all sorts of birds, and of a few no less socially incommunicative, weather-tanned Crackers. Thousands of wild ducks flocked there each winter, to feed on the seeds of wild sunflowers, which covered the low prairies with gold; and there, in equal profusion, thrived bass, and cattails, and bream, and huge yellow pond lilies.

In distinction from the clearly outlined section of the river between Jacksonville and Sanford, known as the Lower St. Johns, this southern part, paralleling the east coast of Florida from Titusville to Fort Pierce, at an average distance of fifteen miles, was called the Upper St. Johns. William Bartram, in 1773, thought wrongly that he had reached its headwaters when, near Titusville, he arrived at Salt Lake, which in fact stands some fifty miles north of the river's sources. Two years earlier, the celebrated engineer, Bernard Romans, had helped to make the first survey of the St. Johns. Yet Romans did not complete his exploration much farther than did Bartram; and Romans furthermore accepted Indian legends to the effect that the St. Johns originated in Lake

Mayacco, which was the Seminoles' name for the present Lake Okeechobee.

No reasonably accurate knowledge of the Upper St. Johns was established, in brief, until 1822, when the naturalist John Eatton Le Conte charted, for the United States government, the course of this river. He then discovered that it "takes its rise in a small lake," and that beyond this lake, "extends a marsh as far as the eye can reach . . . with as level and uninterrupted horizon as the sea itself." This marsh, Le Conte reported further, was "constantly under water, and therefore may be considered as one great spring . . . from which water is slowly but continually oozing out."

These waters, it is now known, are derived from the copious rainfall of South Florida; and that part of the rainfall which does not seep into the northward flowing St. Johns either drains southeast, so as to supply the St. Lucie River, or else goes southward into Lake Okeechobee and the Everglades.

The City of Sanford, which yet forms the gateway to the Upper St. Johns, began abruptly with a warwhoop that, upon the morning of February 8, 1837, surprised a detachment of United States soldiers, at or about the present location of Sanford's Zoo. These troops, who but a few days earlier had disembarked from the steamer *Santee,* under orders to track down the Seminole leader, King Philip, were thus notified as to his willingness to meet them. Yet when the Seminoles crashed through the outer line of pickets, so as to attack the camp, they were thrown back; and the white troops, with the aid of the *Santee*'s six-pounder, drove away the Indians, after losing but one man, in the person of Captain Charles Mellon of Pennsylvania. The fort built later upon the place of his death was named, to commemorate him, Fort Mellon.

William S. Harney, a tall and vividly redheaded lieutenant colonel, who had seen service in the Black Hawk War, was put in command of this stockade, upon Lake Monroe, in the heart of the Indian country. While preparing a counterattack against King Philip, Harney explored the Upper St. Johns lake which has since borne his name; and he made, with the half-breed Seminole warrior, Osceola (whom time has mendaciously romanticized into a talented and noble chieftain) a truce which beguiled Colonel Harney into distributing, among his nominally repentant adversaries, large quantities of shirts, and corn, and tobacco, and whisky. So friendly indeed did Harney and Osceola become that the two slept together in Harney's tent—very shortly after which reunion, the enriched and re-equipped Indians, acting upon moral principles a full century in advance of their era, resumed fighting without compunction.

When the futile Seminole War had at long last dwindled from inanity to inanition, during the early 1840's, white pioneers entered sparsely the areas east of Lake Monroe and south of the crescent-shaped bend of the river beyond Econlockhatchee Creek and among the thousand or so lakes near-by. In time, a trading post came into being at the former site of Fort Mellon; and to this was given the name Mellonville. These early settlers were disturbed not infrequently by bands of Seminoles, who came out of the Everglades so as to scalp the unwary farmer, and steal his livestock, and burn his plantation. With such vigor did these attacks flourish, both in constancy and in ruthlessness, that in 1850, so a St. Augustine paper reported, "a large and respectable meeting of the citizens" of these harried river lands assembled, at

Mellonville, to request protection by the federal government. Armed troops were sent to their rescue; by 1858 the Seminoles had been driven south, permanently; and as a result of their withdrawal, white immigration into the Upper St. Johns valley became more liberal.

Among these first pioneers was small, and alert, and heavy-bearded Jacob Brock. After this steamboat captain had come into Florida to earn a fortune, he so often forgot the pious teachings endured during the days of his youth, in Vermont, that by the middle of the 1840's he had acquired, even among steamboat captains, a notable repute for the lavish and original nature of his profanity. The tradition that it once singed the hair from a brass monkey is believed, however, by most historians, to contain an element of exaggeration.

Captain Brock foresaw the possibilities of tourist travel for the little-known lands about Lake Monroe; and during the early 1850's he builded upon its shore, opposite Mellonville, at the settlement called Enterprise, a neat inn for the entertainment of his steamboat passengers. This he named the Brock House. So accurately had the small captain divined the large growth and the special requirements of the river's traffic that his hotel soon became famous, as "a paradise for sportsmen," now that many hundreds of Northerners, in quest of good hunting or fishing, registered annually at the Brock House, and sought relaxation in its well-stocked barroom.

The favorite among Captain Brock's little steamers plying between Jacksonville and Enterprise was the *Darlington*. After the fashion of most western river steamers, her first deck was given over to freight, and her upper deck to passengers. There was a Special Salon for women and children, in addition to a Grand Salon, which at mealtimes was used as the dining room. Around these halls of splendor lurked many small staterooms. But to Captain Brock's judgment the most pleasing portion of the *Darlington*'s equipment was her powerful whistle, with which, after he had gathered about him his unwarned passengers, he delighted to raise an astounding sudden uproar, by hitting its lever with his malacca cane.

"Hey, but she made you folks jump real lively," he would then remark; for thus subtle is the native, dry, philosophic humor of Vermont.

Just as Captain Brock had transferred his main interests to Florida, from New England, and from Jehovah to Rimmon, so next did he change his loyalty, in 1861, and side with the South. He was, it so happened, at Fernandina, in the March of 1862, when the Federals approached. Very quickly, he assembled, upon the *Darlington*, an odd cargo of military stores, of army wagons, and of forage, intermingled with women and children and mules; and though fired upon, he steamed stubbornly south, toward the St. Johns, until overhauled by his Unionist pursuers. He was then sent north as a prisoner, to Fort Lafayette in New York, and afterward to Fort Warren at Boston, while the captured *Darlington*, becoming a Federal steamer perforce, became also, it may be remembered, the chief agent in adding to the North's navy the swift blockade-running yacht *America*.

Captain Brock's experiences, both martial and penal, during the War Between the States are said to have enriched most advantageously the wide repertoire of his stories suited to an adult male audience; and from this anecdotage he got the profit of a congenial earthly-wise Puritan, after 1865, when he resumed his steamboat service upon the Upper St. Johns, and reopened the Brock House.

Next only to Captain Brock in control of his steamboats ranked his stewardess, "Commodore Rose." She was, upon the authority of Mrs. Calvin Ellis Stowe, "once a slave owned by Captain Brock, but emancipated, as the story goes, for her courage and presence of mind in saving his life in a steamboat accident . . . She knows every inch of the river, every house, every plantation along the shore, its former and present occupants and history." It was observed, also, that Commodore Rose "was not born to bloom and blush unseen. . . . Her every word of command might be heard ringing out, sharp and clear, above the noise and confusion at every landing. Her word was law; her orders were instantly executed by every officer below the captain . . . [She was a] stout-built athlete of two hundred pounds, and with a peculiarly commanding voice, and the look of one whom experience had taught that life was a battle, and they who made the best fight won."

Her sole indiscretion, in brief, as a spinster, appears to have taken the form of twin boys, whom kindhearted Captain Brock regarded with an indulgence virtually paternal.

Commodore Rose did not ever fail to point out to Captain Brock's passengers the impressive hunting lodge of Count Frederick de Bary, which, just north of Enterprise, overlooked Lake Monroe. De Bary, the member of an ancient noble family of Belgium, emigrated from Germany to the United States, in 1851, and became for the makers of Mumm's Champagne their American representative. Since this special champagne was then the most popular brand of that wine which French connoisseurs export, the uncivilized

palate of America very soon built up for de Bary a fortune.
An injudicious habit of sampling that which he sold, however, combined with the cares of finance; and so brought de
Bary to Florida, during the late 1860's, in search of rest and
restored health. He established an extensive hunting preserve
near Enterprise; he planted a large orange grove; and
throughout the winter months he imitated in Florida the
baronial life of his forefathers in Belgium.

Since the number of his guests increased in a logical
ratio to the unlimited supply of champagne at the de Bary
estate, its master attempted to find some means of extending
their pleasures beyond his dining room. He purchased, in
consequence, the small steamer *George M. Bird* for the amuse-
ment of his visitors. Then, when de Bary had made ready to
go back to his summer home in the North, he was urged, by
the captain of his new toy, to allow this steamer, during de
Bary's absence, to be run for the benefit of a properly
assessed public. The count negligently assented.

Upon his return to Enterprise, he found business had
proved so brisk that the impromptu earnings of the *George
M. Bird* assured the nobly born wine peddler as to the easy
profits, in a democracy, to be got out of boats as well as
bottles. He consented therefore to continue as a profession
that which had been a recreation; and his kindness budded,
under the title of the Frederick de Bary Steamship Line, into
one of the most prosperous firms in Florida. At the height of
this service, his line operated a fleet of thirteen steamers, of
which the most luxurious was an iron steam side-wheeler, the
Frederick de Bary.

Count de Bary's nearest neighbor of distinction was
General Henry S. Sanford. Sanford, like many other famous

Floridians of the last seventy-five years or so, was born in New England; and while filling minor diplomatic posts in Europe, he collected reports upon foreign penal codes which the Congress of the United States found valuable enough to have published for the use of American courts. Shortly after Lincoln's inauguration, Sanford was appointed to be the United States minister to Belgium. He was in reality, however, said Secretary of State William H. Seward, "Minister of the United States in Europe," charged with a number of sly missions, such as the covert offering of a commission to Garibaldi, the secret purchase of saltpeter for the Federal army, and the furtive obstructing, through bribes and bluster, of all western Europe's sale of arms to the Confederacy. Even at a period, so very much like any other period, when no government supported by its people could afford to be straightforward, this expert in the secretive was praised more often than he was trusted; and so, when General Sanford was named as ambassador to France the Senate refused to confirm his appointment. Disgruntled in ambition, he gave up his post in Belgium; and in 1871 he sought a career in Florida, where, as the adroit general noted, politicians of perhaps less honesty, and quite certainly of minor experience, had risen to well-paying positions.

General Sanford planned to establish at Mellonville, where he purchased twelve thousand acres, a city named in his honor such as would be to the Upper St. Johns what Jacksonville was to the lower part of the river. "Situated as it is, at the head of navigation . . . of this beautiful and majestic St. Johns," he proclaimed, to potential settlers, "Sanford is the Gate City of South Florida. It is the natural distributing point for its products and for its supplies . . . We have our grip on this great water-way, the St. Johns; with it, we can control prices and easy access to the world's markets. Ocean steamers are bound to come to Sanford."

And even though, in this prospectus, he happened to be more or less wrong in each one of his statements, yet as go prospecti, his protestations assayed a fair per cent of veracity. The modest land agent avoids any and all entanglement with truth in her nakedness.

Thereafter the former diplomat and the architect of a future empire on and about the Upper St. Johns fostered the growing of citrus and of yet other semitropical fruits in the rich lands south and west of the crescent-shaped bend in this river. With an all-comprehensive optimism, he introduced into his experimental gardens, at odd times, the almond, the tamarind, the mango, the fig, the pomegranate, the loquat, the sour sap apple, the custard apple, the maumee apple, the Barbados cherry, the pecan, the peach, the olive, and the banana. Not every one of them prospered, in view of Heaven's grim sloth to perform miracles for the special indulgence of Henry S. Sanford. He then experimented with oranges, and grapes, and guava, and lemons, and pineapples, of all which he imported a wide range of varieties from the East Indies, Spain, South America, Italy, and yet other remote quarters; and he thus made his nursery gardens the most impressive laboratory of its kind to be found in the Western Hemisphere, inasmuch as the sole check upon his success as a fruitgrower was the circumstance that, during the winter months, his fruit trees died.

Not until after his death also, in the early 1890's, was the fact discovered that the soil and climate of Sanford were particularly well suited to the needs of celery. This vegetable replaced the hundreds or so fruits which General Sanford had unsuccessfully tried to raise; and his city now produces about one-third of the celery native to the United States. —Which proves, perhaps, that the rewards of unflagging industry need to be forecast by illogic.

"Yet even his failures . . . have been profitable," wrote the Florida commissioner of agriculture, in 1883, with a not unexampled official charity toward blunders, ". . . inasmuch as they serve to prevent further loss by other experimentators." Moreover, General Sanford had interested a group of English capitalists in his St. Johns River scheme, and he so set afoot the Florida Land and Colonization Company. From its offices in London, this company very lavishly advertised—in pamphlets, in circulars, and in booklets illustrated by the imagination of Great Britain's more fanciful artists—that superior paradise upon earth which was called Sanford.

All this publicity resulted in the enlargement of a few small towns to the south of Sanford, such as Orlando, and to the southeast, such as Titusville and Rockledge. These were served indirectly from the St. Johns by means of a number of steamers—principally, the *Fox,* the *Volusia,* the *Picolata,* and the *Marion.* Except in the dry season, when the Upper St. Johns did not receive enough drainage waters to make it navigable, these steamers connected with larger vessels at Sanford; and from this city transported their freight and passengers to landings upon Lake Jessup (for Orlando), or Salt Lake (for Titusville), or Lake Poinsett (for Rockledge), or at times upon Lake Washington, for places yet farther south. Oxcarts and stages then carried all from the lake landings to the towns.

Orange production in the vicinity of Lakes Jessup and Harney repaid a continuing of steamboat service into the first decade of the twentieth century; but most of the river traffic beyond Lake Harney ended during the early 1890's, when a railroad was builded down the east coast of Florida.

The establishment, by Henry M. Flagler, of new and more luxurious winter playgrounds upon the Atlantic beaches of Florida coincided with a similar development, by Henry B. Plant, of the peninsula's western shore. The railroads of both these northern invaders then combined to make bankrupt the steamboat lines and the tourist traffic of the St. Johns.

Of the two magnates, the disruptive influence of Plant began the more insidiously, when in order to extend the scope of his railroad connecting the North with Jacksonville, he placed upon the St. Johns with éclat a new line of steamers. This, called the People's Line, operated between Jacksonville and Sanford, with the steamers *Chattahoochee* and *Jennie Lane* and, in the best tradition of most other steamboat companies, a vessel named after its proprietor, the *H. B. Plant*. When once, however, in the 1880's, Plant was able to extend his railroad service from Jacksonville to Sanford, and thence onward to Tampa, he ended curtly the career of his river steamers, now that the railroads of the Plant System were ready to take their place.

More rapid transportation facilities to the warmer climate of South Florida then rather hastily removed from the St. Johns those rural and pleasingly bourgeois activities which, for a half century, had made of this river a so famous factor in American life. Orange growers sought acreage south of Sanford; so did the farmers who raised winter vegetables; and the wholesome but simple winter resorts of the St. Johns lost all attractiveness for the tourist now that, a bit southward, so very many huge and fantastic aberrations of archi-

tecture were wooing his pocketbook. In this way did oblivion, as it were, swallow the entire river.

One of the hotels at Palatka was moved piece by piece
to Daytona Beach; the Brock House became a children's
home; yet other winter resorts closed; a great many of them
burned; and so, in time, it was only the exceptional tourist
who returned to the well-nigh deserted St. Johns. Then,
finally, all its steamboat and hotel life reached an unarguable
close, in 1929, with the last trip, to Sanford, of the one lone
remaining river steamer. Upon all the St. Johns valley, beyond Jacksonville, in this way descended an unfamiliar, all-
clogging quietness; and Jacksonville too had been changed,
very far beyond recognition, through a visitation more
ardent.

30

Cora Comes Back

IN 1901, Queen Victoria died, the United States Steel Corporation was organized, and the city of Jacksonville, which was then "modern in a Southern resort fashion"—if Henry James is to be believed—displayed "neither girth nor soul." His young protégé, Stephen Crane, had already phrased the æsthetic delinquencies of this city with a difference, by remarking discourteously: "The town looks like soiled pasteboard that some lunatic babies have been playing with.

The same old women are sitting on the hotel porches saying how well the climate agrees with them."

Jacksonville, at all events, in the May of 1901, had its Big Fire; and so very thoroughgoing was this fire, which destroyed 148 blocks, that its flames could be seen from as far north as Savannah, and at Raleigh, in North Carolina, the smoke was visible. Florida inclines always toward the superlative, even in the producing of a conflagration.

Shortly afterward, when Jacksonville had most vigorously commenced to rearise from out of destruction, a new building began at Madison and Ward streets. No one at first paid to it any particular attention; yet as the passers-by noted, it was of a rather odd shape; and although not big enough to be a hotel, it was remarkably large for a private home. Nowadays, however, all sorts of buildings were being finished, with hurriedness, and with such taste as Heaven had allotted to their designers. The city was reviving; business, from being better, became still better; and in consequence, stanch citizens (such as read Stock Market Reports and Annual Statements with a grave attentiveness) came every morning into their new offices wearing clean-shaven smiles of satisfaction.

"Things are picking up right and left," ran the general verdict; "and the fire may have been a good thing, after all."

Meanwhile, this large house, in the northwest section of Jacksonville, was taking its own form, in a rigid disagreement with Jacksonville's idea of architecture, such as young Stephen Crane, deplorably, had compared to littered and soiled pasteboard. This house, prevailingly colored "a bitter gloomy red," was more like a foreign castle of some sort, with turrets and with never so many stained-glass windows.

Every afternoon, a florid and stout and quite neatly painted
blonde trollop would drive up to its doorway, accompanied
by one or another younger woman, whose profession seemed
no less obvious than ancient; and the two of them would
inspect the workmen's advance.

The building was finished by-and-by; whereupon nur-
serymen in blue overalls began to arrive with small banana
trees and small orange trees, which were to be planted in the
aggressively large courtyard to the rear of the place; and the
results so much pleased the young person who, upon this
special day, was the plump blonde's companion that the girl
clapped her hands, saying:

"Oh, Cora, but the court's lovely! You really gotta call
this joint The Court."

The older woman, still smiling professionally, hesitated
. . . Yet she could not, after all, give to her new place of
business the name of the manor from which it was copied. It
had been perhaps a mistake to have the house built in this
prodigal space-wasting British way, when any other style
would have done as well, so that there were enough bedrooms
for her girls and their clients. She had fourteen bedrooms, as
matters stood; she very well remembered a house with fourteen bedrooms, each filled with guests, so that he had to run
up to London for quiet in which to finish his work; and she
recollected now, for no special reason, the bright, red and
white Mexican blanket which hung over the railing above
the main hallway . . . Then the stout blonde woman nodded
assent. Yes: they would call this new joint The Court. It
would not be fair to him, even though her fourth husband
had always put his own wife second to his profession, to call
this brothel "Brede Place," for all that it so closely copied

Brede, the one home in which she had ever been happy, almost . . .

So The Court got its name.

The Court was being furnished with a brittle pompousness, its small private chapel was in apple-pie order, and a Mexican blanket had been draped over the railing about the main hallway, when, from London, her boxes and trunks reached Jacksonville. Four of the girls, in their kimonos, helped her unpack; and the shrill daughters of joy wondered, like twittering, flocked sparrows, why upon earth, along with so many fine clothes, you should be keeping all these books and papers and old letters?

Their Madam grunted, incommunicatively, now that upon her knees she was rooting toward one trunk's bottom for that which she wanted. It proved to be a portrait, the portrait of a gaunt but rather handsome youngster, with an inadequate mustache—beneath which appeared a boy's lax mouth—and with fair-minded, but uncompromising, large, young eyes.

"Whoever is your skinny fellow, Cora?" the girls chattered; "and, my, but what a funny name for a book, *The Red Badge of Courage!*"

"He was called Stephen Crane," the plump strumpet answered, as she toiled upward through the unhurried process of pushing both her palms, first against the floor, and then against both her knees. "He wrote it. He was my husband, one of my better husbands."

She propped the portrait against the wall.

"So his picture is going to stay here as long as I am here," she added, with a meditative greasy chuckle, "now that I am putting Stevie second to my profession. *L'art pour l'art,* as old poor Oscar used to bleat at us, in Paris."

She had visited Jacksonville, not imperceptibly, some years before the disaster of the Big Fire, during a period when she called herself Cora Taylor; and of the persons who, even in a Biblical sense, knew her during this time a number survive.

"Why, but of course I can remember Cora Taylor," a pre-eminent physician assures us. "I recollect all about her first coming to Jacksonville—the way that she told the story at least, and, God knows, nobody but God does know how much truth she was telling. It seems that after checking out on two or three no-account husbands—Cora was always a little bit vague as to just how many of them—why, she got to living in sin and all sorts of other luxuries on the yacht of a rich bachelor; and they had been drinking their way around a considerable part of the known world. When they got to Jax, then the three of them—for this fellow, it seems, liked to keep a couple of girls handy, in case one of them might get out of repair on him—well, sir, they happened to wind up, about as well soaked as usual, at the Hotel de Dream.

"One of our best places, that was, in those days. It was run by Ethel Dream. Ethel was the wife of a shyster lawyer, who was rather widely and deeply damned, as I recollect it, on account of his divorce practice, by a lot of upstanding fine people here in Jax. Nobody but two or three preachers minded about the Hotel de Dream. A town has to have places like that; and somebody has to run them. But most of our best people, in those days, did not hold with folks who got divorced. So this smart lawyer he put his money, and his wife too, into the Hotel de Dream business. It seems funny that his name is not in my mind any longer, but it was something like Bilgewater, or Mud, or Marshclay . . .

"Well, then, just as I was telling you, at the Hotel de Dream, this night there happened to be a well set-up, well-dressed fellow on the loose. He was a sort of professional politician, or pretty near it anyhow, and I can remember his name all right, but I am going to keep quiet about it, because he has relatives living here in Jax. Every one of them fine people, too, from Connecticut. So Cora got to wandering around, looking for the Ladies Room, I reckon; and she met him, and she introduced him to both her friends; and then Cora and this big, handsome ward-heeler got just a little bit too chummy. I mean, for people in a dining room. Her yachting friend did not like it at all; and what with one thing leading to another, Cora told him she would stay right there in the Hotel de Dream if he would buy the place for her. And he did. Yes, sir, the way Cora told it, he bought the whole place for her, and he made her a present of it, and he got all her things off his yacht, the same night. So there she was, set up in a good well-paying business; and I can remember the tea store chromos of *The Age of Innocence* and *Bubbles,* and the engraving of the fellow in the big Roman helmet, and the pansies on the slop-jar, and the frilled pink covers on her big curlicued brass bed, and the mussed-up dinky little dressing table, and pretty much everything else in her rooms, just as if it were night before last."

Questions were put, and replied to with medical frankness. One regrets that the information thus obtained rings more agreeably when omitted.

"Well, and all that was when I had just started to practice medicine, about a year or two before the Cuban War began, and the New York papers sent down a half dozen or so of their crack war correspondents to look after it. They were all over Jax then—Richard Harding Davis and Sylvester Scovel and Stephen Crane and Frederick Palmer and a whole lot of others I forget. Most all of them put up at the old St. James Hotel. That was a mighty fine place then . . . Another one? Well, no, I reckon not. You see, a doctor has to be right careful not to have folks smelling anything on him. But, still, if both you boys insist . . .

"So, as I was telling you, it was the way I met Stephen Crane. I stopped by the Hotel de Dream, I mean, one night, just after *The Little Minister*, to see a girl—just professionally. When I got washed up and was going away, about twelve o'clock may be, then Cora had a page boy out in the hall, to tell me to come up to her rooms and help entertain a friend. He was right young; he talked slow; and if ever he said anything pleasant about anybody, it was not while I was around. He was rather slouchy; speaking as a medical man, I think that a clean shirt would not have hurt him. No, sir, it would not have hurt his looks at any rate, not for a full week before I ever even saw him."

Yet again, one asked questions; and yet again, the replies appear unavailable; but the account of a superior literary genius, as viewed *en negligé*, continued.

"She and Crane were up there, starting in on some quail on toast, and some watercress salad, and two or it might have been three bottles of champagne; and I just joined in with them. It was on the house, Cora said. She was about the happiest thing I ever saw, that night. I mean, a quiet sort of happiness, not a bit like the way she carried on when Cora was drunk. So Crane and I got to talking; and what with the champagne and all, we kept on talking, with Cora filling up the glasses and just patting him every once in a while, right like a mother whose boy had come home with a Sunday-school prize, until after seven in the morning. You could see she was simply crazy about him. He told me about the sinking of the *Commodore* and the hard time he had in a dinghy afterwards. I believe he wrote a story about that."

"He did, indeed," we both answered, reverently recalling *The Open Boat*.

"—But then you know how it is. A doctor, with his patients to look after, all day and night, may like a good book once in a while, but you can hardly ever get around to it. Always meant to, too. So Crane got to calling me by my first name, Ezekiel Adoniram, just as Cora did. He seemed to think that my name was funny. And he told me what he thought about Lillian Russell, and about Richard Harding Davis, I can recollect. Crane gave his facts, and they very certainly did surprise me. Crane said that . . ."

Here, yet again, some omissions have been found an improvement.

"Anyhow, that was the only time I ever did talk to Stephen Crane. He went away a little while afterwards. And by-and-by, Cora went away too, when she heard he was sick, over yonder in Greece. She was simply crazy about him. So that was the last anybody ever saw of Cora for a long time. Four or five years, may be. She came back then, of course, back to Jax. So does most everybody else, unless they die first . . ."

You may read, in Thomas Beer's superb short life of Stephen Crane, how "in tumultuous Athens, Crane . . . was nursed by a fair, affable woman, older than himself, Cora Taylor, who had fallen in love with him at Jacksonville, and had come after him to Greece." You may read how they were married; and how in this manner, the former proprietress of the Hotel de Dream entered into "the high world of letters English," with the result that, at Brede Place in Surrey, her hot biscuits were exceedingly well thought of, by Henry James and Joseph Conrad and Maurice Hewlett and Lady Randolph Churchill, and by never so many other benighted famous persons who had thought previously that "biscuits" were crackers. Especially loud in their astonishment were Lady Randolph Churchill and Mr. James, because of their incriminating American birth.

Cora Crane proved, to her boy husband, a devoted and efficient wife. One needs always to remember that always, in the phrase of our aforetime quoted medical friend, "she was simply crazy about him." And since his horrid books meant so much to him, she concealed loyally her regret that none of them reached the plane of Miss Marie Corelli. You may read likewise, in the magic-haunted pages of Thomas Beer, how Stephen Crane died, in the June of 1900.

With none of these doings, however, did Jacksonville have any concern, for the former patrons of Cora Crane were not interested in literature pre-eminently. Among them it was known only that the Crane fellow (as is the deplorable custom of authors) had left his widow without one red cent. So Cora had come back to Jax; she was opening a fine new place, over on Madison Street; and you hoped she would make a go of it.

She did make a go of it; and The Court fared prosperingly, under the direction of Stephen Crane's widow, in her reduplication of Stephen Crane's home.

"Yes, sir, and Cora had built up her business, in a short time, to where she felt she ought to have a victoria. She bought a beautiful one, with a nifty black horse; and her coachman, I can remember, was a mighty well-set-up darky, in a pongee livery. It was one of the best-looking turnouts in the whole city. Almost every afternoon, Cora would ride around in it, just smiling a little, you know, but without recognizing any of her married friends, of course, and wearing one of those big Merry Widow hats that they used to wear then, and with one of the girls along with her, so as to remind the boys that The Court was open. Cora was a mighty fine-looking woman still. So she got on, in a way, pretty well, for three years or may be four years. Always in debt, though. After Crane died, she just seemed not to have any sense about money. Then Cora got married again, God only knows why, to a big, hard-slugging bartender, this time. He used to work at The Court, I believe. I was married then, you see, and doing pretty well at medicine, and not having my good times any longer."

The ensuing husband, a putative number five, was called Hammond P. McNeil; and no great while after his marriage, McNeil was arrested upon the charge of having killed one Harry H. Parker, with a revolver, in the bedchamber of one Cora McNeil. This case was dismissed, inasmuch as the only witness to the manner of Parker's death was likewise the wife of the accused, and so could not be compelled to testify. She chose to avoid the witness stand.

Then by-and-by, McNeil applied for a divorce, in the October of 1909, upon the grounds that (still in the same bedroom, it is quaint to reflect, in which hung the ever-appraising and ever-youthful portrait of Stephen Crane) the former wife of Stephen Crane had "habitually beaten and struck" the complainant; and in which bedroom, she, it was furthermore declared, "on or about June 7, 1909, in a fit of her violent and ungovernable temper, assaulted and struck said complainant over the head with a shoe, severely and seriously hurting said complainant."

McNeil yet furthermore resented the vigor with which his wife had "struck me over the head with some blunt instrument and laid open the scalp over my left eye and severely wounded me on the top of the head, so that the wound over the left eye required the service and attention of a surgeon, and three stitches were taken in it to close it . . . In her fits of anger and temper she would hit me with anything she could lay her hands on . . . She told me that she was sorry she hadn't beaten me to death."

Edith Gray, housekeeper at The Court, confirmed most of these charges; and added placidly:

"When Mrs. McNeil gets mad, she . . . is very hard to compose."

The physician—not our afore-mentioned medical friend —who had sewed up McNeil's eye, testified:

"She was considerably under the influence of liquor."

The presiding judge, with a grave imitation of surprise, then inquired, of Edith Gray:

"Is Mrs. McNeil accustomed to drinking liquor?"

With a continuance in the delicate art of understatement for which, even after thirty-and-some years, one cannot but admire Miss Gray, the witness said:

"Only in the way of business."

The divorce was granted; and Cora McNeil died within less than a year, bequeathing her entire estate to a male associate who was not named McNeil. Her debts turned out to be somewhat largely in excess of her property. Upon her headstone, at Jacksonville, in Evergreen Cemetery, was cut, in accord with her last instructions, "/Cora Crane/1868—1910/"

—So that it is not altogether a merry chronicle, this tale of Cora Crane's descent from out of "the high world of letters English" into a series of drunken assaults upon a Jacksonville bartender with the aid of her shoes. The considerate may feel, indeed, that the story of Stephen Crane's widow, so far as it developed in the St. Johns valley, betrays its own self-evident authorship. It is a bleak harsh epilogue to her not ever failing devotion and tenderness in all matters which concerned Stephen Crane such as no other American of his era could have designed.

—Which proves only, if it proves anything, that the whole story must be fiction. All may be judged thus to end, after a time-honored example, in mystery and with a flavor of derision also, as would seem to be the fate of most tales touching the St. Johns valley, under the influence of an enchantment just slightly sinister.

An Epilogue:
IN THE FORM OF AN ALTERCATION

Where the river's lip ran o'er
With dancing, diamond spray,
His tomahawk he brandished wide . . .
Howling, he seized his prey;
But swifter yet the dagger's gleam—
Carlos, a stag at bay,
Was ready for his bloody foe
And burning for the fray.

—"A Legend of the St. Johns River (Carlos
and Oriola)," by M. A. Fry

An Epilogue:
In the Form of an Altercation

HANNA: Moreover, I do not approve of the flippant liberties which have been taken in the Stowe chapter, nor do I subscribe to the interpretation given to Bartram's alleged love for his cousin, Mary Robeson.

CABELL: Your belief as to the idiosyncrasies of William Bartram in amour we have discussed earlier. We agreed, I think, that in a volume designed to instruct and inspire the home circle, it should not be printed.

HANNA: But you have interrupted me. I was about to state, also, my firm objection to ending the book with Cora Crane's story, which impresses me as being alike tragic and farcical. I find, in fact, this abhorrent chapter to be a recital of quite trashy stuff, the sole purpose of which can be to reveal a most sordid episode.

CABELL: It involves human nature, I admit; and that, except in fireside chats, is not always immaculate. So let us now turn toward themes of a more edifying nature, since, thus far, we have reached only the year of grace 1910. What further shall we add concerning the pre-eminent who have lived beside the St. Johns a bit more recently?

HANNA: We might add a great deal, but it would get us in trouble. The surviving members of the family would be certain to object. And where the family is large or possessed of some influence we would do well, I believe, to abstain from inviting unfriendly criticism.

CABELL: I bow, as always, to your superior knowledge of Florida's customs. Indeed, time and again, during the book's composition, I have noted the need laid upon us to avoid granting human frailties to any person who has left descendants as yet living in Florida. He that has begotten a family must be esteemed blameless. It is an odd tribute to the powers of reproduction such as second thought impels me to regard as a latter-day survival of the Timucuans' religion.

HANNA: There too I fear that we may have been indiscreet. Even so, the historian has his duty; he must face the truth as he finds it; and besides, the Timucuans have not left any descendants.

CABELL: It is an omission which does not apply to the English, who are at this instant our allies. We have not submerged them in that flood of awe-struck adulation such as most other American writers are pumping out of Lethe, that ink-colored stream of forgetfulness.

HANNA: What nation has figured to advantage upon the banks of the St. Johns? The French, the Spaniards, and the Indians, no less than the English, have all lied and pillaged and murdered there, to an extent which was limited only by the scope of their opportunities for wrongdoing. Even our own history displays episodes more glorious than was the Seminole War. I incline, in fact, to believe that there must be something in climatic conditions which has led such well-thought-of Americans as Colonel Higginson and Zephaniah Kingsley and Major John Hay and Andrew Jackson—

CABELL: Hush, I entreat you! for I can perceive that you are about to give a loose rein to your customary imprudence.

We needs, then, dismiss from consideration those persons who have animated the St. Johns valley during the last thirty years, inasmuch as their relatives survive in quantities inconvenient to candor. So let us end our book, instead, not quite with Cora Crane's story, since you resent its sordidness, but rather with an elaborated prose passage, in somewhat the manner of Lafcadio Hearn, dwelling upon the ephemeral nature of worldly glory; and expressing, in terms suitably handsome, our polite regret that the St. Johns River, to possess which so very many nations have contended, is not any longer of an importance to justify homicide and perjury. The St. Johns has reverted, for the most part, to that same naïve incultivation which Ribaut first found to encompass it.

HANNA: Indeed, when one stands upon Mount Cornelia, the most lofty upland of the Atlantic coast for a full fifteen hundred miles south of the New Jersey highlands, and surveys the scene about him at the mouth of the St. Johns, he will observe much of nature that remains undisturbed by the four centuries, lacking but two decades, of the European civilization which has been imposed upon this American river.

CABELL: So I infer. I was merely about to suggest that, with perhaps a certain eloquence, we might describe the river's present rusticity, and dwell upon that enchantment, just slightly sinister—

HANNA: But you have interrupted me. I was going on to say that, when one stands upon Mount Cornelia, then to the east a luminous blue ocean breaks on the shallow bar, and thus forms an ever-varying and fascinating, low wall of white. Schools of porpoises sport in the deeper sea, and overhead, thousands of sea gulls screech as they fly in every direction. Flocks of pelicans parade upon the beach, and scores of ducks, cranes, herons, and wild geese stand on the shore or alight upon near-by trees. To the west looms a deep glossy background of primeval forest. Gaunt cypresses reflect their moss-bearded arms for seemingly endless stretches along the St. Johns, in dark quiet vistas which but at mile-long intervals are diversified by any sign of human industry, such as a crude wooden bridge, or a soft-drink stand, or perhaps a tollgate. It would thus appear that merely trivial traces of the Spanish explorer, the French colonizer, the English planter, and the Anglo-American frontiersman have been left upon this river, which, now for nearly four centuries, has been the scene of their varied endeavors.

CABELL: I also have visited Mount Cornelia, where, I admit, not every one of these reflections occurred to me.

HANNA: You should employ your mind, in common with your powers of observation, a bit more constantly; for in matters of this nature, it is practice which begets acuteness.

CABELL: I shall endeavor to do better. Pending my complete reformation, I beg you to continue talking.

HANNA: But I have finished speaking as to those many birds and animals which keep animated the St. Johns; for have we not both visited those forest-thronged, quiet banks which they alone frequent daily? So I need not tell you that very often a panther may be noted swimming across this river, near the mouth of the Oklawaha, where but a half century ago big bustling steamers puffed up and down the broad waterway. In fact, in some of the thicker swamps facing upon the river, bears yet maintain the existence which they enjoyed before the coming of the white man. Snakes drop into the water from overhanging branches, and with the exception of the now extinct green parakeet and the

passenger pigeon, the same variety of birds which greeted the
first European explorers have resumed over the river lands a
supremacy not very often marred by any human intrusion.
Fish hawks make their nests in the broken trees, the mocking-
bird trills from many thickets, and white ibises circle over the
landscape. Bald eagles search for food in the river; and the
large caracara, which Mexico has elected to designate as its
national emblem, finds near the St. Johns an opportunity to
relax from the nervous tension imposed by its odd and dis-
torted position upon Mexico's flag. The harsh call of the
Floridian crane may be heard as he works out his cycle of life
on the flat prairie lands bordering the river; wild turkeys are
still to be seen in the dense forests; and thousands of ducks,
both migratory and indigenous, often darken the sky.

CABELL: Nor do I doubt that the savage past of the
river is recalled somewhat frequently during the night season
by the blood-curdling weird cry of the limpkin.

HANNA: Your surmise is well-founded. And so, dedicated to the preservation of this natural life of the St. Johns,
members of the Audubon Society have caused legal enact-
ments to be passed for its protection. They teach the young
and barbarous of our species to respect their feathered superiors, whilst during field trips up and down the river,
these nature lovers endeavor to catalogue, for their own information and satisfaction, the hordes of birds which seek and
still find happiness alongside the St. Johns. Sanctuaries have
been reserved for the birds and plants of the St. Johns—such
as, for example, a tract of a hundred acres of wild untouched
jungle upon historic Fort George Island. There, Gertrude
Rollins Wilson, sickened by the wanton destruction of wild-
life to every side of her birthplace, has endowed and provided a handsome lodge for the accommodation of botanists,

of ornithologists, and of yet other scientists interested in the Floridian field of their special out-of-door studies. She, most wisely, has placed this preserve under the trusteeship of that college which was founded by her near kinsman.

CABELL: You refer, it may be, to Rollins College, whose faculty you adorn?

HANNA: It is very often my privilege to refer to Rollins College. I needs mention also that yet another historic site upon the St. Johns concerns itself nowadays with studies of the jungle, in an effort to understand the complexities of a civilization which, south of Jacksonville, has more or less abandoned the river. This work is conducted at Orange Park, where Zephaniah Kingsley once studied the behaviorism of jungle slaves with a view of profiting by their sale, and where, still later, Harriet Beecher Stowe endeavored to set free her son from his pathological addiction to alcohol.

CABELL: You allude, I imagine, to the Yerkes Anthropoid Experimental Laboratory, conducted jointly by Harvard and Yale universities, in which upwards of thirty chimpanzees now form, as it were, the hub for many radiating studies of primate reproduction, of genetics, or behavioral adaptation, of hygiene, and of pathology in general?

HANNA: I do, indeed—with some frank wonder that you should be flaunting scientific phrases which, it is plain, you do not wholly understand. Then, yet another part of the St. Johns in which the influence of science is bearing fruit nowadays may be observed in that vast prairielike area northwest of the headwaters of the river and paralleling the stream upon the west for a distance of a hundred miles or more. There thrives an industry which has grown out of the large cattle ranges that have made Kissimmee the center of an investment exceeding $150,000,000, and which has placed

Florida among the states at the head of cattle interests. I find this noteworthy because, prior to the turn of the present century, the Florida woods cow provided a precarious livelihood for but a small per cent of the population.

CABELL: She, after all, was a descendant of the original stock imported by Spaniards; and so had not any reason to pamper Americans.

HANNA: Even though you are stating a fact, yet the irrelevant ancestry of this beast appears to me a weak pretext for interruption.

CABELL: I apologize.

HANNA: And I pardon freely, in view of your innate, your perhaps incurable habit of talking too much. As I was saying then, this cow—a dwarfed and scrawny creature—had maintained somehow, throughout the course of three centuries, an underprivileged existence upon wholly inadequate grazing lands. In dry weather she took to the swamps, or she else found food by wading out neck-deep to small islands in the St. Johns. Where a blooded herd would have perished, she and her shaggy sisters flourished upon tough wiregrass. Her range, said Frederic Remington, in 1895, was "flat and sandy, with mile on mile of straight pine timber, each tree an exact duplicate of its neighbor tree, and underneath the scrub palmettos, the twisted brakes and hammocks, and the gnarled water-oaks."

CABELL: It appears a milieu in which, even for an animal so richly gifted with hilarity as is a cow, life might become monotonous.

HANNA: But a cow is not gifted with hilarity. The cow is a quite stolid creature. You should observe cows more closely.—For, as I was saying, modern methods have been applied to the cows of Florida; and so today, upon the prairies near the headwaters of the St. Johns one finds some of the most important ranges in the country. Hump-shouldered Brahman bulls have been introduced from out of India to improve the local breeds. These bulls proved to be yet better foragers than even the backwoods cow; and since they were accustomed to excessive heat, they quite easily adapted themselves to the Florida sun.

CABELL: Without any negligence, I trust, of their yet other duties?

HANNA: I believe not; for, in point of fact, these diligent foreign bulls have so far increased the average weight of the native cows' progeny that nowadays the fine herds of Florida reveal every trait required by the cattle industry.

CABELL: That is gratifying. It is, for our butchers, an Arcadian state of affairs quite such as it should be, inasmuch as your favorite parable has taught, to I know not how many of your students, that the life of a bull cannot be all romance.

HANNA: But I have never told my students that old Spanish story, nor can I guess to what story you allude. Yet furthermore, those parts of the river in which an evidence of civilization exists—namely, the towns and cities—present a most happy blending of some of the best traditions of the pre-1861 period with the progressiveness of other portions of the country. This combination of ideas, of ideals, and of cultural patterns makes for an almost nonsectional tone to the St. Johns River, and composes an unique aspect of American life. It is a blending due, no doubt, to the fact that these settlements have been the outgrowth of an united effort upon the part of both Southerners and Northerners.

CABELL: Of that there is no manner of doubt—no probable, possible shadow of doubt—no possible doubt whatever!

HANNA: I must ask your pardon for saying so, but really you were not meant to be a singer. This lack of sound musical taste may account for your stubborn and strange unresponsiveness to my notion of including in our book a chapter as to Frederick Delius.

CABELL: That he is highly honored by Rollins College, I know. I have spent, in fact, an entire evening with your Delius Trio of Chamber Music. Even so, I have not ever been quite able to distinguish between Delius and Sibelius, or to remember which one of them composed *Under the Bamboo Tree* beside the unoffending St. Johns River, or to see that it very much mattered if he did.

HANNA: Most obviously, you have not taken the trouble to inform yourself as to the heroic struggles of Frederick Delius against the gentility of an Anglicized German father, who at last despaired of ever making a reputable wool merchant out of Frederick. Delius père concluded that his son might be saved from the infamy of becoming a professional musician only through an exile from concert halls; and so, purchased an option upon an old Spanish plantation, near Picolata, called Solano Grove, to the rural quietudes of which young Frederick Delius, who was then but twenty-two, was dispatched in the spring of 1884. The four-room cottage in which he lived for more than a year still stands.

CABELL: And to hear of this fact enkindles, throughout my entire being, every appropriate emotion, do you let me assure you.

HANNA: There the future world-famous composer attended to his own housework unaided, living almost entirely upon canned food, and he viewed with enthusiasm the charms of Florida. He was drugged by the heavy perfume of orange blossoms; he worshiped the waxen purity of the magnolias; and he became enchanted by the picturesque scenery. His inseparable companion was an old Negro servant, who strumming always upon a banjo, sang tirelessly to the young foreigner a never-ending succession of plantation melodies. Hour after hour, this faithful darkey would sing to Delius, as they rowed about the St. Johns, or sat together upon its banks in the moonlight.

CABELL: Yet many other young Germans have shown this strange tendency to incite discomfort for themselves, and even in some sense to enjoy it. In the place of Delius, I would have urged my so faithful retainer now and then to lay down his banjo, and to desist from singing to me twenty-four hours a day, if not through compassion for my shaken reason, at least long enough to help out with the housework.

HANNA: Frivolity does not alter the fact that Delius later on acknowledged his indebtedness to this, the most impressionable time of his life, by bestowing the title *Florida* upon the first of his compositions ever to be played by an orchestra—under, it is true, the influence of a barrel of beer, with which Delius had bribed them. He yet furthermore introduced into his great tone poem, *Appalachia,* one of these naïve, but impassioned and heart-moving, songs which he had heard beside the St. Johns beginning "Oh, honey, I am goin' down de ribber in de morning."

CABELL: I am indeed sorry to interrupt—

HANNA: Your laughter does not disturb me; for the belief of Delius that a most significant contribution to the field of music has been made by the Negroes of North America is exceedingly well-confirmed by the careers of two men of that race, James Weldon Johnson, and his junior brother, J. Rosamond Johnson, both born in Jacksonville. It is the latter whom you have recalled hazily as the composer of *Under the Bamboo Tree*. Yet the supreme achievement of these two natives of the St. Johns valley is to be found, perhaps, in no one of the hundreds of melodies which they themselves have written, but rather in their great *Book of American Spirituals*. It is widely recognized as being a notable collection of Afro-American folk songs and a superb recording of what many persons regard as the unique gift made by our country to music.

CABELL: I confess that in all this talk about Delius and about Johnsons, I cannot perceive anything relevant to our proposed account of the St. Johns River as it is today.

HANNA: For you still to be talking any such nonsense is but another mark of your arbitrary nature, which resents opposition. I feel strongly that both Delius and the Johnson brothers possess a strong relationship to the St. Johns and are of arresting interest. Moreover, the St. Johns does not lack for its verbal interpreters of present-day life on the river. Among them is Elvira Garner of Sanford, a former student of Rollins College, whose salutary influence has perhaps aided Mrs. Garner to become a well-known writer of children's stories. Like Munro Leaf, and Hendrik Van Loon, and others of the "can't draw" school, her genius has succeeded in investing many samples of what, to the unthinking, might appear mere haphazard ink scratches with a truly remarkable character and movement. Gay, spontaneous, and wholesome, her *Ezekiel* is rich with those rare qualities which possess a permanent value. It is the story of a little darkey who lives on the banks of the St. Johns, with his sister Emancipation and his brother Lil' Plural and the baby Assafetida, and it relates how his "Pappy got a dandy job on de St. Johns Ribber Line."

CABELL: The dénouement appears satisfying. Although I am not familiar with the masterworks of Mrs. Garner, I dare not question that they merit your encomia, and reflect credit upon the curriculum of Rollins College.

HANNA: Then, farther down the river than stands Sanford, and slightly to the west of the river near its chief tributary, the Oklawaha, resides an adopted daughter of the St. Johns, who has so ably interpreted life in this locale that, with her *Yearling*, published in 1938, she won a Pulitzer Prize.

CABELL: Even so, *The Yearling* is a good book; and to receive a Pulitzer Prize, although compromising, is not always a quite definite proof of insignificance.

HANNA: I am certain you speak jestingly, or else, under the spur of envy; for I allude to Marjorie Kinnan Rawlings, whose books have been commended by *Time* magazine. In 1932, she settled in an orange grove on Cross Creek, which carries the waters of Lake Lochloosa into Orange Lake, and from Orange Lake through Orange Creek into the Oklawaha, and thence into the St. Johns. It was thereabouts that, according to *Time*, "Author Rawlings then discovered and took possession of a new United States literary landscape, of a new literary folk (the Florida backwoods people) and of the Cracker idiom, whose Shakesperean and Chaucerian turns had struck her sensitive ear, when she first heard them, like a blow."

CABELL: It appears an unprovoked rudeness upon the part of the idiom such as Mrs. Baskin, one makes no doubt, has learned to pardon with that customary graciousness which, both in social intercourse and in her books, adds luster to the solidity of her talent. I applaud very heartily both your and *Time's* panegyric as to Marjorie Kinnan Rawlings.

HANNA: Moreover, within a few miles of the scene of the Rawlings stories is located, upon the St. Johns, the city of Palatka, which devotes in particular its civic energies to what, all Palatka assures me, is the most magnificent lumber mill upon earth. Lumber, as you may or may not recall, in view of your haphazard regard for history, has always ranked among the chief exports of the St. Johns; and today this river produces, by long odds, the main portion of the cypress lumber milled annually in the United States of America. Impressed by the fact, I have been at pains to spend, at the logging camp of this mill, a number of instructive and delightful hours with Rust Macpherson, who is at the head of this vast enterprise. There I have noted no less than sixteen hundred persons engaged either in felling or in drawing out of the St. Johns River swamps huge cypress logs, which were then rafted down the river. And so it would be well for us, I believe, to describe the main features and the *modus operandi* of this great lumber mill—

CABELL: I can imagine no more futile exercise upon the part of two persons whose ignorance of lumber is equaled only by their lack of interest in it.

HANNA: Let us, then, dismiss the lumber industry of Palatka—even in the teeth of its very many lively attractions, as you must permit me to observe, for the well-balanced. Yet farther down the St. Johns, and within twenty-five miles of its mouth, stands Jacksonville, important as a city, as a shipping port, but perhaps most of all, as a significant blending of the various elements which today represent American life. Not unlike the water front of Cairo on the Nile, its harbor is filled with globe-girdling freighters, pleasure craft, tugs, and fruit- and fish-boats. Eastward, on the north bank, where the river twists into an S, are five miles of wharves terminating at municipal piers. Alike as a focal point of land, of water, and of air transportation in the southeastern parts of the United States, and as the virtual gateway to Florida, this thriving St. Johns River city possesses the largest naval-stores yard, in addition to the most extensive wholesale lumber market, to be found upon our Atlantic coast. More than a half century of intensive work, and the expenditure of some $18,000,000 in 'dredging the river's channel and basin, have made Jacksonville one of the great inland ports of North America. I have here, indeed, some rather striking statistics—

CABELL: Every one of which, even down to the last decimal fraction, with your permission, my dear confrere, we will omit from our book; for to me, I confess, it is less the present than the past of the St. Johns, its gaudy and its well-nigh incredible past, which appears engaging. Upon no other river in the United States have white men lived for so long a while, or so variously; and I choose to regard its history far less as a record of events, and of commerce, and of fruit raising, than as a pageant of strange persons passing, with Time as their drum major, beside its broad brown waters. Nor is it a monotonous pageant, this outlandish parade which, starting with the imperial swagger of Jean Ribaut, ends with a furtive, stumbling, and tipsy Cora McNeil.

HANNA: Now that you have raised the point, Don Pedro Menéndez, and Le Moyne, and de Gourgues, and Martínez, and Master Barrow, and impetuous Oglethorpe, and thrifty, stanch James Grant, indeed have but very little more in common than had the last-named with his seven years' plague, called Denys Rolle.

CABELL: Or than had any one of them with perplexed McGirth, or dry Panton, or timeserving McQueen. It is thus the diversity of the persons with whom we have trafficked that I have found to be the most beguiling element in our year-long commerce on or about the St. Johns River.

HANNA: Then too to these foreign subjects have succeeded our purely Anglo-American Bartram, and Kingsley, and Audubon, and Higginson, and Mrs. Stowe, and J. J. Dickison, and Captain Baya, and Colonel Hart, and the two Broward boys, along with still many other human beings who, beside the St. Johns, have displayed their varied traits— traits very vivid, and, at times, ludicrous, and yet always flavored with pathos, somehow, by that inborn instinct which, when strict logic quits guard, persuades every one of us that the foibles of a dead person ought not to be derided. . . . We have dealt, beyond doubt, with a somewhat motley squad of oddities.

CABELL: Yes: for human nature is not merely undulant and diverse; it is also, as an acute philosopher has pointed out, a rum one. So with this aged moral, my dear friend, let us dismiss the grotesque and highly colored pageant which, as if under the influence of an enchantment just slightly sinister, has trooped toward us from out of our river's fantastic past, and which now evades us.

Acknowledgments at Large

Here to record the benefactors—including, as they do, friends of long standing and casual acquaintances and personal strangers—whose kindness has been utilized to make this book, may evoke, it is feared, a suspicion that, with so much help, the book's nominal authors must have been spared mental exertion. That is not quite true; and in any case, courtesy requires hereabouts an acknowledgment that our collaborators have proved even more amiable than numerous.

To this amiability we stand indebted for several trips on and along the St. Johns. One exploring of its upper reaches was made memorable by the large hospitality of James and Ruby Leach Carson, at their ranch "Caruja," near Kenansville; and was there enriched by their special knowledge and their considerable collection of Floridiana. Another visit to the Upper St. Johns was gilded by the kindness of the W. L. Siegs, at their picturesque cabin, upon the small bluff overlooking those waters which flow into the river from out of Salt Lake. Still other expeditions have been enjoyed upon the boat of the F. E. Roumillats, in company with Francis Harper, a leading authority as to William Bartram, as well as with Nina Oliver Dean, who has written often, but in a vein more imaginative than is ours, about the St. Johns.

A more cordial appreciation of the river's bird life was acquired through sharing in field trips of the Florida Audubon Society, during one of which good fortune afforded to us the companionship of Thomas D. Clark, author of *The*

Kentucky. Some insight as to the process of converting age-old cypress trees into new timber was gained, near Eustis, under the instruction of Rust C. Macpherson, at the logging camp of the Wilson Cypress Company.

Historic sites have been studied, whenever possible, at first hand—very notably during a prolonged trip by motor with Herbert and Carita Doggett Corse, during a similar excursion with Henry and Irma Culver, and through several visits to Gertrude Rollins Wilson, upon Fort George Island, at the mouth of the St. Johns. Informal interviews with residents upon the banks of the river, in places remote from civilization as well as within the radii of city tax collectors, have often produced impressions and statements which we found to be of value.

It follows that an intimate personal study of the St. Johns, league by league, when combined with three decades of association by half of us with its customs, begun during college days upon the old river steamers, has provided, we hope, a fairly complete and well-balanced perspective.

Of an interest no more slender, to this book's compilers, have been their forays into the recorded history of the St. Johns. Chief in providing authentic data, in assaying their proper value, and in prompting a fair-minded use of all, have been Kathryn T. Abbey, author of *Florida, Land of Change*, and Dorothy Dodd, Archivist of the State of Florida, and Watt Marchman, Librarian of the Florida Historical Society, and Julien C. Yonge, editor of the *Florida Historical Quarterly*.

The records and the facilities in general of The National Archives in Washington have been made available through the more than official interest of Elizabeth Drewery and

Philip M. Hamer. No less active has been the co-operation of Seymour Robb and other members of the Library of Congress staff. Use has been made of the John Carter Brown Library of Brown University, of the Florida Historical Society Library, of the St. Augustine Historical Society Library, of the Rollins College Library, and (through the alert courtesies of George A. Zabriskie and A. J. Wall) of the library of the New York Historical Society, as well as of the Public Library of the City of Richmond in Virginia, through the special kindness of Thomas P. Ayers.

Even more extensive aid of this nature came from the Union Catalog of Floridiana, whose editor, Della F. Northey, has shared equally with us in the labors of collecting a card bibliography of the St. Johns, in addition to data relating to some two hundred vessels which, at one period or another since 1562, have been connected with this river. It was a task in which the three of us were assisted by historians, librarians, and students at large, from many parts of the United States, but most notably by John Marvin Sweeney.

A quantity of material not available elsewhere has been procured from the files of the Federal Writers' Project in Jacksonville, through the courtesy of Carita Doggett Corse, as well as from the files of the Historical Records Survey, through the similar kindness of Louise Biles Hill.

The chapter concerning Cora Taylor is based primarily, upon a typescript left uncompleted by Carl Bohnenberger; whereas from George Powell (former attorney for the protagonist of this chapter), from Ames W. Williams (the compiler of a bibliography of the works of Stephen Crane), and from the anonymous physician quoted as to interior conditions at The Court, came yet further aid.

P. B. Cabell, W. T. Cash, Carita Doggett Corse, Henry B. Culver, Richard P. Daniel, T. Frederick Davis, H. D. De-Grove, Jane Taylor Duke, Douglas Southall Freeman, Mary B. Graff, Alfred Hasbrouck, Paul Kruse, Alberta Johnson, Katherine S. Lawson, Philip S. May, Dorothy Dewhurst Parker, Frank W. Pratt, Mary M. Price, Marjorie Kinnan Rawlings, Martha Richmond, Mary Ross, and Elizabeth Howard West, in various ways, have made contributions to this book. Some of these auxiliaries have shared liberally their specialized information as to the St. Johns, while others have pointed out the way toward needed data, or they have aided yet otherwise in a completing of the river's story. For the particular use made of such materials, and their interpretation, we only have been responsible.

Among those who enabled us to explore the cartographic records of the St. Johns, and to reach concerning them more or less valid conclusions, rank mainly John M. Baxter, John C. Cooper, Jr., Verne E. Chatelain, William P. Cumming, W. B. Kyzer, E. G. Thatcher, and Lawrence C. Wroth.

We stay indebted yet furthermore to a number of assistants—including scholars, and businessmen and -women, and professional men and women, and pioneers, and translators, and critics—who by correspondence or interviews, or in other ways, have advanced the progress of this record of the St. Johns River. Among them, we now render our cordial thanks to: Richard F. Adams, Oakes Ames, Margaret Anderson, Stanley C. Arthur, Bion Barnett, William L'Engle Barnett, Burton Barrs, Sr., H. P. Baya, John C. Bills, Jr., James Black, Ben Briggs, Hortense Broward, William Lowndes Calhoun, Madeleine Barnett Camp, Angela Palomo Campbell, Leon J. Canova, Margaret Davis Cate, Joshua C. Chase, D. K. Clippinger, H. C. Conkling, J. Paul Conway,

William E. DeBary, Barney Dillard, Mozelle DuBose, G. A. von Duhn, Annice Davis Elkins, George L. English, Stanley Faye, Elizabeth S. Fowles, Maynard Geiger, George Couper Gibbs, Edwin Granberry, H. James Gut, William Hallowes, Walter C. Hartridge, Rebecca Hentz Hatch, Nina Hawkins, Winifred Herron, Hamilton Holt, J. Hatten Howard, Alfred W. Jones, Stetson Kennedy, Herbert Lamson, Agnes K. Lawson, Alice Lerch, Katherine Litch, William A. Lockwood, Kathryn Slemons Marks, Walter Martin, C. Russell Mason, Walter Scott Mason, Jr., Alton C. Morris, Charles L. Mowat, Donald John Nicholson, W. A. Pratt, Anna and Elizabeth Rand, William M. Robinson, Jr., W. H. Siebert, Frederick Sleight, Dena Snodgrass, J. Edward Spurr, Nathan C. Starr, Juanita Tucker, Gordon Tully, Ralph Wight, Myra Williams, and H. H. Winegar.

Bibliography

T HOUGH in preparing this book all the material listed has been consulted, yet a number of the items hereinafter cited have been left unused, on account of a number of motives. This Bibliography is intended, thus, not merely to include our source material. It may guide those who wish to learn a bit more extensively about human doings alongside the St. Johns River during the last 380 years—and who will be rather amply rewarded by finding out much which we have been counseled by spatial limits, as well as by prudence, to omit.

With no less of prudence do we disclaim any pretension that this is a definitive Bibliography of the St. Johns. A Bibliography which approached completeness would display many hundreds of additional items.

Manuscript and Typescript Materials

BOHNENBERGER, CARL, sketch of Mrs. Stephen Crane, in possession of A. J. Hanna, Winter Park.

Brock House, Enterprise, Florida, registers, 1875-1911, Library of Florida Historical Society, St. Augustine.

BUFORD, RIVERS, "Napoleon Bonaparte Broward," an address, Florida Historical Society.

DE GROVE, H. D., "Early Steamboating on the St. Johns," Library of Jacksonville Historical Society.

HANNA, A. J., biography of Achille Murat, Winter Park.

LE CONTE, JOHN E., two reports, 1822, to Office of Chief of Engineers, U.S. War Department, The National Archives.

MAY, PHILIP S., material collected for a biography of Zephaniah Kingsley, Jacksonville.

McNEIL, CORA TAYLOR (Mrs. Stephen Crane), divorce proceedings, 1909; will and inventory of The Court, 1910, Duval County Court House, Jacksonville.

Panton, Leslie and Company and John Forbes and Company papers, 1788-1832, Florida Historical Society.

Official Publications

COOKE, C. WYTHE, "Scenery of Florida," State of Florida *Geological Bulletin 17*, Tallahassee: State Geological Survey, 1939.

RICHARDSON, JAMES D., *A Compilation of the Messages and Papers of the Presidents* (10 vols.). Washington: Government Printing Office, 1896-1899.

SWANTON, JOHN R., *Early History of the Creek Indians and Their Neighbors*. Washington: Government Printing Office, 1922.

Biographies and Memoirs

ARTHUR, STANLEY C., *Audubon, An Intimate Life of the American Woodsman*. New Orleans: Harmanson, 1937.

AUDUBON, MARIA R., *Audubon and His Journals* (2 vols.). New York: Charles Scribner's Sons, 1898.

BEER, THOMAS, *Stephen Crane, A Study in American Letters*. Garden City: Garden City Publishing Co., 1927.

DELIUS, CLARE, *Frederick Delius*. London: Ivor Nicholson & Watson, 1935.

DICKISON, MARY ELIZABETH, *Dickison and His Men*. Louisville: Courier-Journal Job Printing Co., 1890.

EARNEST, ERNEST, *John and William Bartram*. Philadelphia: University of Pennsylvania Press, 1940.

ETTINGER, A. A., *James Edward Oglethorpe, Imperial Idealist*. Oxford: Clarendon Press, 1936.

FENBY, ERIC, *Delius as I Knew Him*. London: G. Bell & Sons, Ltd., 1937.

GEIGER, MAYNARD, *Biographical Dictionary of the Franciscans in Florida and Cuba (1528-1841)*. Patterson, N. J.: St. Anthony Guild Press, 1940.

GILBERTSON, CATHERINE, *Harriet Beecher Stowe*. New York: D. Appleton-Century Co., 1937.

GRANT, ALASTAIR MACPHERSON, *General James Grant of Ballindalloch, 1720-1806*. London: n.p., 1930.

HARTRIDGE, WALTER, ed., *Letters of John McQueen.* Columbia: Bostick & Thornley, 1943.

HERVEY, JOHN, LORD, *Memoirs of the Reign of George the Second* (3 vols.). New York: Scribner & Welford, 1884.

HIGGINSON, MARY THACHER (editor), *Letters and Journals of Thomas Wentworth Higginson.* Boston: Houghton Mifflin Co., 1921.

HIGGINSON, THOMAS WENTWORTH, *Army Life in a Black Regiment.* Boston: Houghton Mifflin Co., 1900.

KENNY, MICHAEL, *Pedro Martínez, S.J.* St. Leo: n.p., 1939.

LEE, R. E., JR., *Recollections and Letters of General Robert E. Lee.* New York: Doubleday, Page & Co., 1909.

MÉRAS, GONZALO SOLÍS DE, *Pedro Menéndez de Avilés.* . . (translated and edited by Jeannette Thurber Connor). DeLand: Florida State Historical Society, 1923.

MURRAY, AMELIA M., Lady, *Letters from the United States, Cuba, and Canada.* New York: G. P. Putnam's Sons, 1857.

MUSCHAMP, EDWARD A., *Audacious Audubon.* New York: Brentano's, 1929.

ROURKE, CONSTANCE, *Audubon.* New York: Harcourt, Brace and Co., 1936.

STEVENS, HENRY, *Thomas Hariot, The Mathematician, the Philosopher, and the Scholar.* London: n.p., 1900.

STRICKLAND, AGNES, *Lives of the Queens of England* (6 vols. of which Vol. III is devoted to Elizabeth). London: George Bell and Sons, 1903.

STOWE, CHARLES EDWARD, *Life of Harriet Beecher Stowe.* . . Boston: Houghton Mifflin Co., 1889.

WEISS, H. B., and ZIEGLER, G. M., *Thomas Say, Early American Naturalist.* Baltimore: C. C. Thomas, 1931.

WHIPPLE, H. B., *Southern Diary, 1843-44* (editor, L. B. Shippee). Minneapolis: University of Minnesota Press, 1937.

WILSON, FORREST, *Crusader in Crinoline.* Philadelphia: J. B. Lippincott Co., 1941. Pulitzer Prize biography of Harriet Beecher Stowe.

WRIGHT, ROBERT, *A Memoir of General James Edward Oglethorpe.* London: Chapman and Hall, 1867.

Articles in Periodicals and Newspapers

ANDREWS, CHARLES M., "God's Protecting Providence, A Journal by Jonathan Dickinson," *Florida Historical Quarterly*, October, 1942.

BOHNENBERGER, CARL, "The Settlement of Charlotia (Rolles Town), 1765," *Florida Historical Society Quarterly*, July, 1925.

CORSE, CARITA DOGGETT, "Denys Rolle and Rollestown, A Pioneer for Utopia," *Florida Historical Quarterly*, October, 1928.

CORSE, HERBERT M., "Names of the St. Johns River," *Florida Historical Quarterly*, October, 1942.

CRANE, MRS. STEPHEN, "What Hell Might Be," *Smart Set*, November, 1901.

DODD, DOROTHY, "The Secession Movement in Florida, 1850-1861," *Florida Historical Quarterly*, July and October, 1933.

HOWARD, J. HATTEN, "Sternwheeling on Jungle Rivers," *Motor Boating*, January, 1942.

HUHNER, LEON, "Moses Elias Levy," *Florida Historical Quarterly*, April, 1941.

Jacksonville *Florida Times-Union*, advertisements of hotels and steamship lines, 1880's and 1890's.

LEARY, LEWIS, "Philip Freneau on the Cession of Florida," *Florida Historical Quarterly*, July, 1942.

MANUCY, ALBERT, and JOHNSON, ALBERTA, "Castle St. Mark and the Patriots of the Revolution," *Florida Historical Quarterly*, July, 1942.

RICHMOND, MRS. HENRY L., "Ralph Waldo Emerson in Florida," *Florida Historical Quarterly*, October, 1939.

STONE, DORIS, "The Relationship of Florida Archaeology to that of Middle America," *Florida Historical Quarterly*, January, 1939.

WHITMAN, ALICE, "Transportation in Territorial Florida," *Florida Historical Quarterly*, July, 1938.

WROTH, LAWRENCE C., "Source Materials of Florida History in the John Carter Brown Library of Brown University," *Florida Historical Quarterly*, July, 1941.

General Works

BARBOUR, GEORGE M., *Florida for Tourists, Invalids and Settlers.* New York: D. Appleton and Co., 1882. The author, a correspondent of the Chicago *Times,* gathered information for this book while accompanying General Grant on his tour of Florida in 1879.

BARTRAM, WILLIAM, *Travels* . . . New York: Facsimile Library, 1940.

BEAZLEY, C. RAYMOND, ed., *Voyages and Travels Mainly During the 16th and 17th Centuries* (2 vols., of which Vol. I contains all three of the Hawkins voyages from Hakluyt, in addition to the State Papers concerning Hawkins). New York: E. P. Dutton & Co., n.d.

BILL, LEDYARD, *A Winter in Florida.* New York: Wood and Holbrook, 1869.

BRADLEE, FRANCIS B. C., *Blockade Running During the Civil War.* Salem: Essex Institute, 1925.

BRINTON, DANIEL G., *Notes on the Floridian Peninsula,* Philadelphia: J. Sabin, 1859.

BROOKS, ABBIE M. [Sylvia Sunshine], *Petals Plucked from Sunny Climes.* Nashville: Southern Methodist Publishing House, 1880.

BRYANT, WILLIAM CULLEN, *Letters of a Traveller.* New York: G. P. Putnam's Sons, 1850.

CABELL, BRANCH, *The First Gentleman of America.* New York: Farrar & Rinehart, 1942.

CORSE, CARITA DOGGETT, *The Key to the Golden Islands.* Chapel Hill: University of North Carolina Press, 1931.

DAVIS, W. W., *Civil War and Reconstruction in Florida.* New York: Columbia University, 1913.

DELAND, MARGARET, *Florida Days.* Boston: Little, Brown and Co., 1889.

DICKENSON (*sic*), JONATHAN, *God's Protecting Providence* . . . The Third Edition, Printed in Philadelphia: Reprinted in London and Sold by the Assigns of F. Sowle, at the Bible in George-Yard, Lombard-Street, 1720.

GEIGER, MAYNARD, *The Franciscan Conquest of Florida, 1573-1618.* Washington: Catholic University of America, 1937.

GUEDALLA, PHILIP, *Fathers of the Revolution.* New York: G. P. Putnam's Sons, 1927.

HANNA, A. J., *Flight into Oblivion.* Richmond: Johnson Publishing Co., 1938.

HEARN, LAFCADIO, *Leaves from the Diary of an Impressionist.* Boston: Houghton Mifflin Co., 1911.

HRDLICKA, ALES, *Anthropology of Florida.* DeLand: Florida State Historical Society, 1922.

JEFFERSON, THOMAS, *Writings,* Vol. VIII. Washington: Thomas Jefferson Memorial Association, 1907.

KENNEDY, STETSON, *Palmetto Country.* New York: Duell, Sloan and Pearce, 1942.

KENNY, MICHAEL, *The Romance of the Floridas.* Milwaukee: Bruce Publishing Co., 1935.

LANIER, SIDNEY, *Florida, Its Scenery, Climate, and History.* Philadelphia: J. B. Lippincott Co., 1875.

LANNING, JOHN TATE, *The Spanish Missions of Georgia.* Chapel Hill: University of North Carolina Press, 1935.

LAUDONNIÈRE, RENÉ DE, "The Description of the West Indies in General, but chiefly and particularly of Florida," and "The Second Voyage unto Florida, made and written by Captaine Laudonnière, which fortified and inhabited there two Summers and one whole Winter," Richard Hakluyt, *The Third and Last Volume of the Voyages, Navigations, Traffiques and Discoveries, &c.* London: 1600.

LE MOYNE DE MORGUES, JACQUES, *Narrative* . . . Boston: J. S. Osgood and Co., 1875. A translation from the Latin *Brevis Narratio* . . . (1591) published as Part II of Théodore de Bry's *Great Voyages.*

LEY, JOHN C., *Fifty-Two Years in Florida.* Nashville: Publishing House of the Methodist Church South, 1899.

MURAT, ACHILLE, *Moral and Political Sketch of the United States.* London: Effingham Wilson, 1833.

RIBAUT, JEAN, *The Whole and True Discouerye of Terra Florida.* DeLand: Florida State Historical Society, 1927. Facsimile reprint of the London edition of 1563 edited by Jeannette Thurber Connor.

ROBERTS, WILLIAM, *An Account of the First Discovery and Natural History of Florida*. London: n.p., 1763.

[ROLLE, DENYS], *Extract from the Account of East Florida Published by Dr. Stork with the Observations of . . .* London: n.p., 1766.

RONCIÈRE, CHARLES DE LA, *La Floride Française* (2 vols., of which Vol. II contains in full color the engravings made from Le Moyne's paintings). Paris: Les Editions Nationales, 1928.

STOWE, HARRIET BEECHER, *Palmetto Leaves*. Boston: James R. Osgood and Co., 1873.

————— *Uncle Tom's Cabin, A Tale of Life among the Lowly* (2 vols.). Boston: John P. Jewett Co., 1852.

TORREY, BRADFORD, *A Florida Sketch Book*. Boston: Houghton Mifflin Co., 1894.

TOWNSHEND, F. T., *Wild Life in Florida*. London: Hurat and Blackett, 1875.

WINTER, NEVIN O., *Florida, The Land of Enchantment*. Boston: The Page Co., 1918.

YONGE, CHARLOTTE M., *Cameos from English History* (9 vols.). London: Macmillan and Co., 1899.

Regional, State, and Local Histories

ABBEY, KATHRYN T., *Florida, Land of Change*. Chapel Hill: University of North Carolina Press, 1941.

BRINTON, DANIEL G., *A Guide-Book to Florida and the South*. Philadelphia, 1869.

CHATELAIN, VERNE E., *The Defenses of Spanish Florida, 1565 to 1763*. Washington: The Carnegie Institution, 1941.

[CORSE, CARITA DOGGETT, editor] *Florida, A Guide to the Southernmost State*, New York: Oxford University Press, 1939.

DAVIS, T. FREDERICK, *History of Jacksonville, Florida*. St. Augustine: The Record Co., 1925.

GOLD, P. D., *History of Volusia County, Florida*. DeLand: E. O. Painter Co., 1927.

LOWERY, WOODBURY, *The Spanish Settlements Within the Present Limits of the United States* (2 vols.). New York: G. P. Putnam's Sons, 1905.

REYNOLDS, CHARLES B., *Old St. Augustine, A Story of Three Centuries*. St. Augustine: E. H. Reynolds, 1888.

ROMANS, BERNARD, *A Concise Natural History of East and West Florida*, 1775.

SIEBERT, WILBUR H., *Loyalists in East Florida, 1774-1785* (2 vols.). DeLand: Florida State Historical Society, 1929.

WILLIAMS, JOHN LEE, *The Territory of Florida*. New York: A. T. Goodrich, 1837.

Miscellaneous Items

BARRS, BURTON, *East Florida in the American Revolution*. Jacksonville: Guild Press, 1932.

Broward, Napoleon B., Candidate for Governor. Jacksonville: n.p., 1904. A campaign pamphlet.

CALL, RICHARD KEITH, *An Address to the People of Florida*. 1860.

Georgia Historical Society *Collections*, Savannah.

Into Tropical Florida; or a Round Trip upon the St. Johns River. New York: Leve and Alden, 1883. An advertising pamphlet of the de Bary-Baya Merchants Line.

KINGSLEY, ZEPHANIAH, *Treatise on the Patriarchial or Cooperative System of Society* . . . n.p., n.p., 1828.

MOORE, CLARENCE BLOOMFIELD, *Certain Sand Mounds of the St. Johns River, Florida* (2 vols.). Philadelphia: The Lenytype Co., 1894. The small steamer *Alligator* was chartered for Moore's expeditions.

WYMAN, JEFFRIES, "Explorations of the St. Johns River, Florida, Shell Mounds," Peabody Museum *Annual Report*. Boston, 1868.

YERKES, ROBERT M., *Yale Laboratories of Comparative Psychobiology*. Baltimore: The Johns Hopkins Press, 1932.

Maps: Listed in Chronological Order

[1564-1587]. JACQUES LE MOYNE DE MORGUES, *Floridae Americae Provinciae Recens & exactissima descriptio* . . . , immediately preceding text of Le Moyne's *Brevis Narratio* . . .

(1591). Based on explorations of the River of May [St. Johns] made in 1564 by Le Moyne.

[1680-1700?]. Anonymous (Spanish), *Mapa de la Ysla de la Florida*, Map 7 in Verne E. Chatelain's, *The Defenses of Spanish Florida*, *1565 to 1763*, (1941).

[1711]. EDWARD CRISP, *A Compleat Description of the Province of Carolina.* . . . See *Lowery Collection*, pp. 234-235. The explorations on which an inset to this map was based were conducted by Captain Thomas Nairne, Indian agent of South Carolina. V. W. Crane, in his *Southern Frontier* (p. 349), describes the inset as "a crude map based upon the Nairne manuscript map of 1708, which has disappeared."

1715. HERMAN MOLL, *A New and Exact Map of the Dominions of the King of Great Britain on ye Continent of North America* . . . , Map 8 in Moll's *The World Described* . . . , (1709-1720). An inset shows "St. Juans R." in "East Part of Florida" at the mouth, and "S. Juan R." along the course of the stream.

1766-1770. WILLIAM GERARD DE BRAHM, *Map of the General Surveys of East Florida* . . . , Plate VII in John Bartram's, *Diary of a Journey through the Carolinas, Georgia, and Florida*, annotated by Francis Harper, *Transactions* of the American Philosophical Society, XXXIII (new series, Part I), (1942). Based on the first surveys of the St. Johns.

1924. *Historical Map of Florida*, supplement to *American Motorist*, (November, 1924).

1925. CARTER and DAMEROW, *Map of Indian River County, Florida*. Drew Press, Jacksonville.

1941. *Sectional Map of Florida*. Department of Agriculture, Tallahassee.

N.D. *Oklawaha River*. United States Engineer Office, Jacksonville.

Charts

Charts of the St. Johns river by the U.S. Coast and Geodetic Survey:

458 *Lake Monroe to Lake Washington*, 1891
688 *Lake Dexter to Lake Harney*, 1940

687   *Dunns Creek to Lake Dexter, 1940*
686   *Racy Point to Crescent Lake, 1940*
685   *Jacksonville to Racy Point, 1941*
577   *Fernandina to Jacksonville, 1941.*

In the absence of accurate charts of the Upper St. Johns, the records and preliminary drawings of this section of the river, which have been assembled and made by the United States Engineer Office of the War Department, located at Jacksonville, have been consulted through the courtesy of Messrs. J. R. Peyton and Gordon S. Mobley, Jr.

Index

319

THE ST. JOHNS of Florida is the first book in the Rivers of America Series to appear under dual authorship. The combination of a professor of history and a great stylist has produced a book of singular charm with no sacrifice of accuracy. History is here, and the stirring of important events, but it is above all a story of people. As Mr. Cabell says in an amusing epilogue:

" . . . it is less the present than the past of the St. Johns, its gaudy and its well-nigh incredible past, which appears engaging. Upon no other river tory far less as a record of events, and of commerce, and of fruit raising, than as a pageant of strange persons passing, with Time as their drum major, beside its broad brown waters. Nor is it a monotonous pageant, this outlandish parade which, starting with the imperial swagger of Jean Ribaut, ends with a furtive, stumbling and tipsy Cora McNeil."

Florida is not like any other state in the Union, and in Florida the St. Johns is not as other rivers. At a time when the more northerly American settlements were finding nature and man their stern enemies, there was already evident a suavity and sophistication that has never since left these shores. The Spanish, French and English have alternately claimed possession, and all have left their imprint on the land. Here is the story of one of the least known of America's cultures told with affection and wisdom.